I, LIBRARIAN

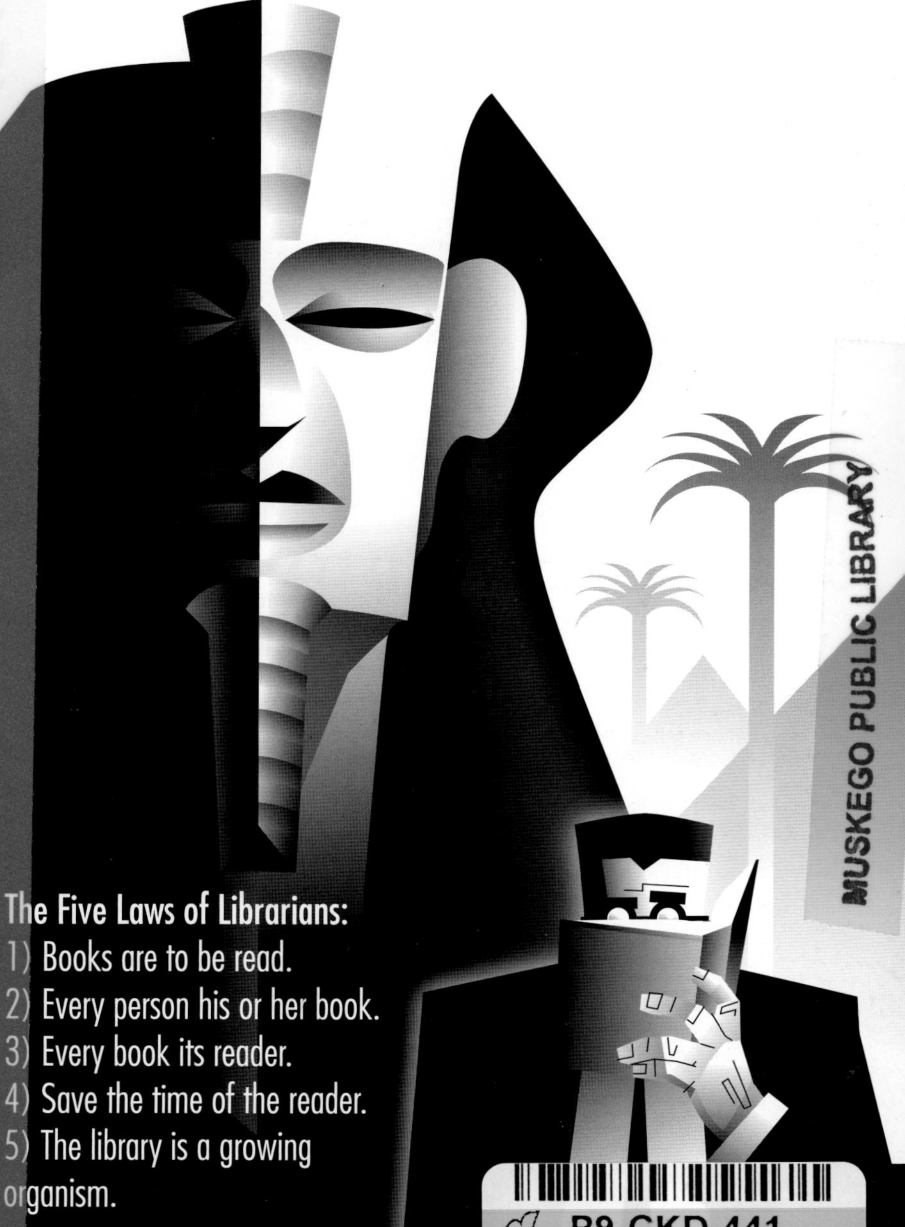

The Five Laws of Librarians:
1) Books are to be read.
2) Every person his or her book.
3) Every book its reader.
4) Save the time of the reader.
5) The library is a growing organism.

Written and Illustrated by
James Turner

Published by
SLG Publishing

President and Publisher
Dan Vado

Editor-in-Chief
Jennifer de Guzman

P.O. Box 26427
San Jose, CA 95159

www.slgcomic.com

Rex Libris Volume One: I, Librarian collects issues #1-5 of the SLG series *Rex Libris.*

First Printing: June 2007
ISBN 978-1-59362-062-2

FINALLY!
THE COMIC BOOK ABOUT A TWO-FISTED LIBRARIAN WE'VE ALL BEEN WAITING FOR

Introduction by Dave Sim

You know it really seems like just yesterday that James Turner's (as it was then called) I, Librarian was just one of the many in vitro comics that I get in the mail every month—a pile of photocopied pages of Rex Libris and another pile of Nil: A Land Beyond Belief. Having been a definite anti-computer-drawn-comics advocate, it surprised me a great deal to find myself caught up in both storylines and eager to read more. I tossed them both in the mail pile and, when the time came, wrote what I thought was a suitably encouraging letter. It was when I was writing the address on the envelope that I did a double take. "This address is VERY familiar." I pulled out the old Cerebus freebie list and sure enough, the address was the same as that of Chester Brown, just off by four digits on the condominium apartment number.

The next time I was talking to Chet on the phone, I asked him, "Do you know the guy in #1011?" He hesitated and said, "I don't KNOW him, but I recognize him. We say hello or we wave. He's my neighbour right across the hall, why?" So I told him about the package and (perhaps unethically) sent him both Rex Libris and Nil to read. Chet liked them both, too. The next time I was in Toronto having lunch, I asked Chet if he wanted me to say something to James in my next letter. "I mean, he's your neighbour. If he turns out to be an annoying fanboy it's going to be your headache. You bought your place, so you can't very well pick up and move because Dave Sim exposed to you an annoying fanboy who lives across the hall." Chester mulled this over and said, "Sure, tell him in your next letter."

Well, since that time we've had lunch or coffee the three of us several times when I've been down visiting and James hasn't proven to be even remotely an annoying fanboy.

So, that's always the most vivid memory I have about James and his books, way back when he was still wondering whether to self-publish or to shop them around to various publishers. Consequently, there is a very dream-like quality to re-reading six issues of Rex Libris, the regularly published Slave Labor Graphics comics title with its own devoted following (it's already gone from a special-order title at the Beguiling to having its own nicely packed little slot in the indy section. How in the heck did James get to issue six, already? Has that much time gone by? And I remember reading each one of them quite vividly, that stage where you're really pulling for the guy and hoping that book is actually the page-turner you remember it being when you were reading it in photocopy form. It's such an intelligent book, informed by James' own background in so many fields of interest. Sensitive as I am to any blasphemous content, I remember laughing comfortably at Thoth's rant towards the end of issue one that there's no place for a god in this day age, that the Big Three have had it locked up for centuries. It's an interesting theme that I'm sure James will revisit: it isn't just the gods but so many elements which once dominated society over uncountable generations which have gradually faded in influence and popularity until they really do find their final limited home in the confines of. . .the library. They aren't forgotten exactly, they're just the subject of books for those interested. If it's not quite immortality it is at least immortality of a kind. The Library at Alexandria no longer exists, but the Middleton Public Library is still here. There's probably a lesson in there somewhere.

James does so many things well in these early issues, has so many memorable moments. It's hard to believe that Simon—Rex's transformed-by-Circe bird companion—only gets introduced on page 4 of issue 2 and yet by page 7 is vivid enough in the reader's mind as a personality that his fantasized conquest line—"Take what you wish, my minions, but the bird seed is mine!" —provokes one of the biggest early laughs. The discussions with B. Barry Horst, the publisher of Rex's comic book adaptations, are among my favourite parts of the books. "Where's the part about the gun?" That's on page twelve. I thought it was at least two issues later. Barry saying that he loves the idea of a sidekick but suggesting that Simon should have a gun. And Rex's appalled reaction: "Simon? With a gun?" And then Barry's counter-suggestion: they'll have to give him boobs, instead.

Jeez. That was all in one issue?

He's also got that 1960s Marvel Comics thing down. Like issue 3's "Leap of Faith". I forget the reason but they can't actually land Rex on this planet so he has to jump from low orbit and free-fall for about forty minutes. I mean you can picture Jack Kirby coming up with that in an issue of the Fantastic Four. "We won't be able to land you on the planet, Ben!" "That's okay Stretcho—just get this thing a low as you can in orbit and I'll jump from there!" And that leads into the big battle with snowflake-based life forms in "Battle on Benzine", the Praetorian Guard of Vaglox. It's not until we're well into the epic battle itself with Vaglox's death machine that James reminds us that this is actually just about an overdue library book (The Principia Mathematica, but still).

Anyway, there really isn't anything more gratifying in this business than to go from a pile of photocopied pages to an on-going comic-book series, to know that there's more in the same vein up ahead, just waiting for James to get around to running it through his computer and getting it down on paper.

I'm glad I was there at the beginning and I'm very glad to be here at one of the first major steps on the way to becoming a comic book legend, the first collected volume. Dive in and enjoy and then join the rest of us Rex Libris fans as we eagerly await the next issue.

Dave Sim
Kitchener, Ontario
3 February 07

CHAPTER ONE
I, LIBRARIAN

BARRY'S BRAIN

Welcome to the first publication of Hermeneutic Press. Rejoice! Yes, rejoice! Why you ask? Because! This is quite possibly the greatest event in the modern history of comics. Never before has Hermeneutic Press published! This is it! The very first time! In all six thousand years of recorded history! Incredible, you say? Believe it! Not only that, but the molecules in the material you hold in your hands comes to you from the inside of a long dead star! What's that you say? Impossible? No! Not for us at Hermeneutic Press! Only the best will do for our readers, and we'll go to the far corners of the universe to bring the best to you!

Now. Let's get something straight, right from the get go: we're in this for the money. That's the bottom line. Instead of investing our hard earned money in fickle things like stocks, real estate, Nortel or Enron, we've invested our nest egg in the economic miracle niche of comic books, where vast fortunes await us. Indeed, few fields are so ridiculously prosperous as the independent comic book industry. Just create a confection of fun frivolity mixed with high octane action, and top it off with an ever-so-light dusting of hyperbole and voila—a new multi-million dollar comic franchise is born into this, the new, Ironic Age of Comics! We just have to sit back and wait for the movie offers to pour in from the studios. The first franchise I think we'll let go for a few million. The commercial tie-ins is where the money is really at. Action figures. Cups. Hats. Key chains. Lamps. Motor oil. We'll push the envelope of commercial exploitation til it bursts like the condoms we're going to endorse. And it doesn't end there! Theme parks will follow, and, eventually, we'll buy a small, remote island from which to plot complete world domination. And we'll owe it all to you, our dear readers, and the magical medium of Visicomboics! You heard me right.

Here at Hermeneutic Press we don't publish just comics. Plain old comics, as the rabbit might say, are for kids. We publish the phenomenal Deluxe Visicomboic™ Comics. We will offer a PHD program in Visicomboicology™ as soon as the B. Barry Horst Wing is added to the University of Wisconsin. Anytime now. Check your watches. Ah! It's time for me to take my medication.

So. Thanks again for purchasing this fine Hermeneutic Press comic. If, however, you are standing in the store reading this and have not paid for it, cut it out. Get out that cash. A few tiny rectangular pieces of paper (or disc shaped pieces of heavy, worthless metal) and you get, in return, several much bigger, not to mentioned stapled, pieces of paper. Sure we don't have any fancy holograms, but those cause eyestrain anyway.

Yours,

B. Barry Horst

WELCOME, ADVENTUROUS READER, TO THE FIRST ISSUE OF REX LIBRIS, PUBLIC LIBRARIAN. HERE YOU WILL FIND, FOR THE **FIRST TIME IN PRINT EVER,** THE TUMULTUOUS TALES OF THE PUBLIC LIBRARY SYSTEM AND ITS UNENDING BATTLE AGAINST THE FORCES OF EVIL. THIS STRUGGLE IS NOT JUST CONFINED TO OUR TERRESTRIAL SPHERE BUT EXTENDS OUT INTO THE FARTHEST REACHES OF THE COSMOS... **AND BEYOND!** THE LIBRARIAN HAS FACED PATRONS SO TERRIBLE, SO HORRIFIC, THAT THEY CANNOT BE DESCRIBED HERE WITHOUT THE RISK OF DRIVING READERS **MAD.** BUT ENOUGH PRATTLE AND PREAMBLE! SETTLE BACK WITH A CUP OF COFFEE AND A DONUT (OR OTHER PASTRY IF YOU PREFER), AND PREPARE TO ENTER THE SECRET WORLD OF...

REX · LIBRIS

"I, LIBRARIAN"

DAZZLING ART BY: JAMES TURNER / BABBLING SCRIPT BY: "JAZZED" JAMES

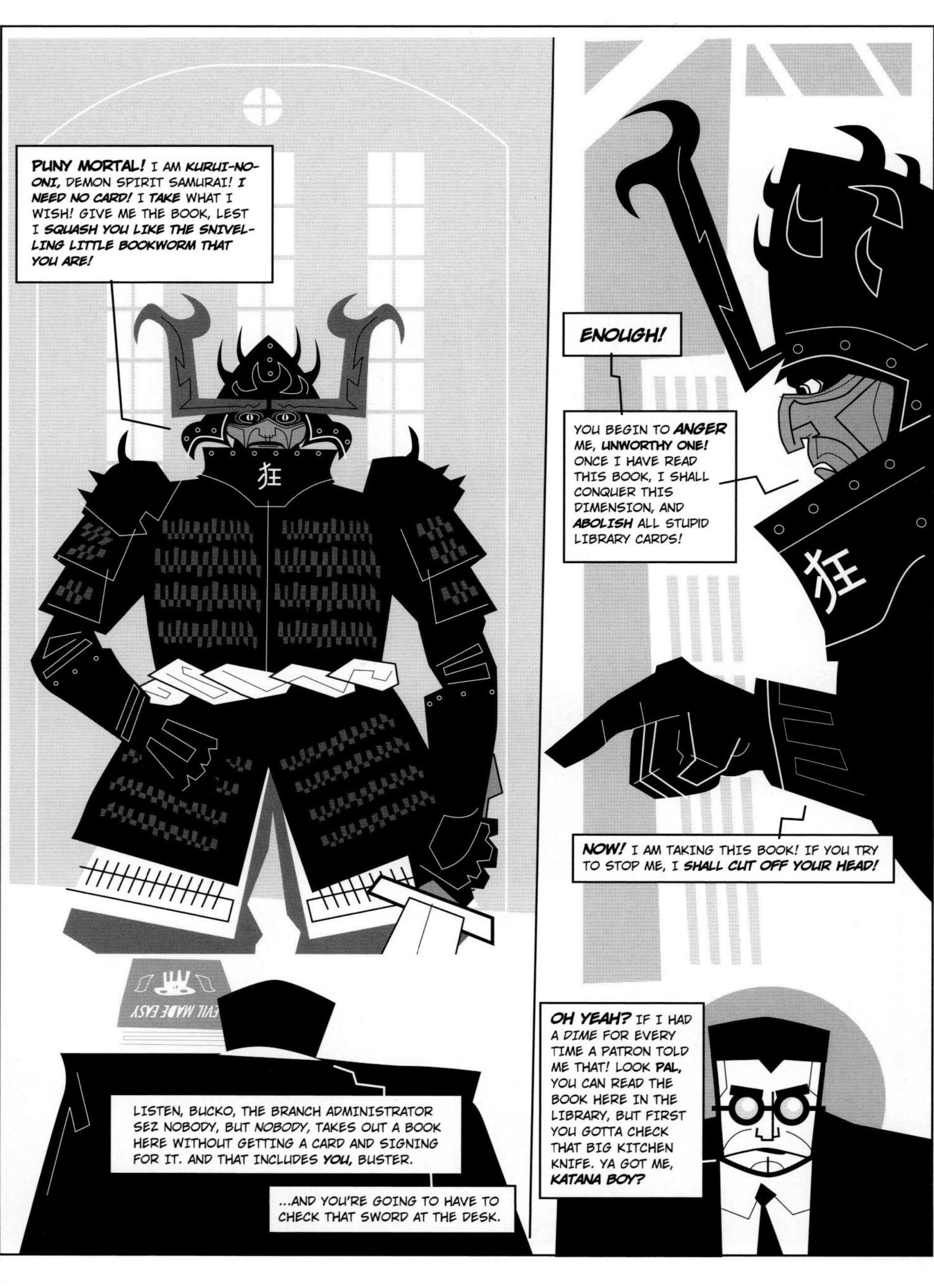

PUNY MORTAL! I AM KURUI-NO-ONI, DEMON SPIRIT SAMURAI! I NEED NO CARD! I TAKE WHAT I WISH! GIVE ME THE BOOK, LEST I SQUASH YOU LIKE THE SNIVELLING LITTLE BOOKWORM THAT YOU ARE!
狂
EVIL MADE EASY
LISTEN, BUCKO, THE BRANCH ADMINISTRATOR SEZ NOBODY, BUT NOBODY, TAKES OUT A BOOK HERE WITHOUT GETTING A CARD AND SIGNING FOR IT. AND THAT INCLUDES YOU, BUSTER.
...AND YOU'RE GOING TO HAVE TO CHECK THAT SWORD AT THE DESK.
ENOUGH!
YOU BEGIN TO ANGER ME, UNWORTHY ONE! ONCE I HAVE READ THIS BOOK, I SHALL CONQUER THIS DIMENSION, AND ABOLISH ALL STUPID LIBRARY CARDS!
狂
NOW! I AM TAKING THIS BOOK! IF YOU TRY TO STOP ME, I SHALL CUT OFF YOUR HEAD!
OH YEAH? IF I HAD A DIME FOR EVERY TIME A PATRON TOLD ME THAT! LOOK PAL, YOU CAN READ THE BOOK HERE IN THE LIBRARY, BUT FIRST YOU GOTTA CHECK THAT BIG KITCHEN KNIFE. YA GOT ME, KATANA BOY?

INSOLENT ONE, YOU SHALL PAY FOR THAT INSULT! I SHALL DRINK THE CHI OF YOUR SOUL FROM THE CUP OF YOUR DECAPITATED HEAD! BEHOLD! THE SWORD OF TABI CAN SLICE THROUGH ANY MATERIAL LIKE IT WAS MADE OF TISSUE PAPER!
HIS WEIGHT... SHIFTING! GOT TO MOVE... NOW!
PREPARE TO DIE! YEAAAAAAAAH!
KRAK!
SWIIIISSSSSSSSSSSSSSSSSSSSSSSSSSSSSSSSH
HEY! THAT'S LIBRARY PROPERTY, YOU WITLESS CLOD!
CRUNCH
THUNK
YOU'LL PAY FOR THAT!

AND YOU CAN START WITH EATING **HOT LEAD,** ME BUCKO!

POK! POK! POK! POK!

PANG!

DAMN! HE'S RIGHT! HE'S **BULLET PROOF!**

PANG!

HAHAHAHAHAHA! I AM IMMUNE TO YOUR PUNY WEAPON!

FLEE BEFORE MY WRATH, PATHETIC LIBRARIAN **WORM!**

SHIT!

I'LL TAKE THAT ADVICE! GOT TO STALL FOR **TIME,** TRY TO **THINK!** I'M A LIBRARIAN-- I'VE READ ABOUT *UNDEAD SAMURAI DEMONS* BEFORE! IF ONLY I COULD REMEMBER **HOW** TO STOP THEM!

RUN, HUMAN COWARD! SOON I SHALL SLAKE MY THIRST ON YOUR SPIRIT! **HAHAHAHA!**

SAY? I SEZ SCREW YOU, HELL SPAWN!
'DESE BOOKS ARE FOR THE ENLIGHTENMENT OF EVERYONE! KNOWLEDGE IS NOT TO BE MONOPOLIZED BY TIN-TOPPED DEMONS! IT MUST BE AVAILABLE FOR ALL PEOPLE!
!!!???
IDEALISTIC FOOL! THEN YOU SHALL DIE!
EGADS!
狂
WOOOOOOOOOOOOOOOOOOOOOOSH!!
MY HAIR! YOU BASTARD!
THAK!
ZUCK! THAT WAS TOO CLOSE! ONLY ONE CHANCE NOW!
HUFF! HUFF! I'VE LOST HIM AMONGST THE BOOK SHELVES FOR THE MOMENT!
THERE!
GOT TO REACH IT--

--...THE MYTHOLOGY SECTION!
FACE ME, MORTAL FOOL!
I MADE IT! NOW LET ME SEE "DANGEROUS DRAGONS"... "DEMON ARMIES AND THEIR ARMOUR"... NOT QUITE IT... "DEMON HOLIDAYS"... NO... "DEMON TAXONOMY"... ER... "DEMON SAMURAI AND HOW TO DEFEAT THEM." PAY DIRT! AND DAMN IF SOMEONE DIDN'T MISFILE IT ON THE SHELF! IT SHOULD BE BEFORE DEMON TAXONOMY, NOT AFTER! SHEESH!
HOW MANY TIMES DO I HAVE TO TELL PEOPLE NOT TO RESHELVE THE FREAKING BOOKS??
SCRIBE! WHERE ARE YOU?
YOU ARE TRYING TO FIND A WAY TO DEFEAT ME AMONGST YOUR PRECIOUS BOOKS, AREN'T YOU?
HERE WE GO! INDEX... FEEDING... MATING ... NATURAL HABITAT... VANQUISHING! PAGE 125! YES! ... 56, 104...
FLIP
FLIP
FLIP
FLIP
FLIP
FLIP
FLIP
FLIP
I KNOW WHERE YOU MUST BE THEN! WITH THE BOOKS ON DEMONS!.... I SHALL FIND YOU! HMM... WHERE AM I? 'CHILDREN'S'... AYAMARU! THESE BOOKSHELVES ARE LIKE A LABYRINTH! AN EVIL, INESCAPABLE MAZE OF MASSED INFORMATION!
125!... "THE DEMON IS OFTEN..."
...SWORD... UNH HUH... ...CAN BE TRICKED...
HMMM!
WELL THAT DOESN'T SOUND TOO HARD TO DO!

SOON...

...THE HISTORY OF WORLD WAR II... INCREDIBLE! HOW DID I MISS THIS!? AN ENTIRE WORLD AT WAR! BLOOD AND SACRIFICE! DEATH ON A SCALE EVEN I HAD NOT CONCEIVED! I MUST READ MORE! MORE!!

900 HISTORY

THERE HE IS! SUCKED INTO THE MILITARY HISTORY SECTION LIKE A MOTH TO A FLAME! HE'S COMPLETELY ENGROSSED! NOW IS MY CHANCE. I HAVE TO STRIKE. IF HE GETS OUT OF HERE, ESPECIALLY WITH THAT BOOK 'EVIL MADE EASY,' WE'LL SOON BE ENGULFED IN THE NUCLEAR FIRES OF WORLD WAR THREE!

I MUST NOT FAIL! THE FUTURE DEPENDS ON ME, AND ME ALONE!

"THE WAR ENDED WITH THE DROPPING OF THE ATOMIC BOMB ON HIROSHIMA AND NAGASAKI."
ONE MORE TIME...
"ATOMIC BOMB!"
OOOO! I HAVE TO HAVE ONE OF THESE!
WORLD WAR II
WORLD WAR II
YANK!
HAW! SHUT YOUR BARBARIC YAWP, YA BLOODY MINDED BUM! HAHAHA!
I DID IT! THE SWORD IS NOW MINE! HAHA!
SCHWIIIIIIPP!!
WAH!? NO! WITHOUT THE SWORD OF TABI, I CANNOT REMAIN ON THIS PLANE OF REALITY! I WILL BE DRAWN BACK INTO THE ABYSS!
THAT'S THE IDEA, SUCKER!
YOUR TIME IS UP, YOU FIENDISH, BARNACLE-BRAINED, ARCH-MALIGNANT MONSTER OF MALICIOUSNESS!
NOW GET THE HELL OUT OF MY LIBRARY!

YAAAAAAAAAAAAH!!!
POOF!
IT'S TO JIGOKU FOR YOU!
JUST BECAUSE I'M A LIBRARIAN DOESN'T MEAN I'M AT ALL TAME.
BUCKO.
FRZAP!
CURSE YOU, SCRIBE! YOU HAVE FOILED ALL MY PLANS! YOU AND YOUR LITTLE BOOKS!
LOSING... COHESION!... BEING PULLED BACK... INTO THE VORTEX!
FISSSSSSSSSSSSSSSSSSSSSSSSSS!
IMPRESSIVE... MOST IMPRESSIVE.

AW MAN! HE STAINED THE CARPET....
BRAVO, MR LIBRIS.
EH?
OH HEY MR BLUMENKOHL! HOPE THE NOISE DIDN'T BOTHER YOU TOO MUCH.
NOT AT ALL.
THE BATTLE WAS BOTH EDUCATIONAL AND... AMUSING. ONE CAN LEARN MUCH ABOUT A MAN BY OBSERVING HIM IN COMBAT. DEMON SAMURAI ARE DANGEROUS BUT STUPID.
YET THEIR SWORD FIGHTING ABILITY IS SECOND TO NONE. YOU MANAGED TO OUT FIGHT IT USING A COMBINATION OF STEALTH AND CUNNING. CHARACTERISTICS THAT OFTEN MAKE THE DIFFERENCE BETWEEN LIFE AND DEATH IN THE SHORT AND PARTICULARLY BRUTAL BATTLE FOR SURVIVAL.
I COULD MAKE USE OF A MAN OF YOUR ABILITIES IN MY ORGANIZATION. SHOULD YOU EVER CHOOSE TO FIND... ALTERNATIVE EMPLOYMENT.
AW... SHUCKS MR. B!
JUST DOIN' MY JOB!
YOU DISAPPOINT ME.
MODESTY IS A TIRESOME CHARACTERISTIC, MR LIBRIS. I WOULD ENDEAVOUR TO OVERCOME SUCH TENDENCIES OF WEAKNESS. THEY UNDERMINE YOUR STRENGTH.

MODESTY MERELY DEFERS THE WRATH OF THE ENVIOUS, MY FRIEND. IT'S A KIND OF SELF-CASTRATION. IT PLACATES OTHERS BUT DOES YOU NO REAL FAVOURS. THERE IS NO POINT IN CURTAILING YOUR ABILITIES OR AMBITION FOR THE SAKE OF SOME PETTY MINDED SIMPLETONS. IF THEY GET IN YOUR WAY, IT BECOMES A SIMPLE MATTER OF DISPOSAL. BY WHATEVER MEANS NECESSARY.

YOU HAVE QUALMS ABOUT SUCH A RUTHLESS PURSUIT OF SELF-INTEREST? HMMM? DISCARD THEM. SOCIAL MORALITY IS A LUXURY RELATED ENTIRELY TO CIRCUMSTANCE, AND NOTHING MORE. THE FEMALE PRAYING MANTIS DEVOURS ITS MATE, FOR EXAMPLE. IT NEEDS THE PROTEIN FOR ITS NEWLY FERTILIZED EGGS. FACED WITH THE BIOLOGICAL IMPERATIVE, HUMAN BEINGS WILL BEHAVE NO DIFFERENTLY. CONTEXT IS ALL.

WELL THAT'S A PRETTY HARD LINE VIEW THERE, MR B. I GUESS YOU'RE A LIBERTARIAN, HUH?

OF COURSE.

THE MODERN WELFARE STATE INFANTILIZES PEOPLE. IT HAMSTRINGS THE TRULY CAPABLE WITH STULTIFYING LAWS TO BENEFIT THE WEAK. SUCH AS OUTLAWING DUELING, FOR EXAMPLE. RIDICULOUS.

MEN SUCH AS US SHOULD NOT BE CONSTRAINED BY SOCIAL CODES. WHAT RIGHT DO OTHERS HAVE TO IMPEDE OUR WILL TO POWER? WE ARE LIKE LIONS, YOU AND I. KINGS AMONG MEN. JOIN MY ORGANIZATION, AND I WILL SHOW YOU WHAT IT IS TO BE A KING, MR LIBRIS.
THE BENEFITS ARE MOST... PLEASURABLE, I ASSURE YOU.

NO CAN DO, MR B, BUT THANKS FOR THE OFFER. THE PUBLIC LIBRARY SYSTEM TREATS ME PRETTY GOOD. GOT FULL DENTAL AND THE ADMINISTRATOR HERE IS SECOND TO NONE. HE GETS THE BEST BOOKS IN THE WORLD. AT MIDDLETON PUBLIC WE HAVE THE LARGEST COLLECTION OF RARE BOOKS SINCE THE LIBRARY IN ALEXANDRIA BURNED DOWN!
SNIFF!

YES.... I HAVE BEEN ADMIRING THE COLLECTION HERE. THERE ARE SOME REMARKABLE BOOKS ON PARTICLE WEAPONS SYSTEMS. THE TESLA METHOD OF OVERCOMING ATMOSPHERIC INTERFERENCE ON ELECTROMAGNETIC FORCE BEAMS IS QUITE INGENIOUS...

OH HELL YEAH. MAJOR ADVANCES. WE GOT THE MOST CURRENT BOOKS ON THE TOPIC.
YOU'D LIKE **TSIPIS.** ACCORDING TO HIM, SUB-ORBITAL PLATFORMS IS WHERE IT'S AT. YOU DON'T WANT A PLANETARY BASED SYSTEM. YOU GET TOO MUCH INTERFERENCE FROM THE ATMOSPHERE. IT MAKES IT MORE DIFFICULT FOR THE ELECTRON BARRAGE TO DISRUPT THE TARGET AND UNRAVEL THE ATOMIC LATTICE THAT GIVES IT FORM.
FASCINATING.
I HAVE ENJOYED OUR LITTLE CHAT, MR LIBRIS, BUT I HAVE AN APPOINTMENT IN PARIS THAT CANNOT WAIT. I PUT THE BOOKS ON **POISONOUS FLOWERS** IN THE RETURN BOX. I THINK YOU WILL FIND THEM ALL ACCOUNTED FOR, AS ALWAYS. I NEVER MAKE MISTAKES, MR LIBRIS, FOR I AM... ***THE MASTERMIND!***
OH YES... DO CONSIDER MY OFFER. MY ORGANIZATION, **W.R.A.I.T.H.** ***(WORLDWIDE REVENGE, AGGRESSION, INTIMIDATION, TERROR AND HUBRIS)*** COULD USE AN ***EXPERT*** LIBRARIAN SUCH AS YOURSELF TO HELP WITH OUR ***EXTENSIVE*** RESEARCH PROJECTS. WE HAVE A FULL BENEFIT PACKAGE AND RATHER STYLISH DECODER RINGS. KEEP IT IN MIND. I WILL BE BACK IN A FEW DAYS.
ALWAYS GOOD TO HAVE YA DROP BY, MR. B! YOU HAVE IMPECCABLE MANNERS. THE KIDS WE GET IN HERE? THEY JUST RUN AROUND HERE LIKE ***CRAZY*** AND CAUSE ALL KINDS ***MAYHEM.*** MAKE MY JOB HARDER THAN THAT SAMURAI DEMON, BECAUSE I CAN'T JUST GO AND SHOOT THE KIDS, YA KNOW? PARENTS GET UPSET.
NOT THAT I'M SAYIN' I KNOW WHAT THAT'S LIKE OR ANYTHING. I MEAN ***HYPOTHETICALLY.***

WHOT A CRAZY GUY, THAT MR. BLUMENKOHL!
LITTLE DOES HE KNOW THAT I CAN NEVER LEAVE MY EMPLOYMENT HERE. TO DO SO WOULD BE... DEATH!
WHAT THE!?
HEY! YOU KIDS! GET A ROOM! THIS IS A LIBRARY, NOT A LOVE NEST.
GASP! LOOK TOMMY, IT IS -- THE LIBRARIAN!
Y-YES, SIR. RIGHT AWAY!
THE LIBRARIAN HAS SPOKEN, SALLY! WE DARE NOT DISOBEY!

"LEMME TAKE A MOMENT OUT TO INTRODUCE MYSELF. MY NAME'S LIBRIS. ***REX*** LIBRIS. LIBRARIAN. AND I WORK AT THE ***MIDDLETON PUBLIC LIBRARY***... THE BEST GOD DAMN PUBLIC LIBRARY IN ***NORTH AMERICA.*** THAT'S NOT HYPERBOLE, IT'S THE ***TRUTH.*** MOST OF THE TIME I MANAGE THINGS IN THE LIBRARY. BUT WHEN SHIT GOES DOWN, WHEN PEOPLE DON'T RETURN THE GOODS ON TIME, IT'S MY JOB TO BRING THE BOOKS BACK, AND IN ONE PIECE. THAT MEANS I CAN'T USE MY FLAMETHROWER. GOTTA GET THE BOOKS FROM THEM WITH FINESSE, USING PIN POINT APPLICATION OF FORCE. AND THAT AIN'T EASY, BECAUSE WE GET SOME PRETTY TOUGH PATRONS. ***GODS. UNDEAD. ALIEN WARLORDS. VAMPIRES. TIME TRAVELERS*** FROM THE PAST... AND FUTURE. I'VE GONE TO HELL AND BACK TO GET BOOKS BACK. BUT I'M EQUIPPED FOR IT. WHY? BECAUSE I HAVE THE MOST FORMIDABLE WEAPON OF ALL--***KNOWLEDGE.*** I'VE READ JUST ABOUT EVERY BOOK HERE IN THE LIBRARY. IF ANYONE KNOWS THE WEAKNESS OF A ***BUGONIAN SLIME MOULD,*** IT'S ME. COURSE NOT ALL OUR TROUBLESOME PATRONS ARE ***SO OBSCURE.*** I'VE TANGLED WITH THE BIG TIMERS TOO. FOUGHT ***SCYLLA*** ONCE. THE DAY SHE CAME INTO THE LIBRARY, SHE MADE ONE HELL OF A MESS. WATER SLOSHING AROUND EVERYWHERE. I DAMN NEAR DROWNED, AND THE DAMAGE TO THE BOOKS -- WAS IN THE ***BILLIONS!*** YOU HEARD ME RIGHT. ***BILLIONS.***"

"I KID YOU NOT. FEW PEOPLE KNOW JUST HOW MUCH A PUBLIC LIBRARY COLLECTION IS WORTH. JUST HERE AT MIDDLETON ALONE, WE HAVE ORIGINAL SCROLLS BY SOCRATES AND ARISTOTLE. JULIUS CAESAR'S FIRST BOOK... WE HAVE THE ORIGINAL HERE. ***THE NECRONOMICON,*** THE BOOK OF THE DEAD... ALL HERE. THE MOST POWERFUL AND FORBIDDEN BOOKS OF KNOWLEDGE THE WORLD HAS EVER SEEN... WE GOT'EM. NOT ALWAYS A GOOD READ, MIND. ***THE NECRONOMICON*** IS FULL OF A LOT OF HYPE, AND IT SAGS IN THE MIDDLE, BUT IF YOU WANNA DO EVIL, THAT'S THE BOOK FOR YOU. COURSE IT CAUSES ME NO END OF HEADACHES. NO ONE EVER RETURNS IT WILLINGLY. SO THEY GET TO DEAL WITH ME. AND I CAN BE MEAN. ***REAL MEAN.***"

"MY ARSENAL OF KNOWLEDGE INCLUDES ROCKET LAUNCHERS, TRACKING DEVICES, ELECTRO-MAGNETIC FIELD GENERATORS, FREEZE RAYS, AND THE USUAL ASSORTMENT OF AUTOMATIC WEAPONRY YOU'D EXPECT IN YOUR TYPICAL LIBRARY. THERE IS NOWHERE IN THE UNIVERSE THAT IS OUTSIDE MY REACH THANKS TO THE ADMINISTRATOR'S TELEPORTATION CRYSTALS. PEOPLE THINK THEY CAN HIDE FROM ME, BUT WE HAVE ALL OUR BOOKS BUGGED. I CAN TRACK'EM ANYWHERE, ANY PLACE, ANY TIME. WE HAVE THE USUAL PROCEDURE: FIRST A FRIENDLY PHONE CALL. I ASK ***REAL*** NICE FOR THE BOOK TO BE RETURNED...

HELLO? IS THIS PLANET BENZINE FIVE? I'D LIKE TO SPEAK TO SUPREME WARLORD VAGLOX, PLEASE... YES, I'LL HOLD...

NON-FICTION

HELLO? SUPREME WARLORD VAGLOX?

THIS IS MIDDLETON PUBLIC LIBRARY CALLING... YEAH. ***LISTEN,*** PAL, YOU THINK I WOULDN'T FIGURE OUT WHAT PLANET YOU'RE FROM? ***HUH?*** YOU THINK WE EARTHLINGS ARE DUMB? ***THINK AGAIN, BUCKO!*** YOU GOT A COPY OF BERTRAND RUSSELL'S **PRINCIPIA MATHEMATICA** THAT IS **ONE MONTH** OVERDUE NOW. AT TWENTY-FIVE CENTS PER DAY, YOU OWE EXACTLY $7.00. THAT'S ***RIGHT...*** DON'T MAKE ME COME OUT THERE...

"OF COURSE THE PHONE CALL DOESN'T ALWAYS WORK. SOME PEOPLE JUST CAN'T TAKE A HINT, YOU KNOW? BUT THAT'S OKAY. I GET TO TRAVEL TO ALL KINDS OF EXOTIC LOCATIONS WHEN I'M TRACKING DOWN BOOKS. THE AMAZON, NEW YORK CITY, LONDON, EVEN OUTER SPACE. THAT'S BEEN THE BIG ONE LATELY, AND THE LIBRARY ADMINISTRATOR TOOK OUT A PROTECTION POLICY FROM UNIVERSAL MAGIC INSURANCE THAT PROTECTS ME IN VACUUM. IT'S LIKE A LITTLE POCKET, OR BUBBLE, OF ROOM TEMPERATURE AIR AROUND ME, ALONG WITH A MINIATURE SOLAR WIND SHIELD. NO BULKY SPACE SUIT FOR REX! UNFORTUNATELY, WE DON'T HAVE THE BUDGET AT MIDDLETON TO TAKE OUT PROTECTION FROM FIRE, DROWNING, OR BULLETS. WE DO HAVE A POLICY THAT PROTECTS US FROM ZOMBIFICATION THO..."

HEY YOU! ***YEAH, YOU!*** YOU HAVE A COPY OF ***'HOW TO DRAW CARTOONS'*** BY JACK HAMM THAT IS ***THREE*** WEEKS OVERDUE! JUST HAND IT OVER NICE AND SLOW AND WE CAN AVOID ANY ***UNPLEASANTNESS....***
GASP! THE LIBRARIAN!
I THOUGHT I'D BE SAFE UP HERE FROM YOU! I... I HAVE THE BOOK. I DON'T WANT ANY TROUBLE! I'LL GET IT, IT'S IN THE SHUTTLE!
NASA
AND DON'T FORGET THE $5.25 YOU OWE IN FINES!....

"THE GRAPHIC NOVELIZATION YOU HOLD IS BASED ON MY AUTOBIOGRAPHY, *"I, LIBRARIAN"* FROM ASTUTE PRESS. I FELT THAT THE STORY, THE **REAL** STORY, OF THE LIBRARIAN, WAS NOT BEING TOLD. SOCIETY DOESN'T APPRECIATE US LIKE IT SHOULD. THERE ARE TV SHOWS ABOUT COPS, LAWYERS, DOCTORS, SOLDIERS, AND SECRET AGENTS AD INFINITUM. MOVIES AND BOOKS, TOO. BUT NOTHING FOR THE LIBRARIAN. EVEN AFTER I'VE SAVED THE WORLD, OH, ABOUT A DOZEN TIMES OVER--AND THAT'S JUST ***ME!*** THERE ARE HUNDREDS, ***THOUSANDS*** OF LIBRARIES IN NORTH AMERICA, AND ***EACH ONE*** HAS SEVERAL LIBRARIANS. IF THEY'VE SAVED THE WORLD EVEN HALF THE NUMBER OF TIMES I HAVE, WHY, WE MAY HAVE SAVED THE EARTH SOME ***SIX THOUSAND TIMES.*** SURELY THAT IS WORTH AT LEAST ***ONE*** BOOK. SO THAT'S WHY I BROKE THE LIBRARIAN CODE OF SILENCE AND WENT PUBLIC WITH MY LIFE STORY. AS SOON AS IT CAME OUT, I WAS CONTACTED BY A COMICS PUBLISHER, ***HERMENEUTIC PRESS,*** WHO WANTED TO DO A COMIC BOOK SERIES BASED ON MY LIFE...

WOW! THIS IS HOT STUFF! YOU WERE BORN IN ANCIENT ROME! ***FANTASTIC!...*** AND DID YOU REALLY FIGHT OFF A **ZOMBIE INVASION** SINGLE-HANDED?
WELL I ***DID*** HAVE SOME HELP FROM MY ***FRIENDS.***
INCREDIBLE!
JUST DOING MY JOB...
B. BARRY HORST

OUTSTANDING! FABULOUS SOURCE MATERIAL! JUST INCREDIBLE. BEST EVER... OF COURSE WE'RE GOING TO HAVE TO CHANGE SOME THINGS...
EH? WHAT DO YOU MEAN?
SONNY, YOU CAN'T JUST PUT OUT THE SAME OLD SAME OLD! PEOPLE WANT TO SEE SOMETHING ***NEW!*** STORIES WITH A ***TWIST.*** A NEW ANGLE. TAKE YOUR STORY FOR EXAMPLE. ALL THIS SAVING THE WORLD STUFF: IT'S BEEN ***DONE!*** DONE TO ***DEATH*** I TELL YOU.
BUT... IT HAPPENED...

LISTEN KID, WE GOTTA JAZZ IT UP A BIT. ***TRUST*** ME. GIVE YOUR STORY THE HOOK IT NEEDS TO BE A BEST SELLER. LET ME THINK... HMM. OKAY... HOW ABOUT THIS: YOU'RE SAVING THE WORLD, BUT, AND HERE'S THE HOOK: YOU HAVE TO DEAL WITH YOUR OWN HOMO-EROTIC FEELINGS... FOR YOUR ***GREATEST ENEMY!***

WHAT THE? HEY, LOOK, I'M NOT GAY...-- *NOT THAT THERE'S ANYTHING WRONG WITH THAT.*
BUT REALLY, THROWING IN A HACKNEYED LOVE STORY ***DOESN'T*** MAKE IT NEW!! PEOPLE BEEN TELLING THE SAME KIND OF STORIES, BASED ON LOVE, REVENGE, SEX, WAR, JEALOUSY, AND SO ON FOR *THOUSANDS AND THOUSANDS OF YEARS!*

YOU'RE RIGHT. THE GAY ANGLE HAS BEEN DONE. THOSE ***ROMANS!*** AND THE SPARTANS! ***WAIT!*** I'VE GOT IT. WE MAKE YOU A COMPULSIVE SEX MANIAC WITH A DRUG ADDICTION AND... AND WE MAKE YOU AUTISTIC! ***ANYTHING*** WITH AUTISM IS A ***BIG HIT!*** IF WE CAN ONLY WORK IN SOME KIND OF TERMINAL ILLNESS...

HMMM...

CAN I HAVE SUPER POWERS?

SUPER POWERS! BRILLIANT! SURE! SUPER POWERS ARE HOT HOT HOT! I SMELL A MOVIE FRANCHISE HERE! ANOTHER CHANCE TO PROMOTE COMICS. YOU SEE...

COMICS AND CINEMA HAVE BEEN IN COMPETITION FOR AGES. BUT THEY HAVE A WEAKNESS FOR SUPER POWER STUFF. IT'S REAL VISUAL, YOU KNOW? IT'S ONLY NATURAL WE DOMINATE THEIR MEDIUM!

YOU'LL NEED A SECRET LAIR OF COURSE... AND A SIDE-KICK. EVERY SUPERHERO NEEDS TO HAVE ONE OF THOSE TO BOUNCE DIALOGUE OFF OF. JUST NEED A NAME... BINGO? BUCKO? BYRON?

UMMM...
HAVE YOU, AH, HAD A LOT OF COFFEE TODAY, BARRY?

8 CUPS, I THINK.

I'VE GOT IT! WE GIVE YOU A SIDEKICK WHO'S A FROG. EXCEPT HE USED TO BE A PRINCE?HE'S BEEN TRANS-FORMED INTO AN AMPHIBIAN BY AN EVIL SPELL!

AND I HAVE JUST THE RIGHT TWIST FOR THE LOVE INTEREST! OKAY, IMAGINE THIS: WE MAKE HER A MAN HATING LESBIAN AT A RIVAL LIBRARY! HUH? ADDS A PROFESSIONAL TENSION, ALONG WITH PERPETUAL, UNREQUITED PASSION, HEIGHTENED BY A KIND OF MUTUAL ANIMOSITY! WHAT DO YOU THINK? IT'S GOLD!

GOOD GRIEF! UH... WELL MR HORST, IT'S ALL STARTING TO SOUND LIKE SOMETHING OUT OF GREEK MYTHOLOGY. WHY NOT JUST HAVE ME MARRIED TO THEODORA, OR EMPRESS WU?

WU? THE ONE WHO MADE HER PALACE OF DELIGHT DIVINE? FANTASTIC THINK-ING, REX! ABSOLUTE DYNA-MITE! YOU'RE A NATURAL!

UH, THANKS, BUT UH, I THINK I'VE HEARD OF THAT 'PRINCE-TURNED-INTO-A-FROG' THING BEFORE, TOO. AND SINCE YOU ARE REAL BIG ON DOING NEW STUFF... MAYBE...

REX, REX, **REX!** GET WITH THE PROGRAM, FELLA! OF **COURSE** YOU'VE HEARD OF THAT BEFORE! COME ON! THERE IS NO **'NEW.'** DO YOU SEE NEW COKE ANYMORE? **NO!** NEW IS A FOOL'S ERRAND, MY FRIEND!
BUT YOU JUST SAID...
LISTEN REX: ALL WE DO IS PUT OLD STUFF TOGETHER IN NEW WAYS. CREATIVITY IS INCREMENTAL, MY BOY! LET ME TELL YOU A STORY...
ONCE UPON A TIME, THERE WERE TWO BRICKLAYERS, OKAY? IMAGINE THESE TWO GUYS...
BROTHERS. **NOW.** THE TWO OF THEM HAVE A PILE OF BRICKS EACH, AND THEY CAN BUILD WHATEVER THEY WANT.
THE FIRST ONE STARTS TO LAY BRICKS. THE SECOND BROTHER *JUST* STANDS THERE AND WATCHES WHILE THIS GOES ON.
FINALLY HE SAYS, *"THAT'S HOW EVERYONE ELSE LAYS BRICKS! HOW ABOUT SOME ORIGINALITY? SOME* ***INNOVATION?"***
THE FIRST BROTHER IGNORES HIM AND KEEPS BUILDING. HE PUTS UP LAYER AFTER LAYER OF BRICKS.
EVENTUALLY, A STRUCTURE STARTS TO TAKE SHAPE. PEOPLE GATHER ROUND. THEY ***GAWK!*** *WHY?* BECAUSE EVEN THOUGH THE ELEMENTS OF THE BUILDING ARE OLD, THE SUM OF THE PARTS IS ***NEW,*** INNOVATIVE, EXCITING, ***FRESH.*** SEE?
YEAH, SURE. I SUPPOSE THE OTHER FELLA NEVER GOT ANYTHIN' DONE.
NO, NOT A BLESSED THING, MY BOY! YOU SEE? TO BUILD YOU HAVE TO USE WHAT HAS GONE BEFORE, OR YOU GO NOWHERE. THE SUM IS GREATER THAN THE PARTS. FROM ORDINARY BRICKS, YOU CAN BUILD AN ***ARCHITECTURAL MASTERPIECE!*** BUT YOU HAVE TO USE THE INNOVATIONS OF THE PAST TO BUILD THE FUTURE. WELL. SORT OF.... NO STORY IS PERFECT, SON!

"MY STORY BEGAN OVER TWO THOUSAND YEARS AGO. FRESH FROM SCRIBE SCHOOL, I MOVED FROM ROME TO ALEXANDRIA, WHERE I OBTAINED ONE OF THE ONE HUNDRED COVETED POSITIONS AT THE GOOD OLD **MEGALE BIBLIOTHEKE,** THE **GREAT LIBRARY OF ALEXANDRIA.** I BECAME THE ASSISTANT OF CALLIMACHUS, ONE OF THE SHARPEST LIBRARIANS IN ALL OF HISTORY, AND HELPED HIM PUT TOGETHER THE ***PINAKES,*** THE LIBRARY GUIDE. STILL HAVE A COPY OF THAT SOMEWHERE. AND IT WAS AT ALEXANDRIA THAT I FIRST DISCOVERED LOVE-- THE YOUNG AND LOVELY ***HYPATIA,*** THE LAST HEAD LIBRARIAN, DAUGHTER OF THE FAMED MATHEMATICIAN... WHATSHISNAME. ***THEON.*** ANYWAY, I WAS LOOKING AT A COPY OF EUDOXOS' ***"DIALOGUE OF DOGS"*** WHEN I SAW HER WITH A COPY OF ***HIPPOCRATES' MEDICAL CORPUS.*** I WAS INSTANTLY SMITTEN. SHE COULD TALK ***NEOPLATONIST PHILOSOPHY*** LIKE NO OTHER. IT MADE ME **HOT.** *REAL* **HOT.** SHE WAS THE IDEAL MADE REAL. SHE WAS ALSO AN ASTRONOMER, KNEW ALL THE STARS. SHE WAS TRULY A CREATURE OF THE ***HEAVENS.*** WE BEGAN A TORRID LOVE AFFAIR, AND EVENTUALLY, IN THE GREEK FASHION OF RELATIONSHIP PERFIDY, TRICKED HER BORING HUSBAND ***SYNESIUS*** INTO MOVING TO HERCULANEUM. HEY, AT LEAST WE DIDN'T CHOP HIM UP AND FEED HIM TO THE SHARKS AS WAS FASHION AT THE TIME.

<HI HYPATIA!>
<OH HELLO, UH... ER... FELLOW LIBRARIAN...!>

"THEN TRAGEDY STRUCK ALL AT ONCE. HYPATIA WAS KIND OF STRONG WILLED AND OUTSPOKEN IN A TOUCHY AGE. SHE GOT ON THE WRONG SIDE OF ***ST. CYRIL,*** A REAL IDEOLOGUE. YA GOTTA UNDERSTAND THE CONTEXT. THE CHRISTIANS WERE FIGHTIN' FOR CONTROL OF THE CITY, AND DIDN'T LIKE WHAT CLASSICAL KNOWLEDGE HAD TO SAY. ***HYPATIA*** WAS IN THEIR WAY. SO ***CYRIL*** GETS THIS TWERP ***PETER THE CLERK*** TO ROUND UP A MOB. THEY GRAB HYPATIA, STRIP HER, STONE HER, AND THEN TEAR HER APART. AFTER THAT, THE MOB MOVED ON TO THE LIBRARY AND BURNED IT TO THE GROUND, BUTCHERING *NINETY-NINE LIBRARIANS* IN THE PROCESS. I WAS THE ***ONLY*** SURVIVOR...."

CRACKLECRACKLEPOPRRRRRRRRRCACKLERRRCRACKLERRRRRPOP!

VESANUM!

MUHAHAHA!

<***NOOOO! YOU BASTARDS!*** YOU HAVE DESTROYED EVERYTHING I HAVE EVER LOVED! ***I'LL GET YOU!***>

<I WILL DEDICATE MY LIFE, TO THE ***ERRADICATION*** FROM THE FACE OF THE EARTH OF YOUR DNA CODE, YOUR CHROMOSOME STRANDS, YOUR INDIVIDUAL GENES, UNTIL ***NOT ONE*** SINGLE, SOLITARY STRING OF GENETIC MATERIAL FROM YOUR NUMBERS REMAINS ON THIS GREEN EARTH, YOU... YOU... YOU DIRTY ***BARBARIANS! DIRTY, DAMN BARBARIANS!***>

"MY PLANS FOR REVENGE DIDN'T WORK OUT AT THE TIME, AS I HAD NO COMBAT SKILLS. BEFORE LONG THE ENTIRE ROMAN EMPIRE HAD FALLEN INTO RUINS. IN THE AFTERMATH OF THESE CUMULATIVE CATASTROPHES, IN BOTH THE PRIVATE AND THE PUBLIC REALMS, I ALMOST GAVE IN TO DESPAIR, EXISTENTIAL ANGST, AND ENNUI..."

<WHY? DAMN THE GODS! HYPATIA WOULDN'T HURT A FLY! SHE'D JUST GET SOMEONE ELSE TO DO IT. NOW SHE IS DEAD! ALL BECAUSE OF THOSE RELIGIOUS ZEALOTS! DAMN THIS END-LESS CYCLE OF VIOLENCE! OH BY THE THUMB OF JUPITER, WHY CAN'T WE JUST GET ALONG? WHY!?>

<WHY?!?>

"IT WAS THEN THAT THE ONE WHO BECAME THE LIBRARY ADMINISTRATOR TOOK ME UNDER HIS WING. I STUDIED SORCERY, SCIENCE, BOTANY, AND THE COMBAT ARTS; I BECAME THE ADMINISTRATOR'S RIGHT HAND MAN..."

<THAT BOOK IS NEEDED FOR THE NEW GREAT LIBRARY, BUCKO! ***HAND IT OVER!***>

<AND THE LITTLE KID TOO: THAT COLOURING BOOK IS ***CONFISCATED!***>

"WE BUILT AN ***UNDERGROUND LIBRARY,*** AND SLOWLY ASSEMBLED A FABULOUS COLLECTION OF TEXTS. I VOWED THAT NEVER AGAIN WOULD THE BOOKS UNDER MY PROTECTION BE DESTROYED BY THE ***IGNORANT.***"

"OUR METHODS AND ETHICS WERE CRUDE, AS BEFIT THE TIME, BUT OUR GOAL WAS JUST. CIVILIZATION IS KNOWLEDGE, EVEN MORE THAN IT IS URBANIZATION, FOR YOU CANNOT HAVE THE LATTER WITHOUT THE FORMER. EVERYTHING BUILDS ON EVERYTHING ELSE. AND THE KNOWLEDGE OF CIVILIZATION IS KEPT IN REPOSITORIES KNOWN AS... ***LIBRARIES,*** AND IF BOOKS BURN, CIVILIZATION BURNS WITH THEM. SO YOU SEE, OUR TASK WAS OF VITAL IMPORTANCE TO THE WORLD! DURING THE RENAISSANCE, WE SET UP A LIBRARY IN THE OPEN ONCE MORE, THIS TIME IN **SALAMANCA.** WE'VE BEEN MOVING ABOUT EVER SINCE, ESTABLISHING NEW LIBRARIES, BRINGING NEW BLOOD INTO THE SACRED ORDER OF THE LIBRARY. AND I HAVE PERSONALLY CRISS-CROSSED THE GLOBE IN SEARCH OF RARE TEXTS, HIDDEN KNOWLEDGE, AND LOST WORLDS THAT MIGHT HAVE LOST BOOKS, AT THE BEHEST OF THE ADMINISTRATOR... WHO PREFERS TO KEEP HIS IDENTITY SECRET AND WORK FROM BEHIND THE SCENES FOR REASONS THAT WILL EVENTUALLY BECOME CLEAR...."

GASP!
HUFF!
<SHANGRI-LA SHOULD BE JUST... AFTER THE... NEXT RIDGE... I'M JUST IN TIME FOR THE BOOK SALE...!>

SPEAKING OF IDENTITY, I COULD NEVER CONVINCE BARRY THAT I WAS OVER TWO THOUSAND YEARS OLD, AND USED TO LIVE IN 'ANCIENT' ROME. HE SAID I DON'T HAVE THE KIND OF ACCENT, OR EVEN THE MANNERS, HE'D EXPECT OF A CITIZEN FROM ANTIQUITY. HAW! FUNNY. FIRST, HE OVERESTIMATES THE CITIZENS OF ANTIQUITY. NOTHING WE LIKED MORE THAN PUTTING PICTURES AND STATUES OF BIG GENTITALIA ALL OVER THE PLACE. USED TO HAVE IMAGES OF PENISES AT EVERY STREET CORNER. COURSE THE VATICAN HAS COVERED ALL OF THIS UP. BUT I REMEMBER! SECOND, I BEEN THROUGH THE LIBRARY ADMINISTRATOR'S CULTURAL TRANSMORGIFIER SEVERAL TIMES OVER THE YEARS. IT IMPRINTS A SET OF MODERN CULTURAL IDIOMS AND MANNERS DIRECTLY ONTO THE CEREBRAL CORTEX USING AN ENGRAM STAMP; HELPS YOU FIT IN AND ACT LIKE A NATIVE, SWEAR WORDS AND ALL. ONLY WORKS IF YOU HAVE THE RIGHT CULTURE SETTINGS ON THE MACHINE. I SET IT WRONG ONCE AND WOUND UP SPEAKING GREEK TO THE CREE. THEY DIDN'T GET ANY OF MY FORUM JOKES EITHER. THAT MADE ME ***MAD. REAL MAD.***"

THE SYBIL VII CULTURAL TRANSMORGIFIER AT WORK:
BZT!
FUTUE TE IPSUM!
GO ZUCK YOURSELF!
PRE
INITIATING CULTURAL TRANSMORGIFICATION
POST
CULTURAL TRANSMORGIFICATION PROCESS COMPLETE

"BUT ENOUGH OF THIS MEANDERING INTERLUDE... I RETURN YOU NOW TO THE STORY..."
REX MARCHES PURPOSEFULLY TOWARDS THE BACK OF THE LIBRARY, THROUGH A LABYRINTH OF BOOKCASES THAT CAN ONLY BE NAVIGATED SUCCESSFULLY BY FOLLOWING THE STRATEGICALLY PLACED GUIDE OF CUNEIFORM NOTCHES IN THE HARD BOOKCASE WOOD. WITHOUT THEM, AN ORDINARY MORTAL WOULD BECOME HOPELESSLY LOST AND STARVE TO DEATH BEFORE REACHING THE DIABOLICALLY HIDDEN 'EMPLOYEES ONLY' DOOR....
EMPLOYEES

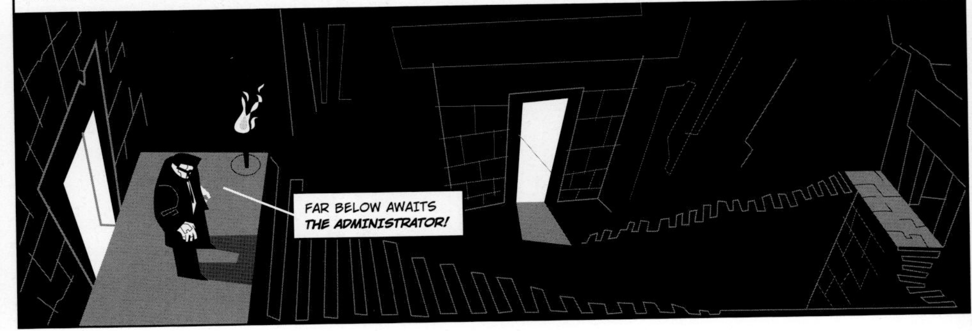

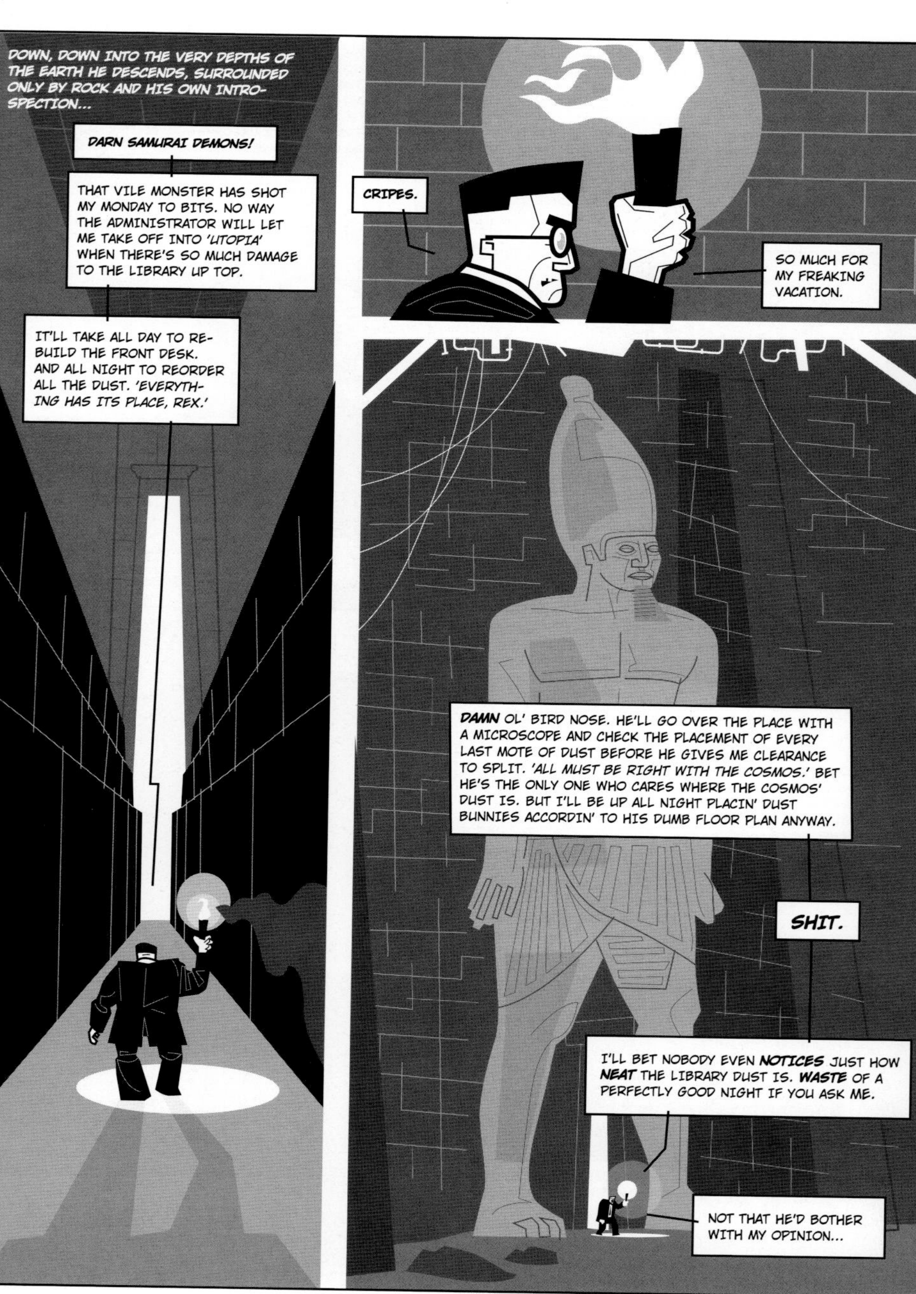
DOWN, DOWN INTO THE VERY DEPTHS OF THE EARTH HE DESCENDS, SURROUNDED ONLY BY ROCK AND HIS OWN INTRO-SPECTION...
DARN SAMURAI DEMONS!
THAT VILE MONSTER HAS SHOT MY MONDAY TO BITS. NO WAY THE ADMINISTRATOR WILL LET ME TAKE OFF INTO 'UTOPIA' WHEN THERE'S SO MUCH DAMAGE TO THE LIBRARY UP TOP.
IT'LL TAKE ALL DAY TO RE-BUILD THE FRONT DESK. AND ALL NIGHT TO REORDER ALL THE DUST. 'EVERYTH-ING HAS ITS PLACE, REX.'
CRIPES.
SO MUCH FOR MY FREAKING VACATION.
DAMN OL' BIRD NOSE. HE'LL GO OVER THE PLACE WITH A MICROSCOPE AND CHECK THE PLACEMENT OF EVERY LAST MOTE OF DUST BEFORE HE GIVES ME CLEARANCE TO SPLIT. 'ALL MUST BE RIGHT WITH THE COSMOS.' BET HE'S THE ONLY ONE WHO CARES WHERE THE COSMOS' DUST IS. BUT I'LL BE UP ALL NIGHT PLACIN' DUST BUNNIES ACCORDIN' TO HIS DUMB FLOOR PLAN ANYWAY.
SHIT.
I'LL BET NOBODY EVEN NOTICES JUST HOW NEAT THE LIBRARY DUST IS. WASTE OF A PERFECTLY GOOD NIGHT IF YOU ASK ME.
NOT THAT HE'D BOTHER WITH MY OPINION...

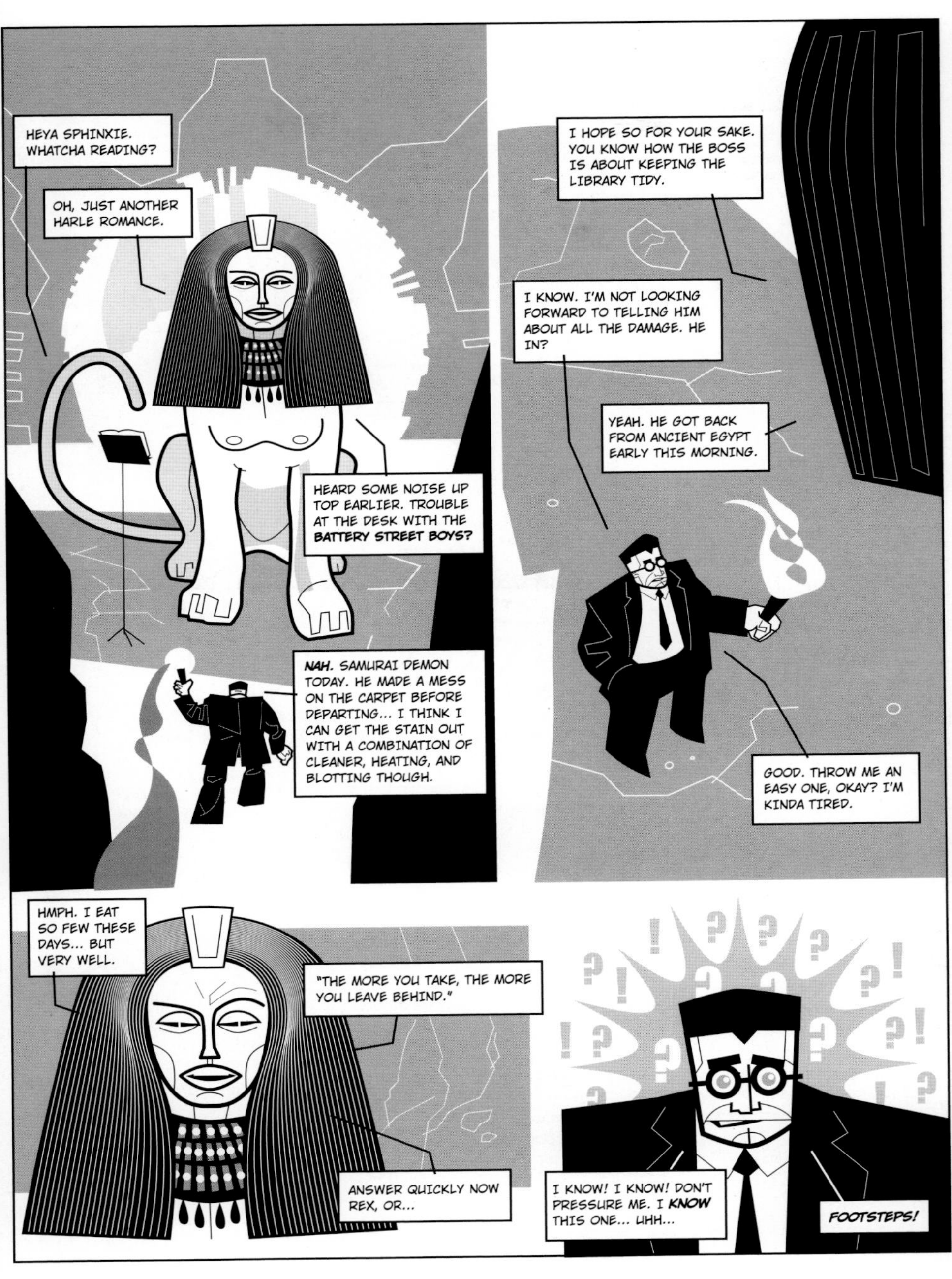
HEYA SPHINXIE. WHATCHA READING?
OH, JUST ANOTHER HARLE ROMANCE.
HEARD SOME NOISE UP TOP EARLIER. TROUBLE AT THE DESK WITH THE **BATTERY STREET BOYS?**
NAH. SAMURAI DEMON TODAY. HE MADE A MESS ON THE CARPET BEFORE DEPARTING... I THINK I CAN GET THE STAIN OUT WITH A COMBINATION OF CLEANER, HEATING, AND BLOTTING THOUGH.
I HOPE SO FOR YOUR SAKE. YOU KNOW HOW THE BOSS IS ABOUT KEEPING THE LIBRARY TIDY.
I KNOW. I'M NOT LOOKING FORWARD TO TELLING HIM ABOUT ALL THE DAMAGE. HE IN?
YEAH. HE GOT BACK FROM ANCIENT EGYPT EARLY THIS MORNING.
GOOD. THROW ME AN EASY ONE, OKAY? I'M KINDA TIRED.
HMPH. I EAT SO FEW THESE DAYS... BUT VERY WELL.
"THE MORE YOU TAKE, THE MORE YOU LEAVE BEHIND."
ANSWER QUICKLY NOW REX, OR...
I KNOW! I KNOW! DON'T PRESSURE ME. I ***KNOW*** THIS ONE... UHH...
FOOTSTEPS!

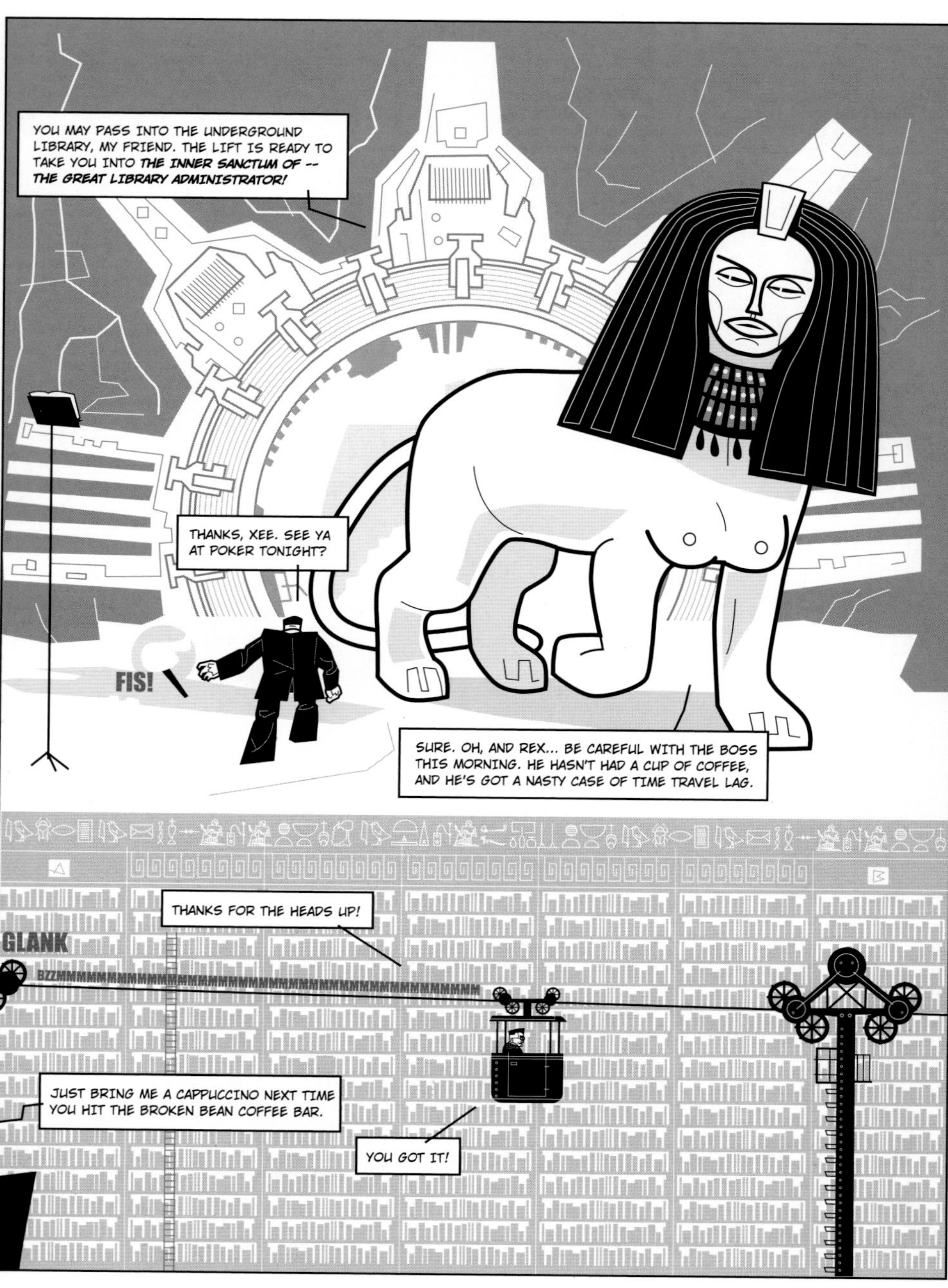
YOU MAY PASS INTO THE UNDERGROUND LIBRARY, MY FRIEND. THE LIFT IS READY TO TAKE YOU INTO THE INNER SANCTUM OF -- THE GREAT LIBRARY ADMINISTRATOR!
THANKS, XEE. SEE YA AT POKER TONIGHT?
FIS!
SURE. OH, AND REX... BE CAREFUL WITH THE BOSS THIS MORNING. HE HASN'T HAD A CUP OF COFFEE, AND HE'S GOT A NASTY CASE OF TIME TRAVEL LAG.
THANKS FOR THE HEADS UP!
GLANK
BZZMMMMMMMMMMMMMMMMMMMMMMMMMMMMMMMMMMMMMMMMMMM
JUST BRING ME A CAPPUCCINO NEXT TIME YOU HIT THE BROKEN BEAN COFFEE BAR.
YOU GOT IT!

GOTTA THINK NOW...
HOW TO BREAK IT TO HIM? I COULD PUT IT OFF. BUT... IT'LL JUST BUG ME, SCRAPE AT THE BACK OF MY MIND LIKE A CHEESE GRATER, UNTIL I DO TELL HIM. ACK. I'LL TELL HIM POINT BLANK.
JUST GET IT OVER WITH...
*!
DANG!
I SHOULDA SOFTENED HIM UP BY BRINGING HIM A LOW FAT LATTE. FRIG! TOO LATE TO GO ALL THE WAY BACK UP NOW THOUGH...
THIS IS IT!
HEYA MR. THOTH! HOW WAS YOUR TRIP?
AH... HETEPSESH! REX. EGYPT WAS...KHUT NUH NEFER WEBET. IT WAS OK. HOT. RATHER SMELLY IN THE CITY. THOTH HAD FORGOTTEN THE BAD SANITATION. THE MIGHTY WESIR WAS IN GOOD HEALTH, THO SADLY THE FOREHEAD FROM WHICH THOTH SPRANG IS STILL HOSTAGE TO THE FORCES OF DARKNESS. BUT ENOUGH OF THE FAMILY ISSUES OF THOTH...

THOTH HAS HEARD OF WHAT REX IS UP TO. THOTH IS *CONCERNED.*

YOU HAVE SIGNED A PUBLISHING DEAL WITH A COMIC BOOK COMPANY. YOUR ONTOGENY WILL BE USED AS FODDER FOR THEIR NARRATIVE. LOYAL **HETEPSESH,** THOTH DOES NOT OBJECT TO POSITIVE COVERAGE OF THE **NOBLE** LIBRARIAN...

BUT ***COMICS?*** THOTH HAS HIS CONCERNS. HEAR THE WORDS OF **MIGHTY THOTH:**

LIBRARIANS HAVE BEEN A RESPECTED CASTE FOR MANY ***THOUSANDS*** OF YEARS, AND HAVE AN CULTIVATED AN ERUDITE PUBLIC IMAGE **WORTH** PROTECTING. THOTH THEREFORE ***FORBIDS*** YOU FROM WEARING A HOOD AND CAPE IN THE LIBRARY! SUCH GARB WOULD **DIMINISH** THE SANCTITY OF THE ***CELESTIAL SCRIPTORIM!***

BOSS! YOU GOT IT ALL WRONG! IT'D BE A BIG BOOST FOR THE LIBRARY. IT'D BE LIKE, PROMOTIONAL, MAKIN' A NEW IMAGE

AHT! THOTH HAS DECIDED. NO TIGHTS. NO SPANDEX. YOU WILL CONTINUE TO WEAR A SUIT AND TIE. NO GETTING CONTACTS, EITHER... I FIND GLASSES GIVE MORTALS AN INTELLECTUAL AIR. THAT BEING SAID, YOU MAY PARTICIPATE SO LONG AS YOU MAKE MIGHTY THOTH LOOK GOOD AND ARE NOT A 'SUPERHERO.' THE GENRE IS ENTIRELY OVERDONE, UNWORTHY OF A SERVANT OF THE GOD WHO CREATED WRITING. RUSSIAN TRAGEDY WOULD BE A BETTER GENRE.
NOW... GET THOTH A RASPBERRY CHOCOLATE LATTE WITH THE CREAM AND CHOCOLATE SPRINKLES. THOTH COMMANDS, LIBRARIAN! OBEY! SPRINKLES! THOTH HAS SPOKEN!

AW, BUT BOSS, I ALWAYS WANTED TO BE A SUPERHERO, HAVE SUPERPOWERS, MAYBE A UTILITY BELT...

BAH!
YOU AND EVERY OTHER MORTAL ADOLESCENT SINCE THAT HOT HEADED HERCULES PUNK. "I WANNA BE HERCULES!", "NO, I WANNA BE HERCULES. YOU CAN BE THE HYDRA!"
ENOUGH!
THE GENRE IS BURNT LIKE A NAKED MAN IN THE SAHARA AT NOON. SUPERPOWERS ARE FOR GODS AND THEIR CHILDREN, HETEPSESH, NOT LIBRARIANS.
THOTH HIMSELF USED TO BE A GOD... UNTIL THE UNGRATEFUL EGYPTIANS DUMPED THOTH AND THE REST OF THE PANTHEON AND THREW THE LOT OF US OUT, ALL FOR YAHWEH'S SKINNY CARPENTER KID. HUMBUG!

AND WHO WAS HE? A LOWLY PEASANT! NO EXPERIENCE BEING A GOD. NO HISTORY OF MIRACLES. NO TEMPLES. HE DIDN'T EVEN BELONG TO THE LOCAL GOD UNION! NO CREDENTIALS FOR BEING WORSHIPPED. NONE! AND NO YAHWEH LISTED ON THE BIRTH CERTIFICATE, EITHER. AND WHAT OF THOTH? THOTH HAD A RESUME SEVERAL THOUSAND YEARS LONG. THOTH INVENTED WRITING! ATTENDED THE CROSSING OVER OF THE DEAD CEREMONY FOR MILLENNIA, THE WHOLE BIT. AND THEY DUMP THOTH, WITHOUT SO MUCH AS A THANK YOU, FOR A DIFFERENT GOD FRANCHISE!
JUST WHAT IS AN OUT OF WORK GOD SUPPOSED TO DO, ASKS THOTH? THE JOB POSITION DOES NOT COME UP VERY OFTEN. IT ISN'T, "OH, WE NEED A GOD FOR DAIRY GROCER. CAN GREAT THOTH START WEDNESDAY?" NOT EVEN BIG BOOKSTORES CHAINS WANT THOTH TO BE THEIR GOD. THE FOOLS!
STUPID MONOTHEISM! IT PUT MORE HARD WORKING GODS OUT OF WORK THAN ANY OTHER EVENT IN HISTORY! EVEN THE FLOOD! THE ONLY JOBS LEFT ARE IN INDIA, AND THEY HAVEN'T HIRED A NEW GOD IN HUNDREDS OF YEARS!
AND THERE IS NO CHANCE OF BREAKING INTO THE BIG THREE... THEY ARE LOCKED DOWN TIGHT. NO ADDING THOTH TO THE TRINITY. NO ROOM FOR THOTH IN THE DANG MANGER, OH NOOOO. THOTH IS TOO "OLD SCHOOL."
THOTH IS TOO "PAGAN." FEH. THE BIG THREE ARE ALL IN CAHOOTS ANYWAY. SURE, THOTH GRANTS YOU THERE ARE SOME SUPERFICIAL DIFFERENCES, BUT DON'T TELL THOTH THAT THEY AREN'T ALL OWNED, IN THE END, BY THE SAME GOD. IT'S A GOD MONOPOLY!
UH-OH. HE'S STARTING TO GET STEAMED. HE ALWAYS GETS LIKE THIS AFTER HE GOES BACK TO ANCIENT EGYPT. GOTTA DERAIL...
OH SILVER ATEN, STRAIGHT AND TRUE, WOULD YOU LIKE A MUFFIN WITH YOUR LATTE?
WHAT?
YES... YES A MUFFIN. BUT WHAT KIND?
...BLUEBERRY. THOTH SHALL HAVE A MUFFIN, AND IT SHALL BE BLUEBERRY!
SO THOTH COMMANDS!
YOU GOT IT, BOSS!
WAIT!
THOTH ALMOST FORGOT...

ONE OTHER THING: DO YOU REMEMBER SUPREME WARLORD VAGLOX FROM PLANET BENZINE FIVE?
YEAH. HE BORROWED A COPY OF BERTRAND RUSSELL'S PRINCIPIA MATHEMATICA. WHY?
WELL HE HASN'T RETURNED IT.
WHY DAT BUM...!
INDEED. IT IS TIME FOR YOU TO PAY HIM A NOT SO FRIENDLY VISIT, REX LIBRIS.
YOU GOT IT BOSS. I'LL GET THE BOOK BACK AN' GIVE HIM A FEW LUMPS FOR GOOD MEASURE. HE WON'T FORGET AGAIN.
EXCELLENT. I EXPECT NO LESS... BUT YOU WILL HAVE TO BE CAREFUL, FOR VAGLOX IS A POWERFUL WARLORD. TAKE A BOOK WITH A FULL ARSENAL OF WEAPONS. THOTH UNDERSTANDS THE MENTALITY OF WAR-LORDS: HE WILL FIGHT WITH EVERY MEANS AT HIS DISPOSAL. IF YOU MUST, KILL HIM, BUT GET THAT BOOK BACK IN ONE PIECE.
NOW... HERE. TAKE THIS TRAVEL CRYSTAL. IT FALLS A WEE BIT SHORT OF BENZINE FIVE, BUT WILL GET YOU WITHIN 5,000 KILOMETRES OF THE PLANET SURFACE, WITHIN THE MAGNETOSPHERE. ACTIVATE IT IN EXACTLY TWENTY HOURS TIME AT AN ANGLE OF 45 DEGREES TO YOUR PERSON-AL KARMA CRYSTAL, AND YOU WILL LAND ON A SMOOGONIAN SPACE FREIGHTER. IT IS NOT GOING TO BENZINE FIVE, BUT WILL PASS CLOSE TO IT. YOU CAN JUMP FROM THERE. ANY QUESTIONS?
AH, BOSS, NO DISRESPECT OR NUTHIN, BUT JUMPING FROM ORBIT... ISN'T THAT AKIN TO, LIKE, SUICIDE?
NOT TO WORRY. THE PLANET HAS A VERY LOW GRAVITATIONAL FIELD--
I DUNNO BOSS--
ENOUGH! YOU MUST TRUST THOTH! AS FOR GETTING BACK, WELL NOW. THAT... IS A TRICK-IER PROBLEM. THOTH IS SURE YOU WILL FIGURE SOMETHING OUT.
OH YES... ONE LAST THING... THOTH FELT A DISTURBANCE IN THE DUST EARLIER. SOMETHING MUST HAVE HAPPEN-ED IN THE LIBRARY. YOU MUST TELL THOTH WHAT WENT ON WHEN YOU RETURN, REPAIR ANY DAMAGE TO LIBRARY PROPERTY, AND REFORMAT THE DUST. THE COSMOS MUST BE ORDERED, DUST AND ALL, OR THE FORCES OF CHAOS, ANARCHY, AND DECAY WILL REIGN SUPREME! SETH, AND HIS FOREHEAD, MY FATHER, WILL RETURN, AND THE EARTH WILL BE CLOAKED IN DARKNESS AND DEATH.
NOW... GO!
NEXT ISSUE: THIS LABYRINTH OF LITERATURE

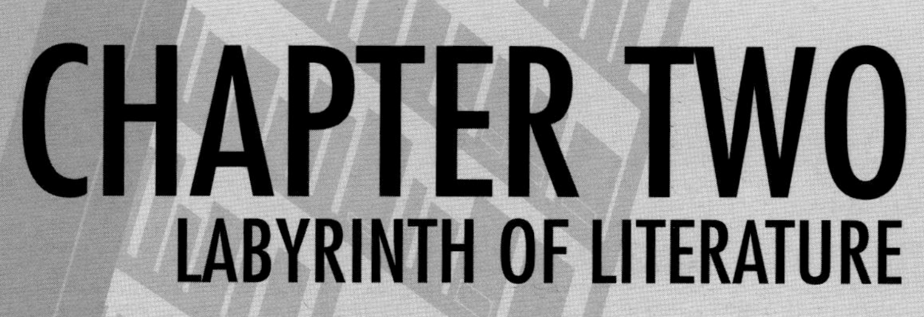

CHAPTER TWO
LABYRINTH OF LITERATURE

Welcome back, faithful readers. We've had some unbelievable feedback on the first issue of Rex Libris! At least, I hope we will. As I write this, the first issue has yet to go to print, so I really have no idea what people will think. But I have a column to write, and I'm not about to let the limitations of my place in the flow of time stand in my way!

So I hired a psychic to look into the future to see how people reacted to the first issue. Sure, I could have had her look at winning lottery numbers, or stock market prices, but then, what would I write about in this column? Exactly. I'd be on a beach in Cuba enjoying my lottery winnings, and Rex would be up crap creek. I just can't do that to the guy.

Unfortunately, the psychic reading turned out to be a bit of a bust. She didn't reach the future. Instead, she contacted the dead. Turns out she's a specialist in talking to people from the great beyond. Fat lot of good that does us. Who cares what some long dead putz thinks about Rex Libris? He isn't likely to pop out to a shop and buy it, is he? Half of the spirits she contacted don't even read modern english, so from them all we got feedback on was the pictures. Fortunately, the psychic understands many languages so she was able to do some translating. Something got a bunch of dead Sumerians riled up real bad on page 24, but it seems we'll never know what it was that set them off, as sadly nobody speaks ancient Sumerian these days. The Aztecs Atlxochitl and Acamapichtli liked the contrast between black and white, but felt the whole thing just wasn't decorative enough. Axayacatl didn't like the grey tones and Tixoc didn't think there was enough graphic violence or heart plucking. Now, I don't mean to knock the aesthetic sensibilities of the Aztecs, as I love their visual style, but come on. Dead Aztec warriors and priests are just not part of the demographic we're trying to reach.

We did get a few interesting comments from Petrarch, and Murasaki Shikibu (creator of the first novel back around 1000 AD) had a few things to say, but sadly no one understood a word of it. If only I'd tape recorded her comments for later translation. That's hindsight for you.

The most common complaint we got was that the comic is overpriced. Well ***of course*** it would seem that way to someone who's been ***dead for two hundred (or more) years.*** Haven't these spirits ever heard of inflation? Yet another reason not to market to dead people.

It wasn't all bad. The Egyptian Zoser corrected a few mistakes we made with the Hiero-glyphics. We're going to use him as a freelance translator for the ancient Egyptian in upcoming issues. I just hope he knows his grammar better than I know mine. That's it for my brain tissue this issue. See you next time!

Yours,

B. Barry Horst

B. Barry Horst

WELCOME ONCE AGAIN, FAITHFUL READERS, TO THE TUMULTUOUS TALE OF LIBRARIAN ***REX LIBRIS*** AND HIS UNENDING BATTLE AGAINST THE FORCES OF IGNORANT **EVIL.** BORN IN ANCIENT GREECE, HE HAS WORKED TO PRESERVE KNOWLEDGE AND WISDOM FOR THOUSANDS OF YEARS AGAINST **ALL** FORMS OF PERFIDY, FROM **BOOK-BASHING BOOGEYMEN** TO **MOANING UNDEAD LEGIONS** WHO IGNORE THE ***"QUIET PLEASE"*** SIGN. NOT EVEN SUPERPOWERED DELINQUENT ALIEN CHILDREN CAN ABSCOND WITH BOOKS WITHOUT SIGNING THEM OUT? WHILE REX IS ON THE JOB. FOR THE FIRST TIME, THE **SECRET** WORLD OF LIBRARIANS AND THEIR DAILY STRUGGLE TO PROTECT CIVILIZATION AND THE VERY KNOWLEDGE IT IS FOUNDED UPON IS ***REVEALED!*** FOR THIS IS THE WORLD OF?

REX · LIBRIS

"LABYRINTH OF LITERATURE"

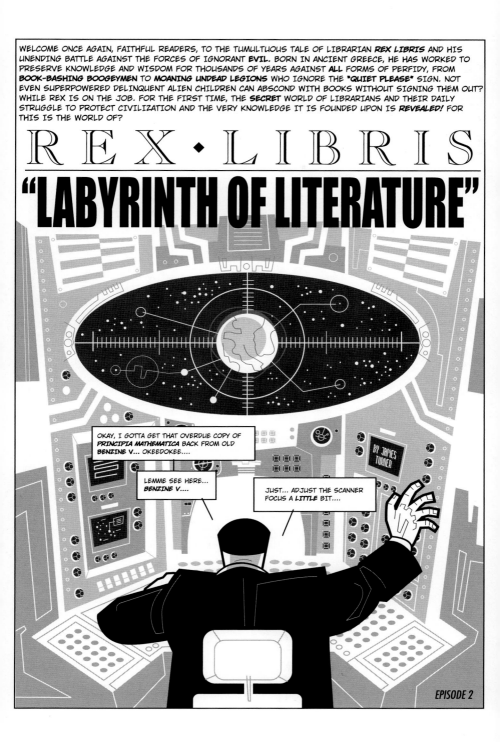

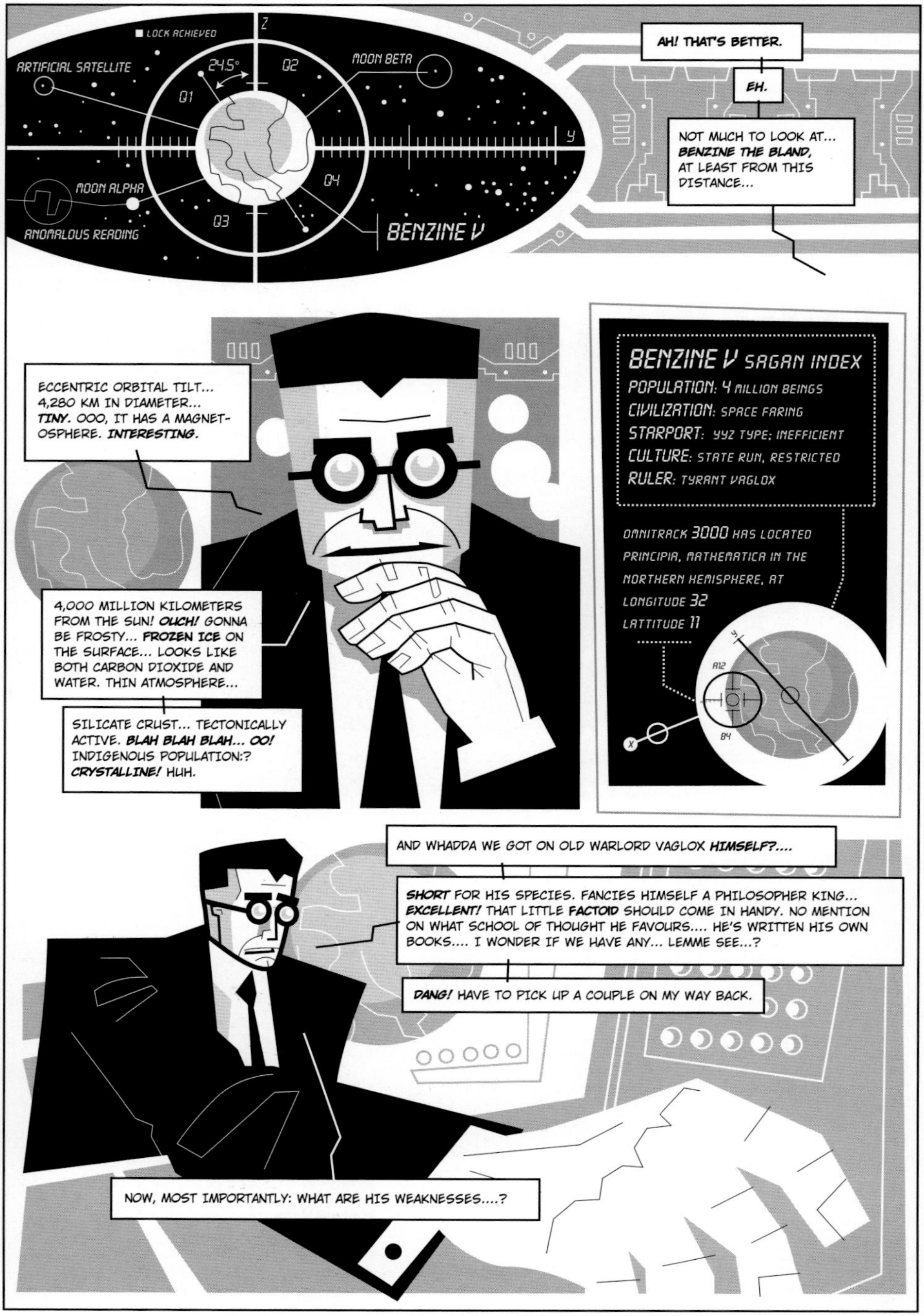

LOCK ACHIEVED
ARTIFICIAL SATELLITE
24.5°
Q1
Q2
MOON BETA
Q3
Q4
MOON ALPHA
ANOMALOUS READING
BENZINE V
Z
Y

AH! THAT'S BETTER.

EH.

NOT MUCH TO LOOK AT... **BENZINE THE BLAND,** AT LEAST FROM THIS DISTANCE...

ECCENTRIC ORBITAL TILT... 4,280 KM IN DIAMETER... **TINY.** OOO, IT HAS A MAGNET-OSPHERE. **INTERESTING.**

4,000 MILLION KILOMETERS FROM THE SUN! **OUCH!** GONNA BE FROSTY... **FROZEN ICE** ON THE SURFACE... LOOKS LIKE BOTH CARBON DIOXIDE AND WATER. THIN ATMOSPHERE...

SILICATE CRUST... TECTONICALLY ACTIVE. **BLAH BLAH BLAH... OO!** INDIGENOUS POPULATION:? **CRYSTALLINE!** HUH.

BENZINE V SAGAN INDEX
POPULATION: 4 MILLION BEINGS
CIVILIZATION: SPACE FARING
STARPORT: YYZ TYPE; INEFFICIENT
CULTURE: STATE RUN, RESTRICTED
RULER: TYRANT VAGLOX

OMNITRACK 3000 HAS LOCATED PRINCIPIA, MATHEMATICA IN THE NORTHERN HEMISPHERE, AT LONGITUDE 32 LATTITUDE 11
A12
B4
X
Y

"ONCE I GOT THE RESEARCH OUT OF THE WAY, I HEADED DOWN TO THE ***TELLURIC CURRENT COLLECTOR.*** IT'S A HUGE UNDERGROUND CHAMBER, KINDA LIKE THE ONES THEY USE TO COLLECT NEUTRINOS... ONLY WE USE IT TO COLLECT THE EARTH ENERGY THAT POWERS OUR BOOKS AND TELEPORTATION CRYSTALS. IT CAN TAKE ALMOST A HUNDRED YEARS TO POWER UP A PAIR OF CRYSTALS ENOUGH TO TRANSPORT MY BODY WEIGHT. I THINK THAT'S WHY ***MR. THOTH*** IS ALWAYS BUGGING ME TO GO ON A DIET. HE WANTS TO SAVE OUR BUDGET. 'CUT OUT THE SNACKS AND THOSE GELATIN THINGS,' HE SAYS. PERSONALLY I THINK IT'S THE DONUTS THAT ARE ADDING ON THE POUNDS, AND THE SWEET COFFEES FROM THE ***INFINITE CUP COFFEE*** STORE DOWN THE STREET. ANYWAY, WHERE THE HECK WAS I?"

BZZZRAP!
BZZZRPA!
GZZZZTHRZZK!
OH YEAH....

HMM. YES! **BOOK 3** HAS THE SNOW SHOES AND ICE CLIMBING GEAR...

"YOU MIGHT THINK THAT LIBRARIES ARE BUILT WILLY NILLY, BUT THAT'S NOT SO. **ALL** OF THEM ARE BUILT ON **LEY POINTS,** WHERE **TELLURIC CURRENTS** OF **UNIVERSAL LIFE ENERGY** CONVERGE. AND THE CONVERTER HARNESSES THE ENERGY THROUGH ITS NUMEROLOGY-BASED GEOMETRICAL STRUCTURE, AS SET OUT BY PYTHAGORAS. SURE, IT CAUSES US TO BE INFESTED BY **PARANORMAL FLOTSAM** FROM TIME TO TIME, BUT THAT'S THE PRICE YOU PAY FOR SITTING ON A LEY POINT. SOUNDS FLAKEY, LIKE **PSEUDOSCIENTIFIC GOBBLEDEGOOK,** I KNOW. YOU PROBABLY THINK THIS IS THE VERY SORT OF BUNK **CARL SAGAN** DECRIED. NOT SO. THIS IS ALL CUTTING EDGE, REAL, ***MEGA QUANTUM PLUS THEORY.***

"FROM THE TCC CHAMBER I HEADED OVER TO THE CREW QUARTERS TO LET MY ROOMIE KNOW I WAS OFF TO **BENZINE V.** (NOTE THAT NOT ALL MEMBERS OF ORDO BIBLIOTHECA LIVE UNDER THE THEIR BRANCH, BUT ME, I LIKE BEING BY MY BOOKS. BESIDES, IT'S PRETTY SNAZZY: I USED OFF-WORLD ENGINEERING TO BUILD IT, COMPLETE WITH WINDOWS BACKED BY ARTIFICIAL SUNLIGHT PANELS. MAKES IT FEEL LIKE A REAL ABOVE GROUND HOME. ONLY MINE IS BOMBPROOF.)"

HEY LITTLE BUDDY! **QUAGIS?** WHERE YOU AT?

I'M IN THE STUDIO!

"I GOT ALL THE JUNK I'VE BEEN COLLECTING FOR THE LAST TWO THOUSAND YEARS HERE. LET ME TELL YA, IT ADDS UP. THAT'S THE POSITIVE THING ABOUT HAVING AN UNDERGROUND HOME: UNLIMITED CLOSET SPACE. I JUST GOTTA HOLLOW OUT ANOTHER CAVERN IN THE LIMESTONE. IF I MOVED, I'D NEED A DOZEN SIXTEEN WHEELERS TO HAUL MY CRAP. IT TOOK EIGHT TO GET ALL MY STUFF HERE, AND THAT WAS **DECADES** AGO NOW...."

HEY! *YOU'VE STARTED* **ANOTHER** *PIECE!*
WATCHA PAINTIN' THIS TIME?
NOT SURE. HAVEN'T WRITTEN THE ESSAY THAT'LL GO WITH IT YET. I'LL LET YOU KNOW, THOUGH....
WHATEVER IT IS, THE NOVELTY OF IT BEING PAINTED BY A TELEKINETIC TALKING BIRD IS GONNA MAKE ME A **FORTUNE.** A COUPLE OF THESE PUPPIES AND I'M SINGING PRETTY ON THE **RIVIERA!**
SIMONIDES, I'VE **TOLD** YOU ***BEFORE*** ABOUT THAT!

YOU KNOW YOU'RE NOT SUPPOSED TO SHOW YOURSELF IN PUBLIC. IT'S PART OF THE SETTLEMENT. WE'RE IN A MONOTHEISTIC AGE OF REASON. IF YOU GO AN' SHOW YOURSELF, YOU'LL UNDERMINE SCIENTIFIC INQUIRY AND THE WHOLE ENLIGHTENMENT. NOT TO MENTION THEY'LL FINE MR. THOTH FOR THE VIOLATION. THE LIBRARY WILL GET SHUT DOWN. YOU WANT THAT, SIMON? HUH?
...NO, YOU KNOW I DON'T....
GOOD! AND I DON'T WANT TO CATCH YOU SENDING ANY MORE LETTERS TO JERRY SPRINGER, YA GOT ME?
THIS AIN'T FAIR!
FOR PETE'S SAKE, SIMON!
LIFE AIN'T FAIR!
YOU DON'T SAY!
IT'S NOT LIKE I'VE SPENT THE LAST TWO THOUSAND YEARS AS A FREAKING BUDGIE! *
AND FOR THE LAST TWO YEARS YOU HAVEN'T EVEN LET ME OUT OF THE HOUSE! CRIPES!
I TRY AND CONQUER THE WORLD, AND YOU GUYS COME DOWN ON ME. I TRY WRITING, AND YOU GUYS COME DOWN ON ME. NOW I TRY AND PAINT AND WHAT HAPPENS? WHAT ELSE?
*SIMON IS NOT ACTUALLY A BUDGIE. -ED.
LOOK, I KNOW YOU'VE GOTTEN A BIT OF A RAW DEAL SINCE BEING TURNED INTO A BIRD BY CIRCE AND ALL, BUT IT'S NOT LIKE THERE'S ANYTHING I CAN DO....
YOU GOT HER A JOB IN THE LIBRARY! SHE'S UPSTAIRS RIGHT NOW COVERING YOUR BREAK! WHYDJA TAKE HER IN!?
WELL THEY WERE GONNA BURN HER AS A WITCH--
SHE IS A WITCH! THE OLDEST, MEANEST, BIGGEST WITCH THAT HAS EVER LIVED! SHE TURNED ME INTO A BIRD, REX!! A BIRD!!!
I HATE BIRDS, REX! I HATE THEM!
IT WAS YOUR FAULT-- !?! YOU DO? HOW CAN YOU HATE BIRDS? THEY'RE SO CUTE. ALL FEATHERY AND CHIRPY....

YOU'D HATE BIRDS TOO IF YOU HAD TO SPEND CENTURIES AS ONE. CIRCE DIDN'T GET RID OF MY SEX DRIVE -- OH NO, THAT'S STILL THERE. ONLY AS A BIRD I HAVE NO REAL PROSPECTS... UNLESS I RULE THE WORLD OR I'M A FAMOUS ARTISTE, HOW AM I GONNA SCORE HOT CHICKS?
WELL NOT EVERYONE IS THAT SUPERFICIAL, SIMON. YOU'LL FIND...
BAH!
ONE OF THESE DAYS I'M GONNA TRY AND TAKE OVER THE WORLD AGAIN, AND THIS TIME I WON'T SCREW IT UP!
I DON'T GET YOU AND THE WHOLE CONQUER THE WORLD THING. IT SEEMS LIKE AN INVITATION TO A REAL BIG HEADACHE.
REX, BEING A BRUTAL, DESPOTIC, BAD BOY WARLORD REALLY HELPS ASSEMBLING HAREMS.
BUT YOU'RE A BIRD! WHAT'LL YA DO WITH A HAREM OF FOXY LADIES?
HAVEN'T THE FOGGIEST.
PRIMAL, ANIMALISTIC URGES AREN'T BIG ON RATIONALITY. SPEAKING OF WHICH...
YOU GOTTA GET ME OUT OF HERE! I'M GOING STIR-CRAZY ON TOP OF EVERYTHING ELSE!
TALK TO CIRCE FOR ME! SEE IF SHE'LL SEE REASON!
ARE YOU NUTS? AND GET TURNED INTO A GOAT OR SOMETHING?
YOU CROSSED HER, YOU GO TALK TO HER.
YOU AND YOUR CRAZY SCHEMES. SHE DID WARN YOU....
WHY DON'T YOU JUST FIND A NICE FEMALE OF YOUR OWN PHYLUM AND SETTLE DOWN? A NICE CHICKADEE, OR A HUMMINGBIRD OR SOMETHING.
I TRIED THAT. THEY'RE ALL BIRD BRAINS.
'TWEET TWEET TWEET.' THAT'S ALL THEY SAY.
I USED TO BE A TRAVELING PHILOSOPHY SALES-MAN. A HANDSOME ROGUE! NOW LOOK AT ME!
SAY --
YOU ARE GOING ON A MISSION, AREN'T YOU? I CAN ALWAYS TELL. TAKE ME WITH YOU!
SIMON, YOU KNOW I CAN'T DO THAT ANYMORE. MR. THOTH IS REAL STRICT ABOUT WASTING TELEPORTATION CRYSTAL ENERGY ON EXCESS MASS....
FIRST, JUJYFRUITS AREN'T ESSENTIAL MASS, AND SECOND, I TOOK OVER THREE COUNTRIES IN SOUTH AMERICA BEFORE I GOT STOPPED LAST TIME.... NEXT TIME I WON'T MAKE THE SAME MISTAKES. MAYBE I'LL TRY ANOTHER TACK AND RUN FOR GOVERNOR OF CALIFORNIA....
OH MAN. SIMON, YOU AND YOUR HERO RULER CRAP. SPARTA DIED A LONG TIME AGO, MY FRIEND!

SPARTA BEAT THE CRAP OUT OF ATHENS, REX, AND WE DID IT WITH GOOD OLD **LYCURGIAN IDEALISM.** WE COULD DO ANYTHING WE PUT OUR MIND TO! WE COULD GIVE **HISTORY ITSELF** DIRECTION!
YEAH, YEAH. HARNESS EVERYONE TO PULL THE IDEALS-- OF ***ONE*** TYRANT. PUT THE WORLD ON A YOKE! BAH! IT'S SUCH A WASTE OF HUMAN POTENTIAL.
IN THE END, IT'S A RECIPE FOR DISASTER. YOU ***KNOW*** THAT! WE'VE BOTH ***SEEN*** THE RESULT....
SIMONIDES: FEH. I WASN'T GONNA DO ANYTHING **THAT** EGOMANIACAL WITH ***MY*** LITTLE EMPIRE. JUST AN ENLIGHTENED DESPOTISM TO IMPRESS THE LADIES. A COUPLE YACHTS, A FEW PALACES, A HAREM, A NICE CAR.... YOU KNOW. I'D BE A **LEE KUAN YEW** KIND OF TYRANT. I'LL TAKE SOME CITY STATE SLUM AND TURN IT INTO A GLITTERING JEWEL OF PROSPERITY. I'LL BET LEE WAS A SPARTAN AT HEART-- AT VERY LEAST A ***HOBBESIAN REALIST.***
REX: I DUNNO, SIMON. THAT EMPIRE-BUILDING BINGE YOU WENT ON AS AN EXPRESSION OF YOUR MONUMENTAL EGO LEFT A TRAIL OF DESTRUCTION IN ITS WAKE. IT'S A WONDER NO ONE WAS *KILLED*--
SIMONIDES: I PLANNED IT ALL OUT USING NUMEROLOGY TO THE LAST DECIMAL POINT. ENSURED NOBODY WOULD GET HURT. I HAVE A LIGHT STOMACH.
FORWARD IN THE NAME OF OUR GREAT GENERALISSIMO ***SIMONIDES!***
TAKE WHAT YOU WISH, MY MINIONS, BUT THE BIRD SEED ***IS MINE!***
TAK TAK TAK!
GLANK GLANK GLANKITY GLANK!

REX: THAT LIGHT STOMACH MIGHT IMPEDE YOUR QUEST FOR WORLD CONQUEST.

SIMONIDES: PERHAPS. I JUST HAVE TO WORK OUT THE NUMEROLOGY FINELY ENOUGH... GIVE ME TIME. I'M IMMORTAL. *VITA LONGA, ARS BREVIS...*

WHATEVER.
AWRIGHT. HMM... YA KNOW...
SOME OF THESE PIECES AIN'T HALF BAD, SIMONIDES. BIT OF A MIRO FEEL TO 'EM. ONE OF THESE DAYS I SHOULD TAKE YA TO SEE HIS MUSEUM ON MONTJUIC....
ANYHOW... WE COULD SELL THESE.
YOU MIGHT NOT NEED TO CONQUER THE WORLD AFTER ALL....
REALLY?
SURE!
BUT
ONLY AS A MYSTERIOUS ARTISTE WHO NEVER, EVER APPEARS IN PERSON. YOU'LL HAVE TO TALK THROUGH ME.
I COULD DO PHONE INTERVIEWS. THEY'D NEVER KNOW I WAS A BIRD...
YEAH.... SURE. WHATEVER--
-- DON'T YOU DARE CRAP ON MY SUIT!
HEY, YOU KNOW I HAVE NO CONTROL OVER THAT...

SURE YOU DON'T.
COME ON, I'VE ONLY GOT ABOUT TWO HOURS LEFT BEFORE THE EARTH'S ORBIT CARRIES US TO THE TELEPORTATION POINT. I GOTTA FIND MY 'PORTIN' CAP.
YOUR OLD FIGHTER PILOT CAP? THE ONE YOU LINED WITH TINFOIL? THAT THING MAKES YOU LOOK LIKE A NUT.
DON'T MOCK IT, BUCKO. THAT TINFOIL LINING REALLY WORKS. OTHER-WISE THE TELEPORTING GIVES ME A HEADACHE. I CAN MAKE A LITTLE ONE FOR YOU IF YA LIKE....
NO THANKS!
SUIT YOURSELF.
I KNOW I LEFT MY CAP IN HERE SOMEWHERE...
FLIIIIIIIIIIING!
8
COULDN'T FIND IT FOR ME LAST TRIP-- HAD TO PORT REAL FAST, NO TIME TO LOOK. AND I GOT A NASTY HEADACHE.
BUT NOT THIS TIME.
AHA!

BINGO!

AM I EVER GLAD I FOUND DIS HAT!

THIS ROOM IS A MESS!!

JESUS, REX! HOW CAN AN **ORGANIZATION** PROFESSIONAL **KEEP** SUCH A MESSY CLOSET?

HEH. TWO THOUSAND YEARS OF ACCUMU-LATION TAKES ITS TOLL, LIL' BUDDY!

GAH. YOU LOOK **TOTALLY** ***RIDICULOUS!***

EH. I DON'T CARE A **FIG** ABOUT FASHION. 'SIDES, I GOT A LIL' GALACTIC BAND ***RADIO*** BUILT INTO THE EAR PIECES...

MEANS I DON'T HAVE TO MISS HOCKEY GAMES WHEN I GO ON A MISSION.

AND JUST IN CASE VAGLOX **AIN'T** GONNA BE COOPERATIVE...

MY MEANS OF LESS POLITE ***PERSUASION....***

...AH....
SO?
SO... **WHAT?**
WHERE'S **MY** GUN?
HUH?
HAHAHAHA!
AH.... **NO.**
OH COME **ON!** WHY NOT?
WOULDN'T BE **PRUDENT.**
WE GOT ABOUT AN HOUR TIL 'PORT.
I GOT SOME WINE GUMS ON ME. SO. ALL WE GOTTA DO NOW IS STOP BY THE CIRC DESK. I GOTTA TALK TO **CIRCE....**
HOORAY!!
I **KNEW** YOU'D COME AROUND EVENTUALLY.
GIVE HER A GOOD TALKING TO, I SAY.
THAT'S NOT WHAT I WAS GONNA TALK TO CIRCE ABOUT. NOT EVERYTHING REVOLVES AROUND **YOU,** YA KNOW.
IT **DOESN'T?**
DON'T GIVE ME ANY OF THAT **FICHTE** CRAP. I'M NO EMANATION OF YOUR EGO!

"OF COURSE, MY PUBLISHER, B. BARRY HORST, HAD A FEW IDEAS WHEN IT CAME TO MY BUDDY, SIMONIDES.... A LITTLE BIT OF FACT MASSAGING, WHICH IS QUITE FREQUENT IN AUTOBIOGRAPHIES..."

IT DOESN'T MATTER!
THAT'S THE GREAT THING ABOUT BOOBS! GUYS DON'T LOOK PAST THEM. AND THEY SELL, REX, THEY SELL LIKE LEMONADE IN THE SAHARA!
DON'T BE NAIVE! THIS ISN'T LITERATURE, IT'S ENTERTAINMENT! COMICS! PROTO-FILM! AND DO YOU KNOW WHAT THE MOST IMPORTANT THING IN COMICS AND FILM IS, REX? DO YOU?
UH... PLOT? CHARACTERIZATION?
NO! BOOBS!
AND BY GOD, THE BIGGER THE BETTER!
B. BARRY HORST
HOW DO YOU SAVE A FLAGGING TV SHOW? ADD BOOBS! THEY'RE A FLOTATION DEVICE IN MORE WAYS THAN ONE! THE WORSE THE RATINGS, THE BIGGER THE BOOBS! HELL, HOWARD HUGHES BASED ENTIRE MOVIES AROUND MAMMARY GLANDS, MY MAN! AND HE WAS A GENIUS! YOU CAN'T ARGUE WITH GENIUS!
PLOT, CHARACTER... BAH! THAT'S ALL SECONDARY STUFF! I'VE STUDIED THIS CLOSELY, MY FRIEND. VIOLENCE AND BOOBS IS WHERE IT'S AT.
BARELY ARTICULATE HERO FELLAS ARE IN TOO, COME TO THINK OF IT. YOU COULD TALK LESS, REX. A LOT LESS!
SEE, WE GOT GOBS OF MEANINGLESS VIOLENCE IN THIS COMIC, BUT WE CANNOT AFFORD A BOOB GAP! OUR COMPETITION IS DEPLOYING MASSIVE ASSETS AGAINST US! SERIES LIKE THE REVENGE OF THE STRIPPER AND THAT NEW ONE, FOXY SIZZLE, THE PORN STAR WHO DOUBLES AS A SECRET AGENT FOR THE CIA.
WE CAN'T ALLOW THEM TO GET AN EDGE ON US! DID KENNEDY ALLOW A MISSILE GAP WITH THE SOVIET UNION? NO! THEY STOOD UP FOR WHAT WAS RIGHT AND TRUE AND JUST, AND SO MUST WE, REX!
WHOA, WHOA WHOA. HOLD ON A SECOND!
ISN'T THAT PANDERING, BARRY?
NOT IF EVERYONE DOES IT! I'M WARNING YOU NOW, REX: IF WE DON'T GET DOWN INTO THE JELLO AND WRESTLE WITH WHAT'S OUT THERE, WELL, THIS COMIC IS GONNA TANK!
A LITTLE MEGALOMANIACAL FLAT CHESTED BIRD WHO CAN'T HANDLE HIS FIREARMS JUST DOESN'T CUT IT! WE NEED SOME MAMMARIES, REX! BIG ONES!

HMM... NOT SURE OLD FOUILLOY WOULD AGREE...
BUT...... YOU KNOW, HYPATIA HAS THEM...
!? HAS WHAT?
MAMMARY GLANDS.
OH GOD.
OH NO.
MY MAIN CHARACTER HAS FLIPPED HIS LID!
REX.... YOUR EX... WELL, HYPATIA'S DEAD, REX. DEAD AND BURIED AND DECOMPOSED... LONG, LONG AGO. IT'S GOTTA BE ABOUT FIFTEEN HUNDRED YEARS NOW.
YOU GOTTA GET OVER IT!
NO, NO, NO. NOT THAT HYPATIA. I'M TALKING ABOUT THE LIBRARY TECH, HYPATIA KRUPSKAYA. SHE STARTED JUST BEFORE I LEFT FOR BENZINE FIVE. SHE'D JUST FINISHED HER MASTER'S IN LIBRARY AND INFORMATION SCIENCE AND GOTTEN BACK FROM SAS TRAINING. VERY BRIGHT GIRL. HER MOTHER WAS A LIBRARIAN...
ARE THEY REALLY BIG?
ARE WHAT REALLY BIG?
HER BOOBS.
OH! I DON'T THINK IT'D BE RIGHT FOR ME TO COMMENT--
HUH! FINE THEN. THEY'LL HAVE TO DO FOR NOW.
WELL DON'T JUST SIT THERE LIBRIS! GET ON IT, MAN! GET ON IT! THERE'S NO TIME TO LOSE!
"BARRY CAN SOUND A LITTLE MERCENARY WHEN HE GETS GOING, BUT HE'S AN OLD PRO IN THE PUBLISHING FIELD. KNOWS MORE ABOUT WHAT SELLS THAN I DO. ANYHOW, BACK TO THE STORY. NO SOONER HAD SIMONIDES AND I REACHED THE GROUND FLOOR OF THE LIBRARY AND STARTED TO WEAVE OUR WAY THROUGH THE MAZE OF BOOK SHELVES THAN WE RAN INTO A PATRON ON THE VERGE OF PANIC...."
OH, THANK ST. LAURENCE!
A LIBRARIAN!
IT'S NICE TO BE UP HERE AGAIN. BEEN AWHILE SINCE YOU--
AKT! SSSSSHHH!!!
HELLO!
CAN I HELP YOU, MA'AM?

OH YES, YES! **PLEASE!** I'VE BEEN LOST FOR HOURS NOW! THESE SHELVES JUST GO ON AND ON?IT'S LIKE THE **LIBRARY OF CONGRESS ARCHIVES,** ONLY ***WORSE!***
I THINK I MADE A WRONG TURN BACK SOMEWHERE IN ROMANTIC FICTION... THEN I SAW... OH, YOU'RE GOING TO THINK I'M ***CRAZY.....***
MINIME! NOT AT ALL, MA'AM!
WELL....
I THOUGHT I SAW... A SCARECROW, A **TIN** MAN, A GIRL, AND A DOG HOPPING DOWN AN AISLE. LIKE RIGHT OUT OF THAT BOOK! AND BEFORE THAT I COULD HAVE **SWORN** I SAW A MAN... THE VERY EMBODIMENT OF **SHERLOCK HOLMES...** DASH BETWEEN THE SHELVES AFTER SOME MALEVOLENT GENTLEMAN IN A TOP HAT AND CLOAK... SHEER **MADNESS!**
I'VE ONLY BEEN LOST A FEW HOURS AND I FEEL LIKE I'M **LOSING** MY MIND!
CHUCKLE! CHORTLE! OH, **NO** MA'AM! NOT AT ALL! THERE'S A **LOGICAL** EXPLANATION! IT'S ***QUANTUM PLUS!***

YOU SEE... WHAT YOU'VE BEEN SEEING ARE JUST PHYSICAL MANISFESTATIONS OF PARANORMAL EMANATIONS EXTRUDED FROM THE MENTAL ENERGY CAPTURED IN THE LITERATURE ON THE SHELVES.
THESE CORPOREAL EXTRUSIONS OF THE METAPHYSICAL HAPPEN ON OCCASION BECAUSE WE ARE SITTING UPON A LEY POINT, AN ENERGY HUB, FOR THE TELLURIC CURRENTS THAT FLOW IN THE ETHER EMBEDDED IN THE EIGHTH DIMENSION -- ACCORDING TO THE LATEST STRING THEORY. OR IT COULD BE IN THE NINTH.
THEY AREN'T SURE. THAT'S STRING THEORY FOR YA. ONE OF 'EM IS THE DIMENSION OF THOUGHT. MENTAL ENERGY, MANA, SPIRIT, CONSCIOUSNESS, 'N' SO ON.
EVERY NOW AND THEN WE GET A TELLURIC FLARE, AND SOME FICTIONAL CHARACTER OR PLACE ESCAPES FROM THE EIGHTH, OR NINTH, DIMENSION -- FOR A TIME, TILL THE CURRENTS EBB OR THE PSYCHIC ENERGY OF THE FICTION FRAGMENT DISSIPATES. THEY USUALLY DON'T LAST LONG.
IT'S ALL QUITE LOGICAL, JUST LIKE THE BEHAVIOUR OF MATTER ON A QUANTUM SCALE. ALL BASED ON GOOD, CLEAN, HONEST, SCIENTIFIC PRINCIPLES.
NOW MOST OF THESE PARANORMAL FRAGMENTS OF CREATIVITY ARE BENIGN AND HARMLESS. THAT ELEPHANT FELLOW IN THE CHILDREN'S SECTION, FOR EXAMPLE. NICE CHAP.
DO BE CAREFUL TO STAY OUT OF THE WAY OF NASTY TYPES, LIKE OH, MORLOCKS, OR FIRE BREATHING DRAGONS, OR CERBERUS, OR MAN-EATING CANNIBALS. THEY GENERALLY AREN'T THAT PLEASANT.
IT DOES DEPEND ON THEIR MOOD. I TEND TO CARRY SNACKS FOR THE DRAGONS.... WHATEVER YOU DO, NEVER EVER MENTION CHARACTERS YOU MEET WHO ARE NOT YET IN THE PUBLIC DOMAIN. WE LIVE IN A VERY LITIGIOUS AGE.

CRAP.
IS THAT A DEAD BODY OVER THERE?
UNH. NOTICED THAT, DID YOU?
I... THINK THAT'S MR. JENKINS.
HUH. SO THAT'S WHERE HE'S BEEN.
HE USED TO COME IN EVERY DAY BACK IN THE TWENTIES. THEN ONE DAY HE JUST STOPPED. ALWAYS WONDERED WHAT HAPPENED TO HIM.
HAVE TO CLEAN THAT UP... HE'S LOOKING A LITTLE GNARLY....

THERE'S AN IMPORTANT LESSON HERE: ALWAYS, ALWAYS CHECK IN WITH THE LIBRARY CIRCULATION DESK BEFORE YOU GO OFF INTO THE STACKS ON YOUR OWN. THAT WAY WE KNOW TO SEND OUT A SEARCH PARTY IF YOU DON'T COME OUT BY CLOSING TIME.
REMEMBER DAT!
SAINTS ALIVE! OH, HOW FOOLISH I HAVE BEEN! I'LL CHECK IN WITH YOU LIBRARIANS FIRST FROM NOW ON!
SIGH...
THAT POOR, POOR MAN. WHAT A DREADFUL FATE, TO DIE ALONE, WITH ONLY DUSTY BOOKS TO KEEP HIM COMPANY...
JEEZ, LADY, I WOULDN'T GO AND PUT IT LIKE THAT. HE DIED IN THE HUMOUR SECTION AFTER ALL.
YOU MAKE IT SOUND LIKE THERE'S A BETTER WAY TO GO THAN IN THE COMPANY OF STEPHEN LEACOCK....!
OH.... I'M SORRY I DIDN'T MEAN TO--
THAT'S ALL RIGHT.
DID YOU FIND THE BOOK YOU WERE LOOKING FOR?
WHY, YES... I HAD IT A MOMENT AGO... AH, HERE IT IS...
"THE STORY OF O"
OH!
HEH!
LET'S CHECK THAT PUPPY OUT THEN. NEXT STOP....

...THE CIRCULATION DESK!
LET'S GO!
HOLD IT!
YOU HEAR SOMETHING?
NO... WHY?
...NUTHIN.
MUST BE A TELLURIC STORM GOING ON... IT'S NOT USUALLY THIS CRAZY WITH PARANORMAL ENERGY IN HERE!

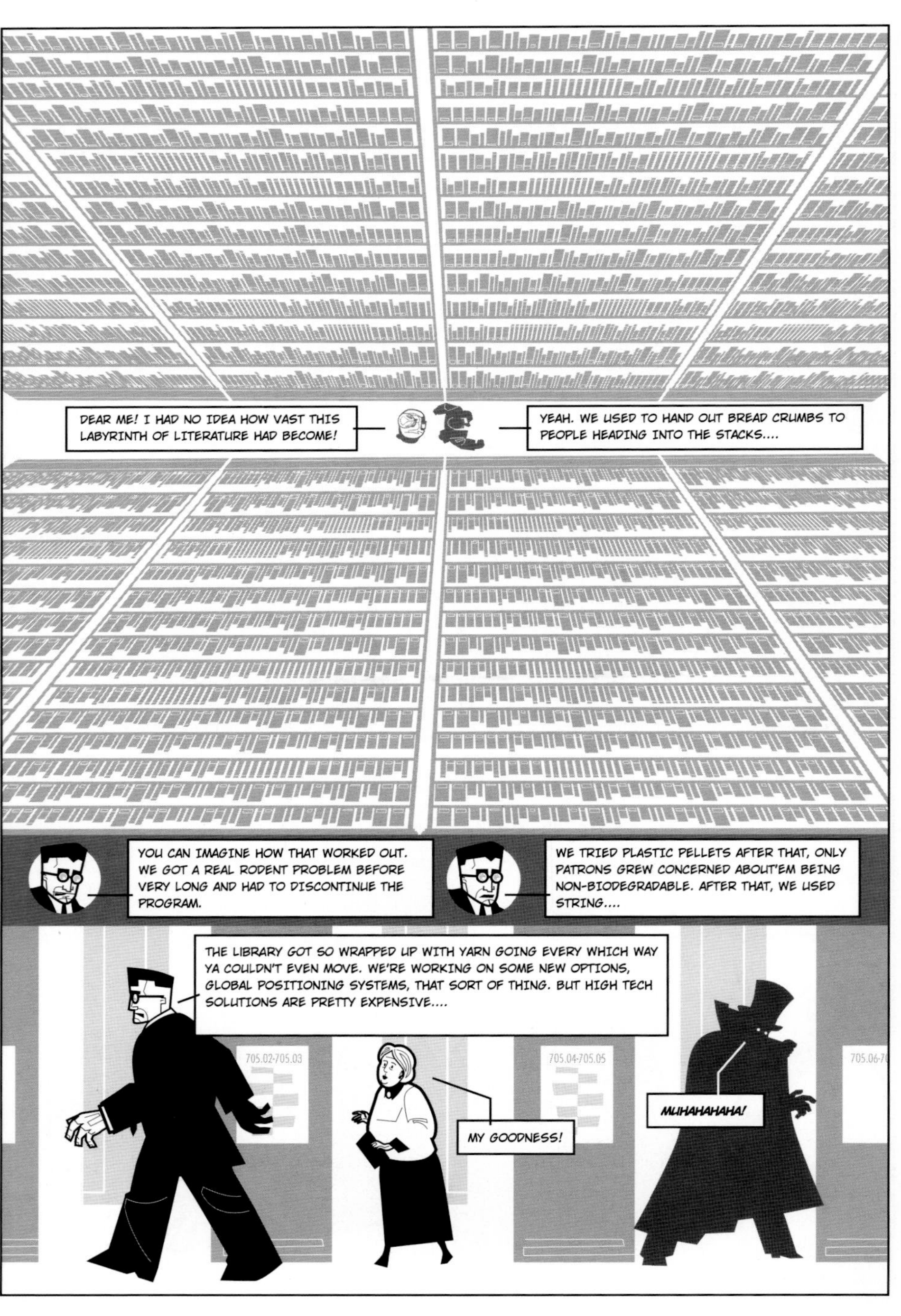
DEAR ME! I HAD NO IDEA HOW VAST THIS LABYRINTH OF LITERATURE HAD BECOME!
YEAH. WE USED TO HAND OUT BREAD CRUMBS TO PEOPLE HEADING INTO THE STACKS....
YOU CAN IMAGINE HOW THAT WORKED OUT. WE GOT A REAL RODENT PROBLEM BEFORE VERY LONG AND HAD TO DISCONTINUE THE PROGRAM.
WE TRIED PLASTIC PELLETS AFTER THAT, ONLY PATRONS GREW CONCERNED ABOUT'EM BEING NON-BIODEGRADABLE. AFTER THAT, WE USED STRING....
THE LIBRARY GOT SO WRAPPED UP WITH YARN GOING EVERY WHICH WAY YA COULDN'T EVEN MOVE. WE'RE WORKING ON SOME NEW OPTIONS, GLOBAL POSITIONING SYSTEMS, THAT SORT OF THING. BUT HIGH TECH SOLUTIONS ARE PRETTY EXPENSIVE....
705.02-705.03
705.04-705.05
MY GOODNESS!
MUHAHAHAHA!

WAIT! THAT EVIL LAUGH! MUST ACT -- NOW!
GET DOWN, LADY!
WHAAAA? -- AAHH!
EAT LEAD YOU MALEFIC PODEX!
!?!
HUH!
SORRY LADY, I COULDA SWORN I HEARD....
!?
NEVERMIND... I MUST BE GOIN' NUTS.

"ALAS, I WAS NOT GOING NUTS AND EVIL WAS, INDEED, AFOOT. YET THIS PARTICULAR INCARNATION WAS CRAFTY AND KNEW BETTER THAN TO FACE ME DIRECTLY. SINCE I KNEW THE TELLURIC CURRENTS WOULD NATURALLY EBB, AND THE FIEND WOULD INEVITABLY DISSIPATE BACK INTO THE BOOK FROM WHICH HE SPRANG, HE DID NOT SEEM A PRESSING CONCERN. AT LEAST, THAT WAS MY BLITHE BELIEF AT THE TIME. HOW THE HECK WAS I SUPPOSED TO KNOW OTHERWISE? I MEAN, THAT'S WHAT ALL THE OTHER ETHEREAL EMANATIONS DID. WHY SHOULD THAT GUY BE ANY DIFFERENT? WHATEVER. I GOT THE LADY OUT OF THE LITERATURE MAZE -- IN RECORD TIME... WITH TEN MINUTES TO SPARE TILL TELEPORT."
TA-DAA!
BACK SAFE AND SOUND AND A LITTLE WISER.
HEAVENS!
I THINK I NEED A LITTLE SIT DOWN AFTER ALL THAT EXCITEMENT!
I UNDERSTAND. I WILL BE JUST OVER AT THE CIRCULATION DESK IF YOU NEED ANY HELP.
THANK YOU YOUNG MAN!

SOON....
OH, HEY HYPATIA! WHERE'S CIRCE?
SHE'S OUT IN THE STACKS. SHUSHING PEOPLE. SHE'S A LITTLE ON THE ZEALOUS SIDE IF YOU ASK ME.... GIVES US A BAD NAME.
AH. YES. WELL. IT IS OUR MANDATE TO SHUSH.
SO... HOW DO YOU LIKE THE NEW CIRCULATION DESK?
AH YES... WHY DO WE HAVE A NEW CIRCULATION DESK?
SAMURAI DEMON SMASHED THE LAST ONE. THIS ONE HAS SOLID OAK PANELLING.
IT'S NICE. LITTLE DUSTY.
DON'T TOUCH THE DUST! I HAVE IT ALL ARRANGED.
WHATEVER....
BUILT IN KEYBOARDS FOR THE COMPUTERS. SOFT LIGHTING PANELS. WATERPROOF. FLAME PROOF. TWO INCH THICK, REINFORCED LEAD COATED STEEL PANELS. IT CAN WITHSTAND A DIRECT HIT FROM A ZOGGAN BLOB BAZOOKA. TOOK ALL LAST NIGHT TO EXTRUDE MY DESIGN PLAN INTO REALITY. USED MY VACATION PAY.
HUH.
IN
AND IT'S GOT SMOKE DISPENSERS.
WHAT?
SMOKE DISPENSERS. THE DESK. AT THE BASE OF THE PANELS.
UH...WHY?
IN CASE THE PATRONS GET ROWDY. GIVE US A SCREEN. BUY US ENOUGH TIME TO REACH THE TASERS.

OOOH-KAAAY....
YOU CAN NEVER TELL WHEN DEALIN' WITH THE PUBLIC. VERY UNPREDICTABLE, YA KNOW?
TRUE.
HOW DID THE SAS TRAINING GO, HYPATIA?
IT WAS -- *!?
SIMON....
SIMON!
YES, HYPATIA?
GET
OFF
MY
HEAD
NOW.
HMPH!
TWITTER TWITTER!
SHOULDN'T HE BE IN A CAGE?
DON'T WORRY, HE'S NOT STAY-ING. WE'RE 'PORTING TO BENZINE IN A FEW MINUTES.
WHERE?
A CAGE! REALLY!
AH, JUST A PLANETARY SYSTEM NEAR BELLATRIX. THE LOCAL WARLORD HAS AN OVERDUE BOOK. I'M TAKIN SIMON ALONG. KEEP HIM OUT OF TROUBLE.
OUT OF MY HAIR WOULD BE GOOD ENOUGH.

HEH. YEAH.
I CAN GUARANTEE THAT FOR AT LEAST A FEW HOURS.....
JUST THE BOYS ON THIS MISSION EH? LOOKS LIKE YOU HAVE ALL THE FUN.
OH HO! EAGER, ARE WE? EXCELLENT. YOU'LL HAVE PLENTY OF MISSIONS TO GO ON, BELIEVE ME. YOU'LL BE HAPPY TO STAY IN THE LIBRARY BEFORE LONG, WHERE IT'S NICE AND WARM!
THAT ISN'T WHAT I HEARD....
CIRCE SAYS YOU MONOPOLIZE MISSIONS.
HAHAHAHA!
SHE DID NOW, DID SHE? HEHE!
WHAT SHE DIDN'T TELL YOU IS THAT SHE'S GROUNDED!
SHE TURNED A PARTICULARLY OBNOXIOUS PATRON INTO A PIG. AS MUCH AS I SYMPATHIZE, WE JUST CAN'T HAVE THAT SORT OF THING HAPPENING AT THE MIDDLETON PUBLIC LIBRARY. NO TRANSFORMATIONS! PERIOD.
INTERESTING, THO'. I DIDN'T KNOW SHE WAS MISSING BOOK COLLECTION MISSIONS.
I CAN USE THIS LITTLE TIDBIT OF INFORMATION. ONLY.... HMM.

OH YEAH. BEFORE I FORGET: A BIG WHITE FURRY GUY CAME BY EARLIER. HE LEFT SOME COFFEE AND BUTTER TARTS FOR YOU.
NAMASTE! I AM METOHKANGMI! YETI! WHERE IS ONE THAT IS REX OF THE LIBRIS?
ARE YOU -- KAFF! -- SHEDDING??
I LEFT THEM ON THE COUNTER....
EGADS!
PECAN BUTTER TARTS!
AND PIPING HOT FRESH COFFEE!
THEY'RE GOOD!

THAT FIEND KNOWS MY EVERY WEAK-NESS!
DAMN YOU YETI! WHY DO YOU TORMENT ME SO?
THESE BUTTERTARTS BRIM WITH THE VERY CALORIES OF EVIL!
INEXORABLY DRAWING ME IN TO A CARBOHYDRATE-FUELED HELL OF HIGH CALORIC SIN!
YOU DON'T HAVE TO EAT THEM YOU KNOW.
OH, THAT'S RIGHT. (MUNCH MUNCH!) TAKE THE BUTTER-TARTS SIDE, WHY DON'TCHA?

I JUST MEANT —
WAIT!
SOMETHING'S WRONG!
I'VE ONLY EATEN ONE BUTTERTART! BUT THERE ARE ONLY TWO LEFT!
SIMON IS TOO SMALL TO HAVE EATEN AN ENTIRE ONE. WHICH MEANS--
SOMEONE ELSE COULD NOT RESIST THEIR SEDUCTIVE POWER!
HEH!
HEY DID I TELL YOU ABOUT MY TIME AT THE SAS TRAINING COURSE? FUN FUN FUN!
OH YEAH. HOW'D THAT GO?
I'M SORRY MISS KRUPSKAYA. BUT I DON'T THINK THAT'S ENTIRELY APPROPRIATE CLOTHING FOR URBAN COMBAT-- AOOOF!!
TELL IT TO THE BOOT, BUSTER!
IT WAS GREAT. MY PREVIOUS SPETZNAZ TRAINING PREPARED ME FOR IT WELL. THEY DIDN'T APPRECIATE MY BUSTIER, THOUGH.

WHY HELLO, YOU TWO! ISN'T IT A LOVELY AFTERNOON?
AH!
HEYA CIRCE. YA SEEN SIMONIDES? HE WAS HERE A SECOND AGO.
WHY YES, REX DEAR. HE CAME AND FOUND ME IN THE BOOK STACKS. IT SEEMS HE'S SPEAKING TO ME AGAIN. AT LAST. HE CAN BE SO VERY STUBBORN.
I WAS MAKING A POINT!
REX! TELL HER! TELL HER SHE OUGHT TO TURN ME BACK INTO A HUMAN BEING!
OH, SIMON, YOU SILLY BIRD. I CAN'T DO THAT. THE SPELL WILL WEAR OFF NATURALLY. WHAT'S A FEW THOUSAND YEARS TO AN IMMORTAL? YOU'LL LOOK BACK ON YOUR AVIAN TIME SOME DAY AND LAUGH AND LAUGH....
COME ON, SIMON! LET'S GO! WE GOTTA 'PORT!
"I GOT SUITED UP AND PREPPED THE TWO CRYSTALS....."
OKAY!
CIRCE: YOU'RE IN CHARGE OF THE LIBRARY TILL I GET BACK. THERE'S AN AFTER SCHOOL HOMEWORK GROUP COMING IN AT FOUR, SO BE READY FOR 'EM. AND IF PROFESSOR RAMSAY CALLS, TELL HIM WE GOT THAT BOOK HE WANTED ON ANGELS IN. HE'LL UNDERSTAND.
I GOT MY PAGER ON. THE NUMBER IS ON THE DESK. BEEP ME IF YOU HAVE ANY TROUBLE.
SO LONG, SUCKERS!
EVERYTHING WILL BE FINE HERE, REX. YOU BOYS BE GOOD NOW.
WAIT A SEC, REX! THAT'S NOT QUITE A FORTY FIVE DEGREE--
BANG!

POOF!
-- ANGLE!
WHAT THE?
AW, CRAP!
I DROPPED THE CRYSTAL!!
AH -- THIS COULD BE A PROBLEM...!

I'M ON IT! I'M ON IT!
HURRY!

GOT IT!!
GOOD WORK! OKAY, GRAB ON, I'M GONNA GIVE IT ANOTHER GO!
SAPERE AUDE!
BANG!

CHAPTER THREE
LEAP OF FAITH

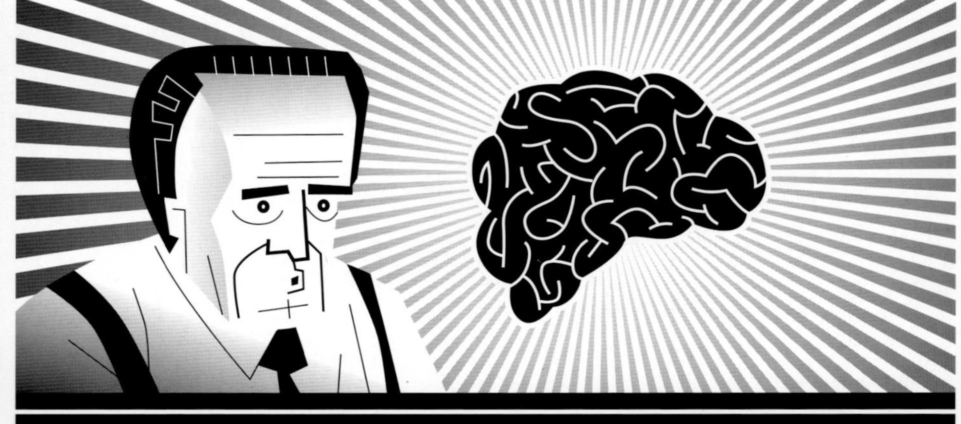

BARRY'S BRAIN

Welcome back, faithful readers. Here we are at issue three of Rex Libris, and we (the Hermeneutic Press collective, that is) haven't gone out of business yet. Incredible you say? Believe it! Rex lives, and in this exciting issue he head rushes a planet, then follows up by kicking the ass of alien snowmen. It's action like you've never seen action before! Except, of course, as you saw it in the previous two issues of Rex Libris. But other than that, it's totally unlike anything else! He's a hard act to follow.

Some ask me, Barry, why do you write this column? You're an editor, not a writer. And you know what, faithful readers? This is true! Yet, somehow, I can't stop myself.

There have been a lot of innovations in the comic book industry over the last few years, but it looks like we've really shaken things up with the debut of Rex Libris. That's right! The comic book world will never be the same again, not after our amazing, innovative comic book commentary track. Note that there were a few problems with it. Many people felt they had to read the commentary at the same time they first read the comic. Yet who watches a movie for the first time with the commentary track on? It's simply unheard of. Well. Maybe some kids hopped up on drugs do it. Those crazy kids! Remember, there are stranger things, and people, out there than even the ones you see in Hermeneutic Press publications!

Of course, we have discontinued the commentary track, mainly because we simply can't think of anything else to say at this time. If I could talk endlessly off the cuff I'd be doing commentary for CNN. But fear not, gentle readers! The commentary track may appear again at any time, to fill your endless appetite for Hermeneutic Press minutae, and to deliver an exclusive, inside look into the thought process behind comic book making! You'll only find it here, at Hermeneutic! Forget Demonic Comics! Pass over Makerel Mush! Ignore Green Knight! Cover your eyes with Dizzy Visage! Make yours Hermeneutic!

Pontificate!

B. Barry Horst

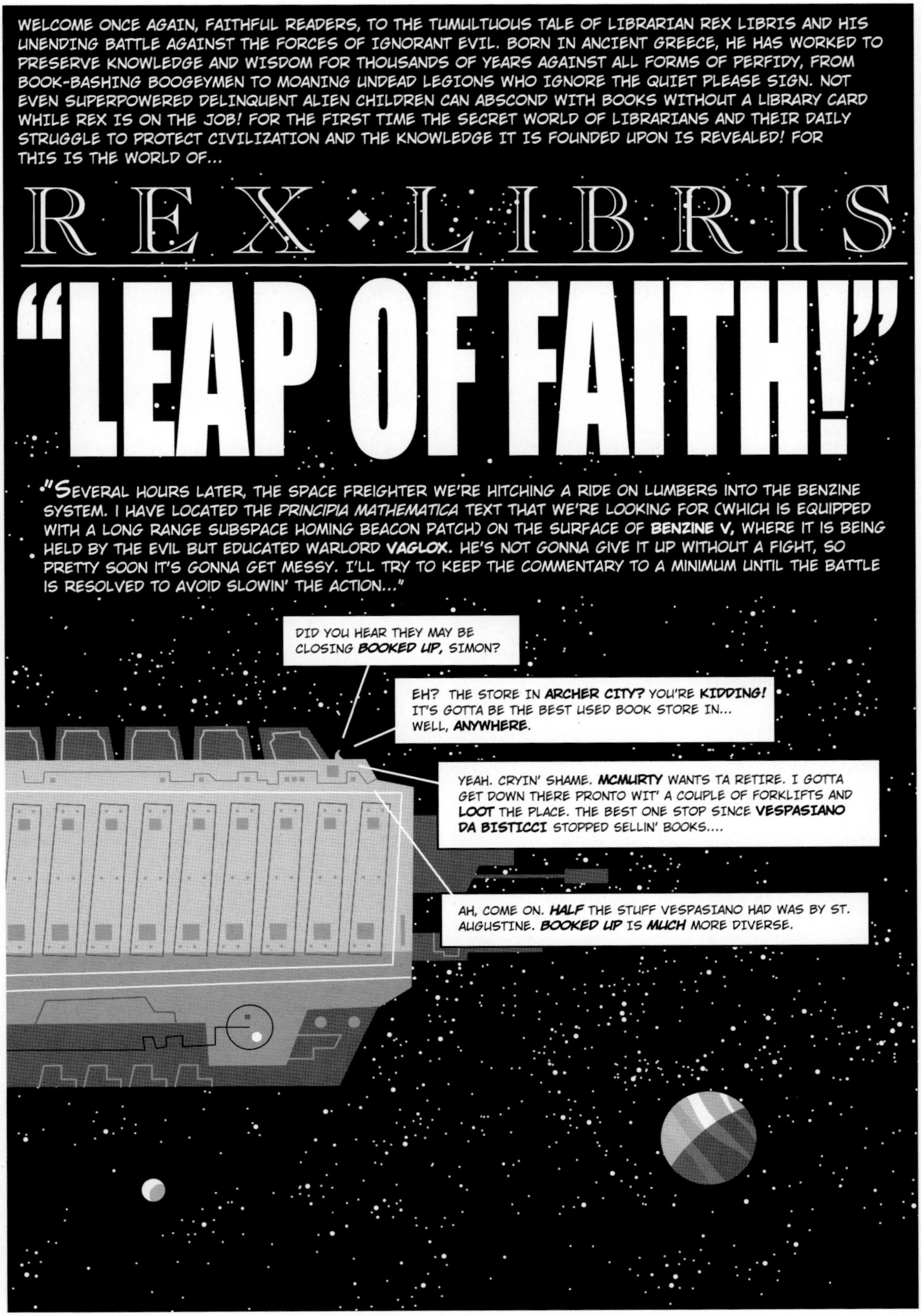

WELCOME ONCE AGAIN, FAITHFUL READERS, TO THE TUMULTUOUS TALE OF LIBRARIAN REX LIBRIS AND HIS UNENDING BATTLE AGAINST THE FORCES OF IGNORANT EVIL. BORN IN ANCIENT GREECE, HE HAS WORKED TO PRESERVE KNOWLEDGE AND WISDOM FOR THOUSANDS OF YEARS AGAINST ALL FORMS OF PERFIDY, FROM BOOK-BASHING BOOGEYMEN TO MOANING UNDEAD LEGIONS WHO IGNORE THE QUIET PLEASE SIGN. NOT EVEN SUPERPOWERED DELINQUENT ALIEN CHILDREN CAN ABSCOND WITH BOOKS WITHOUT A LIBRARY CARD WHILE REX IS ON THE JOB! FOR THE FIRST TIME THE SECRET WORLD OF LIBRARIANS AND THEIR DAILY STRUGGLE TO PROTECT CIVILIZATION AND THE KNOWLEDGE IT IS FOUNDED UPON IS REVEALED! FOR THIS IS THE WORLD OF...

REX · LIBRIS

"LEAP OF FAITH!"

"SEVERAL HOURS LATER, THE SPACE FREIGHTER WE'RE HITCHING A RIDE ON LUMBERS INTO THE BENZINE SYSTEM. I HAVE LOCATED THE *PRINCIPIA MATHEMATICA* TEXT THAT WE'RE LOOKING FOR (WHICH IS EQUIPPED WITH A LONG RANGE SUBSPACE HOMING BEACON PATCH) ON THE SURFACE OF **BENZINE V,** WHERE IT IS BEING HELD BY THE EVIL BUT EDUCATED WARLORD **VAGLOX**. HE'S NOT GONNA GIVE IT UP WITHOUT A FIGHT, SO PRETTY SOON IT'S GONNA GET MESSY. I'LL TRY TO KEEP THE COMMENTARY TO A MINIMUM UNTIL THE BATTLE IS RESOLVED TO AVOID SLOWIN' THE ACTION..."

DID YOU HEAR THEY MAY BE CLOSING ***BOOKED UP,*** SIMON?
EH? THE STORE IN **ARCHER CITY?** YOU'RE **KIDDING!** IT'S GOTTA BE THE BEST USED BOOK STORE IN... WELL, **ANYWHERE**.
YEAH. CRYIN' SHAME. **MCMURTY** WANTS TA RETIRE. I GOTTA GET DOWN THERE PRONTO WIT' A COUPLE OF FORKLIFTS AND **LOOT** THE PLACE. THE BEST ONE STOP SINCE **VESPASIANO DA BISTICCI** STOPPED SELLIN' BOOKS....
AH, COME ON. ***HALF*** THE STUFF VESPASIANO HAD WAS BY ST. AUGUSTINE. ***BOOKED UP*** IS ***MUCH*** MORE DIVERSE.

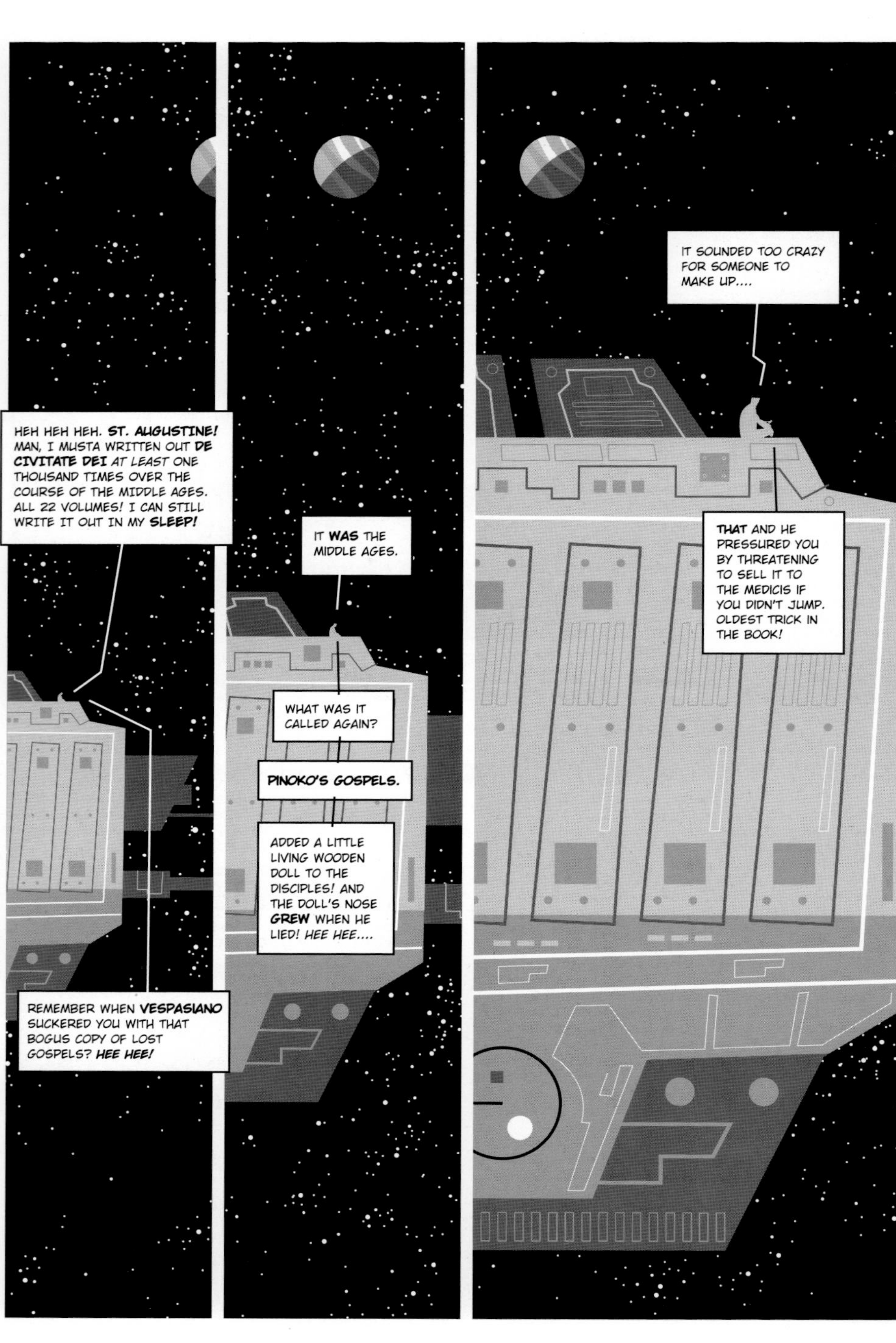
HEH HEH HEH. ST. AUGUSTINE! MAN, I MUSTA WRITTEN OUT DE CIVITATE DEI AT LEAST ONE THOUSAND TIMES OVER THE COURSE OF THE MIDDLE AGES. ALL 22 VOLUMES! I CAN STILL WRITE IT OUT IN MY SLEEP!
REMEMBER WHEN VESPASIANO SUCKERED YOU WITH THAT BOGUS COPY OF LOST GOSPELS? HEE HEE!
IT WAS THE MIDDLE AGES.
WHAT WAS IT CALLED AGAIN?
PINOKO'S GOSPELS.
ADDED A LITTLE LIVING WOODEN DOLL TO THE DISCIPLES! AND THE DOLL'S NOSE GREW WHEN HE LIED! HEE HEE....
IT SOUNDED TOO CRAZY FOR SOMEONE TO MAKE UP....
THAT AND HE PRESSURED YOU BY THREATENING TO SELL IT TO THE MEDICIS IF YOU DIDN'T JUMP. OLDEST TRICK IN THE BOOK!

VESPASIO WAS A REAL CONVINCIN' SALES FELLA, THAT'S FER SURE.
MADE ME FORGET THE ETERNAL MAXIM, "BUYER BEWARE."
SALES GUYS ARE JUST LIKE POLITICIANS. GIMME A DUKE ANY DAY.
BAH!
YOU'RE CONFUSING CAUSE WITH EFFECT. POLITICIANS ARE LIKE SALESMEN BECAUSE THAT'S WHAT WORKS. THE CAUSE IS HUMAN NATURE, NOT THE NATURE OF POLITICIANS. POLITICIANS WOULD BE LESS ANNOYING IF PEOPLE WERE, YA KNOW?
BESIDES, HOW MANY DEATH SENTENCES DID DUKE LORENZO PUT ON YOUR LIFE?
FIVE.
I ALWAYS KNEW WHERE I STOOD WITH HIM.
HEH. I MAY HAVE BEEN SUCKERED A FEW TIMES OVER THE YEARS, BUT I SEEM TO REMEMBER YOU WERE PRETTY KEEN ON BURNING GALILEO AT THE STAKE AWHILE BACK. AND YOU BOUGHT INTO THE PILTDOWN MAN. AND YOU THOUGHT YOGIC FLYING WAS THE WAY OF THE FU--
POINT! POINT CONCEDED!
SHEESH.
BUT I BET THIS VAGLOX TYRANT WILL BE A STRAIGHT FORWARD KINDA GUY. WON'T TALK US TO DEATH AT LEAST.

NO, HE'LL PROBABLY JUST HAVE US **SHOT OUTRIGHT.** A LITTLE DISINGENUOUS DISCUSSION IS BETTER THAN RESORTIN' TA WANTON DESTRUCTION **RIGHT AWAY,** AT LEAST IN **MY** BOOK.

IF IT LEADS SOMEWHERE.

HEH.

SO HOW ARE YOU GOING TO CONVINCE THIS FELLA TO RETURN THE BOOK, ANYWAY?

I GOT IT ALL **WORKED OUT.** FIRST, I'M GONNA GO WITH **REVERSE PSYCHOLOGY.** CONVINCE HIM OF THE ERROR OF HIS WAYS, APPEAL TO HIS BETTER NATURE, ALL THAT SORTA THING.

AND IF **THAT** DOESN'T WORK, I'M GONNA BEAT THE CRAP OUTTA HIM.

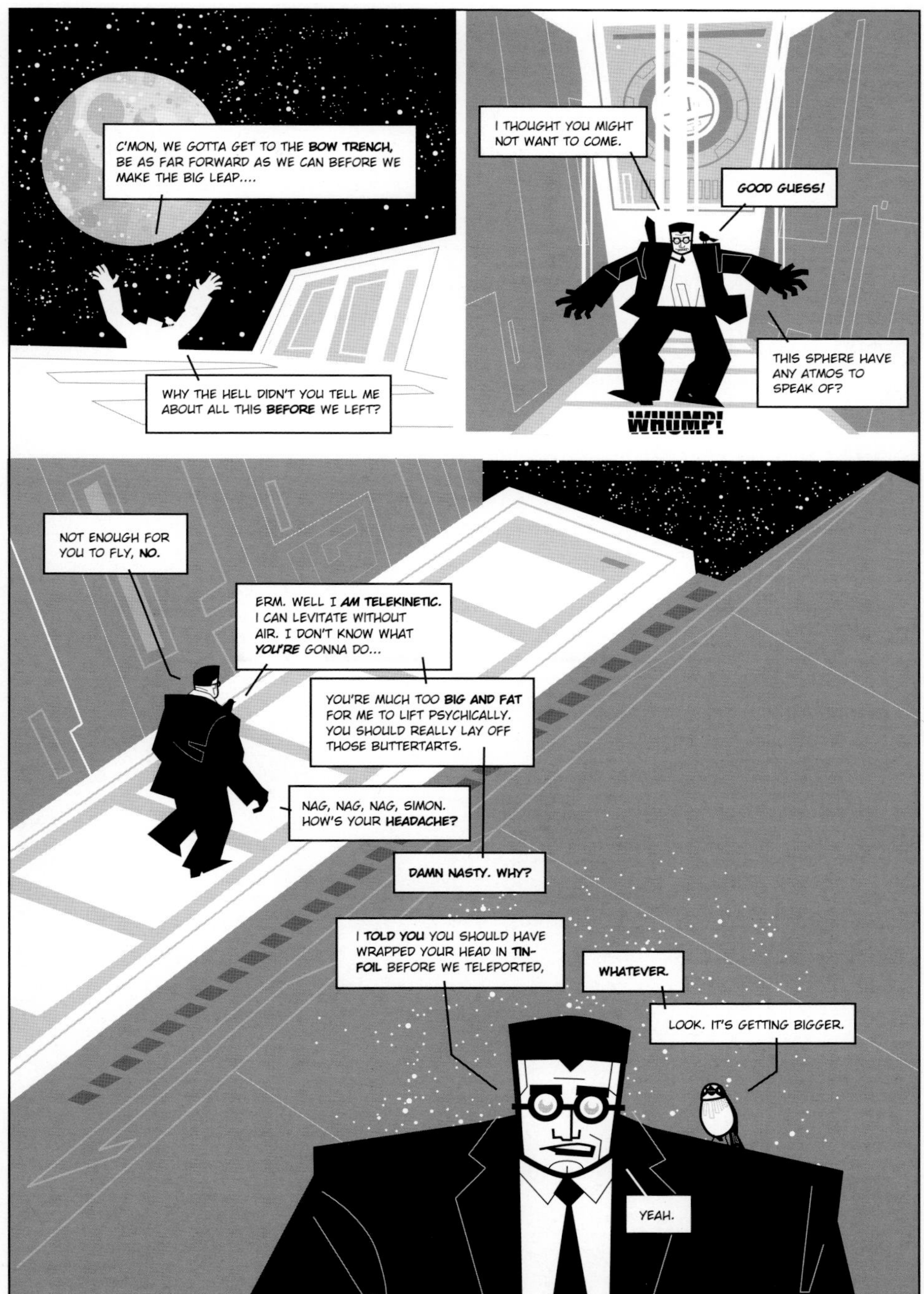
C'MON, WE GOTTA GET TO THE **BOW TRENCH,** BE AS FAR FORWARD AS WE CAN BEFORE WE MAKE THE BIG LEAP....
WHY THE HELL DIDN'T YOU TELL ME ABOUT ALL THIS **BEFORE** WE LEFT?
I THOUGHT YOU MIGHT NOT WANT TO COME.
GOOD GUESS!
THIS SPHERE HAVE ANY ATMOS TO SPEAK OF?
WHUMP!
NOT ENOUGH FOR YOU TO FLY, **NO.**
ERM. WELL I ***AM TELEKINETIC.*** I CAN LEVITATE WITHOUT AIR. I DON'T KNOW WHAT ***YOU'RE*** GONNA DO...
YOU'RE MUCH TOO **BIG AND FAT** FOR ME TO LIFT PSYCHICALLY. YOU SHOULD REALLY LAY OFF THOSE BUTTERTARTS.
NAG, NAG, NAG, SIMON. HOW'S YOUR **HEADACHE?**
DAMN NASTY. WHY?
I **TOLD YOU** YOU SHOULD HAVE WRAPPED YOUR HEAD IN **TIN-FOIL** BEFORE WE TELEPORTED,
WHATEVER.
LOOK. IT'S GETTING BIGGER.
YEAH.

I'VE NEVER RUSHED A PLANET BEFORE. THIS IS GONNA *HURT*.
PITY THEY DON'T MAKE PORTABLE, PERSONAL VERSIONS OF THOSE CAR AIRBAGS.

THEN AGAIN, IT PROBABLY WOULDN'T MAKE MUCH OF A DIFFERENCE. BENZINE V IS A BIT BIGGER THAN YOUR AVERAGE VOLKS-WAGON.
YEAH.
YA READY THERE, LITTLE BUDDY?
AS I'LL EVER BE.
ON A COUNT OF THREE....
ONE...
TWO...
TWO AND A HALF...
THREE!
BANZAI!
SAPERE AUDE!
YAAAAAAAAH!!
"TO SLIP THE SURLY BONDS OF EARTH...
"...AND SMACK INTO THE EYE OF GOD!"

SO....
WHAT?
ARE WE THERE YET?
QUIET, YOU.
HOW LONG IS THIS GONNA TAKE, REX?
I ESTIMATE THAT AT OUR CURRENT VELOCITY, WE'LL HIT THE SURFACE IN ABOUT FORTY MINUTES....
GREAT....
WAIT! WHAT'S THAT? OH MY GOD REX, IT'S A PLANET!...
IT'S COMING RIGHT AT US!
YEAH, YEAH. ...SMARTASS.

I DON'T KNOW ABOUT THIS, REX....
TAP!
TAP!
AS YOUR PUBLISHER, I HAVE TO SAY I'M NOT BUYING THIS WHOLE *JUMPING-FROM-ORBIT* THING.

IT'S NOT THAT I DOUBT YOU, BUT...
IT ALL JUST SEEMS RATHER ***UNBELIEVABLE.***

I DON'T UNDERSTAND.
YOU'VE NEVER DOUBTED EVENTS IN MY AUTOBIO BEFORE, BARRY. NOT EVEN MY BIG BATTLE WITH THE BUXOM SPACE AMAZONS, OR THE FIGHT WITH THE FOUL CREATURE OF KARMA CLOTTING CHOLESTEROL.

REX, SPACE AMAZONS CAN DO ***ANYTHING*** SO LONG AS THEY'RE BUXOM. AND FEW PEOPLE KNOW ABOUT KARMA CHOLESTEROL CREATURES, SO WE CAN GET AWAY WITH 'EM DOING WHATEVER WE WANT. BUT ***THIS?*** IT'S JUST ***BASIC PHYSICS.*** NOT-SO-IRRESISTIBLE FORCE MEETS IMMOVABLE OBJECT.
IT'S JUST *TOO* ***OBVIOUSLY*** IMPLAUSIBLE. JPL WOULD NEVER BUY IT.

THAT DOESN'T MAKE ANY SENSE, BARRY, I GOT ***ON*** THE SHIP USIN' A **TELE-PORTATION CRYSTAL.** I'M ACCOMPANIED BY A TWO THOUSAND YEAR OLD TELE-KINETIC **TALKIN' BIRD,** AN' I'M PURSUIN' AN ALIEN WARLORD WHO'S DIS BIG, GLOWIN CRYSTAL ON LEGS. I COULDN'T GET MORE *OUT THERE* IF I ***WAS*** MAKIN' IT UP.

IN FACT, THE VERY RIDICULOUSNESS OF IT ALL IS WHAT VALIDATES IT: NO ONE COULD MAKE UP SOMETHIN' SO NUTTY. ***AN'*** IT'S A ***COMIC BOOK*** FER CRIPES SAKE.
NONE OF 'EM HAVE REALISTIC PHYSICS.

TRUE, BUT THIS ISN'T JUST ***ANY*** ORDINARY COMIC BOOK, REX. IT'S ***AUTOBIOGRAPHICAL.*** WE DON'T WANT TO LOSE SUSPENSION OF DISBELIEF WITH A STORY BASED ON ***FACT.***
IT'S NOT WHETHER YOU REALLY ***DID*** JUMP FROM ORBIT *BUT WHETHER OR NOT PEOPLE CAN* ***BELIEVE*** YOU JUMPED FROM ORBIT.

MAYBE WE CAN GIVE YOU SOME KIND OF MAGICAL SPACE CUSHION OR SOMETHING.

NO....
MUST THINK FAST! NEED A SUITABLE MUMBO-JUMBO ALTERNATIVE TO SMOOTH OL' BARRY OVER, OR HE'LL FORCE **THAT** TIRED OLD 'SPACE CUSHION' LITERARY DEVICE ON ME!
EASTERN MYSTICISM?
BRILLIANT!
YOU CAN USE THAT TO EXPLAIN **JUST ABOUT ANYTHING!** AND IT IS **HOT, HOT HOT!**
WELL BARRY...
YOU'RE FORGETTING ABOUT MY YEARS OF STUDY OF THE SECRET, EASTERN NINJA ACROBAT ART OF, UH, **ODORU**. FALLING. **BARITSU** IS DERVIED FROM IT. FAR MORE EFFECTIVE THAN SILLY 'SPACE CUSHIONS.'
I'VE SAID IT BEFORE, AND I'LL SAY IT AGAIN: YOU'RE A **NATURAL**, REX! THIS IS BETTER THAN MY MAGIC SPACE CUSHION IDEA. PLAUSIBLE SOUNDING **AND** SPIRITUAL AT THE SAME TIME. **FABULOUS!**
THAT WRAPS THAT UP THEN. SORRY ABOUT THE INTERRUPTION.
NO WORRIES. YA GOTTA JOB TA DO.
GLAD YOU'RE SO UNDERSTANDING. **WELL!** I'D BETTER LET YOU GET BACK TO FALLING, EH? LET'S SEE WHAT THE ART OF **ODORU** CAN DO! I CAN'T WAIT!
OH, I CAN STAY AND CHAT.
YOU DON'T HAVE TO DO THAT, REX. I KNOW YOU WERE **VERY** BUSY THERE, ON BENZINE..
NAH... I DON'T HAVE TO GO BACK **RIGHT** AWAY. NICE AND WARM HERE. GOTTA BE... WHAT, **ROOM TEMPERATURE?**
NO NO, I'M HOLDING UP THE WHOLE STORY WITH MY SILLY INTERRRUPTION AND QUIBBLING ABOUT REALISM. WHAT WAS I THINKING!? OFF YOU GO! I WON'T INTERRUPT AGAIN, I PROMISE.
WAIT, I JUST REMEMBERED SOMETHING.
THAT MAGICAL SPACE CUSHION MIGHT NOT BE SUCH A BAD....

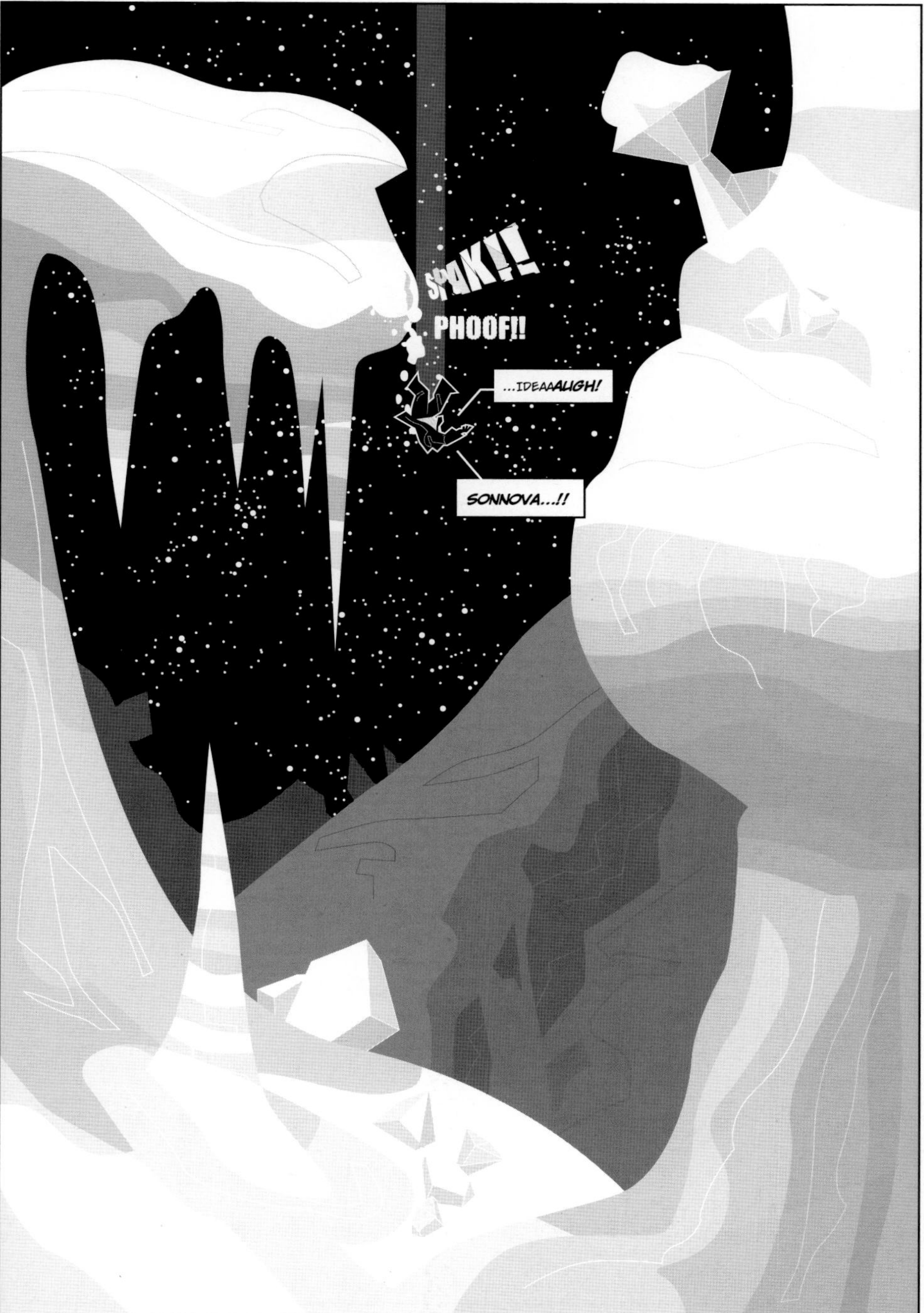
SPAK!!
PHOOF!!
...IDEAAAALIGH!
SONNOVA...!!

YOU ALL RIGHT THERE, REX?
PIF!
KLOMPHF!
PIF!
PIF!
MGLFFKT!
PFFHT! UNH!??
WHOOPS!
WATCH IT! YOU'RE GOING OVER A CLIFF!
PLOF!
AAAAAAAAAAAUGH!!
REMEMBER TO HIT AND ROLL, REX!
BZZZT!
BZZZT!
BRRRZZZT!
BZZZT!
BZZZT!
BZZZT!
GRRRZZZZZT!

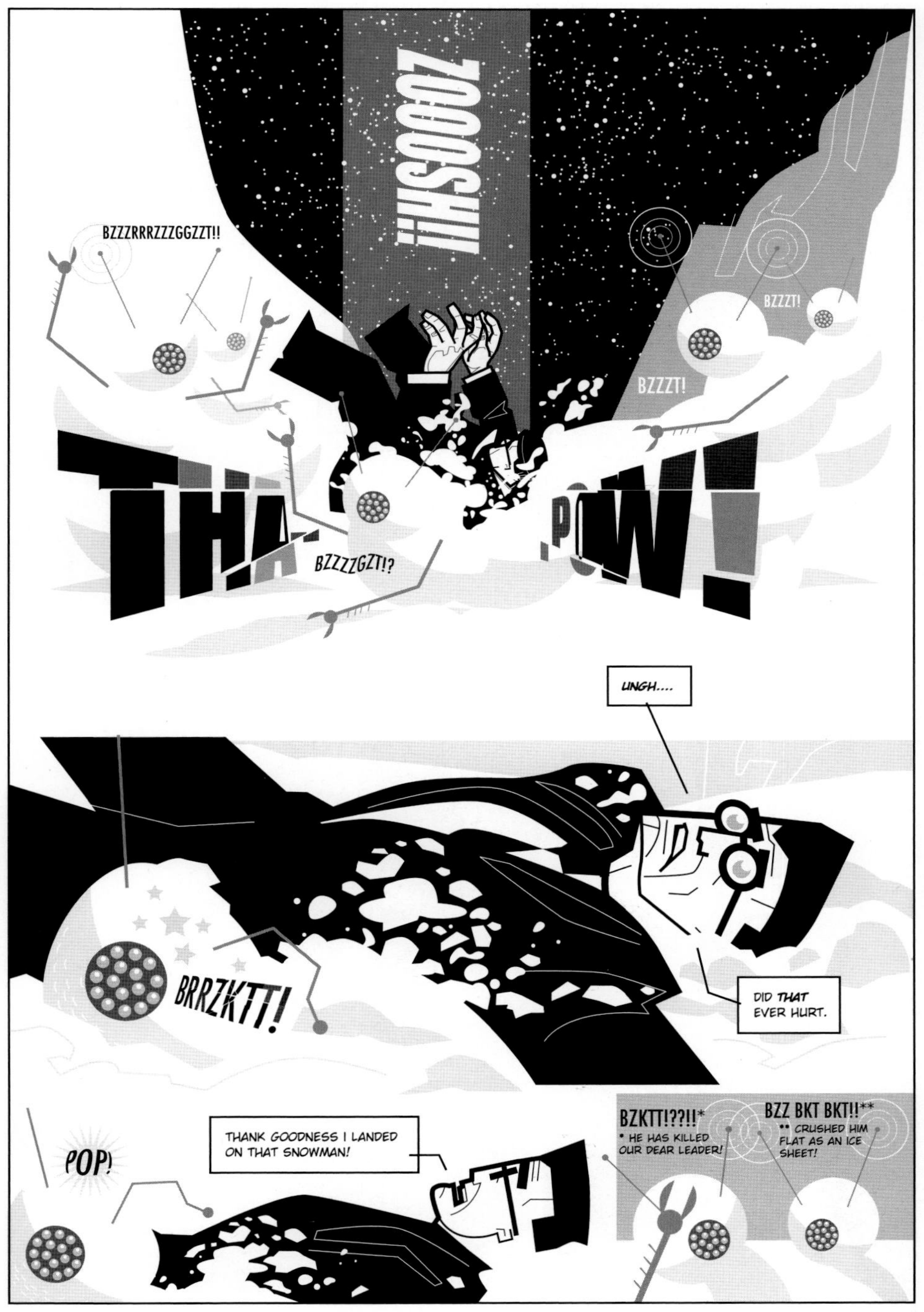
ZOOOSH!!
BZZZRRRZZZGGZZT!!
BZZZT!
BZZZT!
THA-POW!
BZZZZGZT!?
UNGH....
BRRZKTT!
DID THAT EVER HURT.
POP!
THANK GOODNESS I LANDED ON THAT SNOWMAN!
BZKTT!??!!*
* HE HAS KILLED OUR DEAR LEADER!
BZZ BKT BKT!!**
** CRUSHED HIM FLAT AS AN ICE SHEET!

BzZKT!*
* WE HAVE BEEN FOUND! WHAT DO WE DO?
GRZZZT!**
** IT HAS KILLED OUR DEAR LEADER!
BzZrZRZkT!***
*** IT IS HIDEOUS! A MONSTROSITY!
NOW THAT'S WHAT I CALL A FALL FROM GRACE!
WHAT THE!?
WOW! SOME KINDA SNOWFLAKE BASED LIFEFORM!
THAT WAS AN ACCIDENT, YA KNOW....
FZZZZKT!*
* KILL IT! AVENGE OUR BELOVED TYRANT! USE THE BLACK MARKET WEAPONS WE BOUGHT!
SNIP! SNIP! SNIP! SNIP! SNIP!
GRZKZKT!*
* ALLOW ME THE HONOUR, FIZFIZT!
CHIKSNIK!

BZZZT!*
* WAIT! I, FZZP, SHALL AVENGE OUR FALLEN LEADER!
GZBZT!**
** NO, NO, THE HONOUR MUST BE MINE!
LOOK! A WHOLE LOT MORE OF 'EM, AND THEY'VE OPENED UP A BOX OF SPACE GUNS!
WAITASEC, SPACE FROSTY!
BZGZGZZT!*
* IT IS MAKING WILD AND THREATENING GESTURES! IT MEANS TO MELT US ALL!
ABSIT INVIDIA! LET'S TALK THIS OUT!
I COME IN PEACE!
AH... OOT ZOP IK PLOMT! KAPEESH?
SPEAKEE GAL SEVENEE?
MEE TOODOL PLOP MOOGA-SUSH!
DAMMIT SIMON! WHY DON'T THEY SAY ANYTHIN'!?
IT'S TOO LATE FOR TALK! YOU SQUISHED ONE, AN' NOW THEY'RE LOOKING FOR PAY-BACK! TAKE 'EM OUT, QUICK!!
NO!
IT'S ALL A MISUNDERSTANIDING! AN UNFORTUNATE CONFLUENCE OF UNRELATED EVENTS LEADIN' TA UNNECESSARY TRAGEDY! WE DON'T NEED TA ADD TO IT.
'MEMBER, "IT'S BETTER TO JAW-JAW THAN TO WAR-WAR."

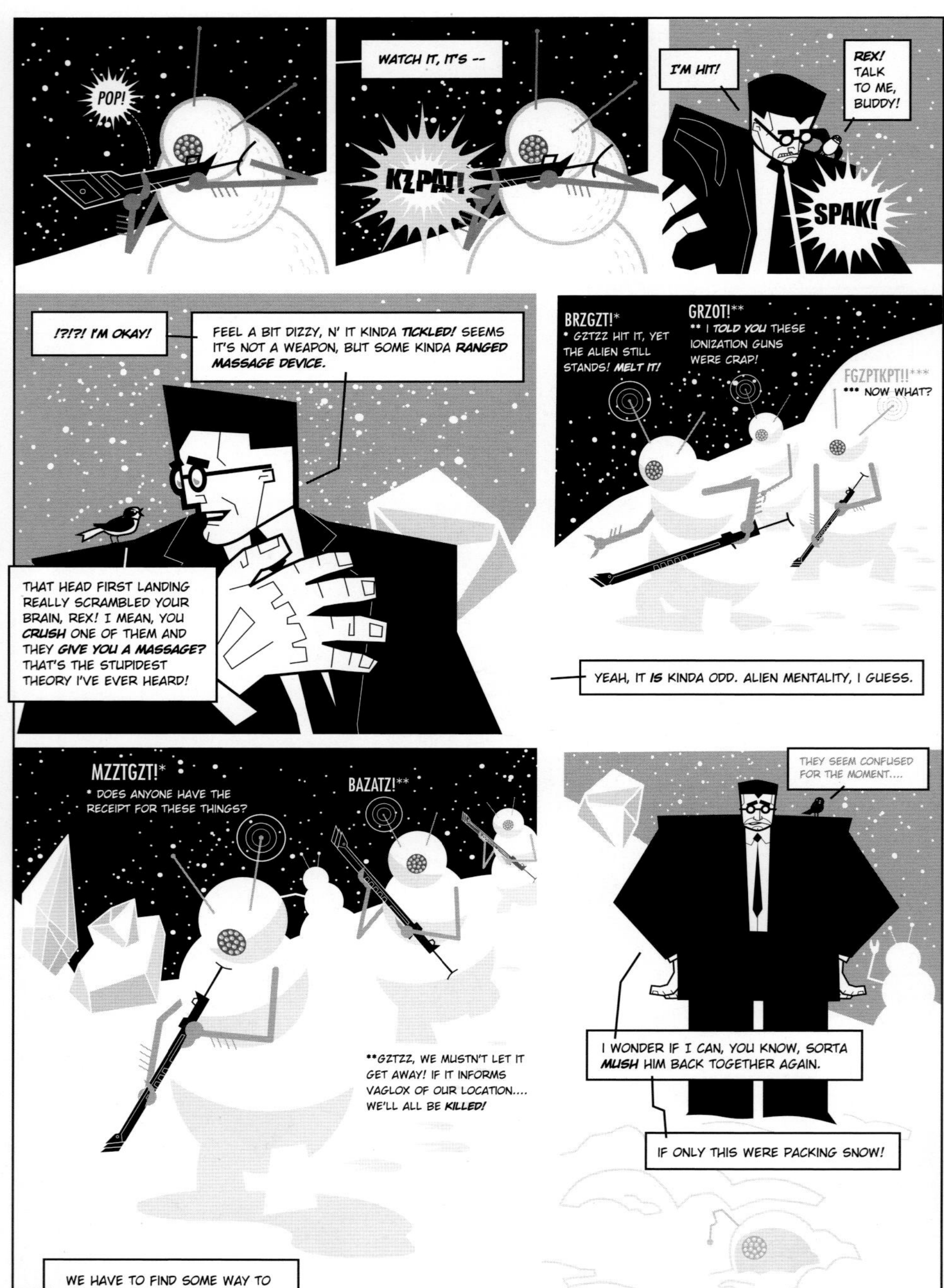
POP!
WATCH IT, IT'S --
KZPAT!
I'M HIT!
REX! TALK TO ME, BUDDY!
SPAK!
!?!?! I'M OKAY!
FEEL A BIT DIZZY, N' IT KINDA TICKLED! SEEMS IT'S NOT A WEAPON, BUT SOME KINDA RANGED MASSAGE DEVICE.
THAT HEAD FIRST LANDING REALLY SCRAMBLED YOUR BRAIN, REX! I MEAN, YOU CRUSH ONE OF THEM AND THEY GIVE YOU A MASSAGE? THAT'S THE STUPIDEST THEORY I'VE EVER HEARD!
BRZGZT!*
* GZTZZ HIT IT, YET THE ALIEN STILL STANDS! MELT IT!
GRZOT!**
** I TOLD YOU THESE IONIZATION GUNS WERE CRAP!
FGZPTKPT!!***
*** NOW WHAT?
YEAH, IT IS KINDA ODD. ALIEN MENTALITY, I GUESS.
MZZTGZT!*
* DOES ANYONE HAVE THE RECEIPT FOR THESE THINGS?
BAZATZ!**
**GZTZZ, WE MUSTN'T LET IT GET AWAY! IF IT INFORMS VAGLOX OF OUR LOCATION.... WE'LL ALL BE KILLED!
WE HAVE TO FIND SOME WAY TO COMMUNICATE WITH THEM.
THEY SEEM CONFUSED FOR THE MOMENT....
I WONDER IF I CAN, YOU KNOW, SORTA MUSH HIM BACK TOGETHER AGAIN.
IF ONLY THIS WERE PACKING SNOW!

ANTENNAE
RADIO TRANSMITTER ORGANELLE
HEAD
COMPOUND EYE
THORAX
MAIN HYDRAULIC PUMP RESEVOIR
HARD OUTER CRUST SNOW SHELL
ARM
CLAW
WHISKERS
ABDOMEN
BRAIN ENCASED IN PROTECTIVE SHELL
PSEUDOPOD
FASCINATIN', THE IDEA OF SNOWFLAKE-BASED LIFE. DESE FELLAS MUST USE RESERVOIRS OF LIQUID TO HYDRAULICALLY POWER THEIR COMPACTED SNOW LIMBS.
ELECTRICITY CONDUCTING SNOWFLAKE CRYSTAL TISSUES
HARDENED EXTERIOR CRUST MEMBRANE
TEMPERATURE MODERATED SUBCUTANEOUS LIQUID WATER HYDRAULIC MUSCLE
CLOSE TO ABSOLUTE ZERO, ELECTRICITY FLOWS WITHOUT RESISTENCE, SO THEIR BODIES ARE NATURAL SUPERCONDUCTORS. THEY PROBABLY LIVE OFFA STATIC ELECTRICITY IN THE CRUST OF THE PLANET! ALL BASIC COMIC BOOK SCIENCE, LIL' BUDDY.
BAH! YOU'RE JUST GUESSING, LIBRIS!
YEAH, BUT EDUCATED GUESSING.
AN' SADLY AN' THEORETICALLY, ONCE THE BRAIN SAC HAS BEEN RUPTURED AN' THE CONTENTS SPLATTERED ALL OVER THE LANDSCAPE, I DON'T THINK THERE'S ANYTHIN' WE CAN DO FOR 'EM.
YEAH, RUPTURED BRAIN SAC'LL DO THAT, I GUESS.
BZZGZERZT!*
* LOOK! BIZZT APPROACHES IT FROM BEHIND!
BZRAP!
GAAAAAAAAAAH!! PERFIDY!

BZGZBZGZ!*
*AHAHA! I, MIGHTY BIZZT, HAVE FELLED THE BEAST! SEE HOW WEAK AND FEEBLE IT IS! HAHAHA!
BZG!**
GZT!***
MZBZGT!****
GRZGZT!*****
GRZGZT!******
I KNEW IT! THESE ALIENS ARE HOSTILE!
****** NO, I WANT TO KILL IT! GET OUT OF MY WAY!
** SHIT! IT'S EASY!!
*** THE ALIEN IS WEAK! LET ME AT IT! I SHALL DEFEAT IT!
GET UP, REX! GET UP OR WE'RE BOTH DEAD!
***** NO, ME!!
**** LET ME ZAP IT!
YEAH, YEAH.
TEACH ME FOR LETTIN' MY GUARD DOWN.
BZGZBZGZ!*
BZB!**
BZBZBZGZ!***
GZAT!****
GINGZ!*****
GZRZGZT!******
ZZGRZTTFZ!*******
IF VIOLENCE BE YOUR REPARTEE, I GOT A LITTLE SOMETHIN' TO SAY....
* LET IT COWER BEFORE MIGHTY BIZZT! WHO RULES NOW? MIGHTY BIZZT RULES,!
** DON'T HOG ALL THE GLORY, BIZZT! LET ME ZAP IT BEFORE IT DIES!
*** WAIT FOR ME! I WANT MY TURN!
**** LET IT SUFFER IN THE GRASP OF THE GREAT GRZAZZT!
*****I SHALL TEACH THE ALIEN A LESSON IN MANNERS WITH MY GRIP OF ICE!
****** I WANT MY TURN! STAND ASIDE, SLUSH BRAIN!
******* I'M NEXT, I'M NEXT!

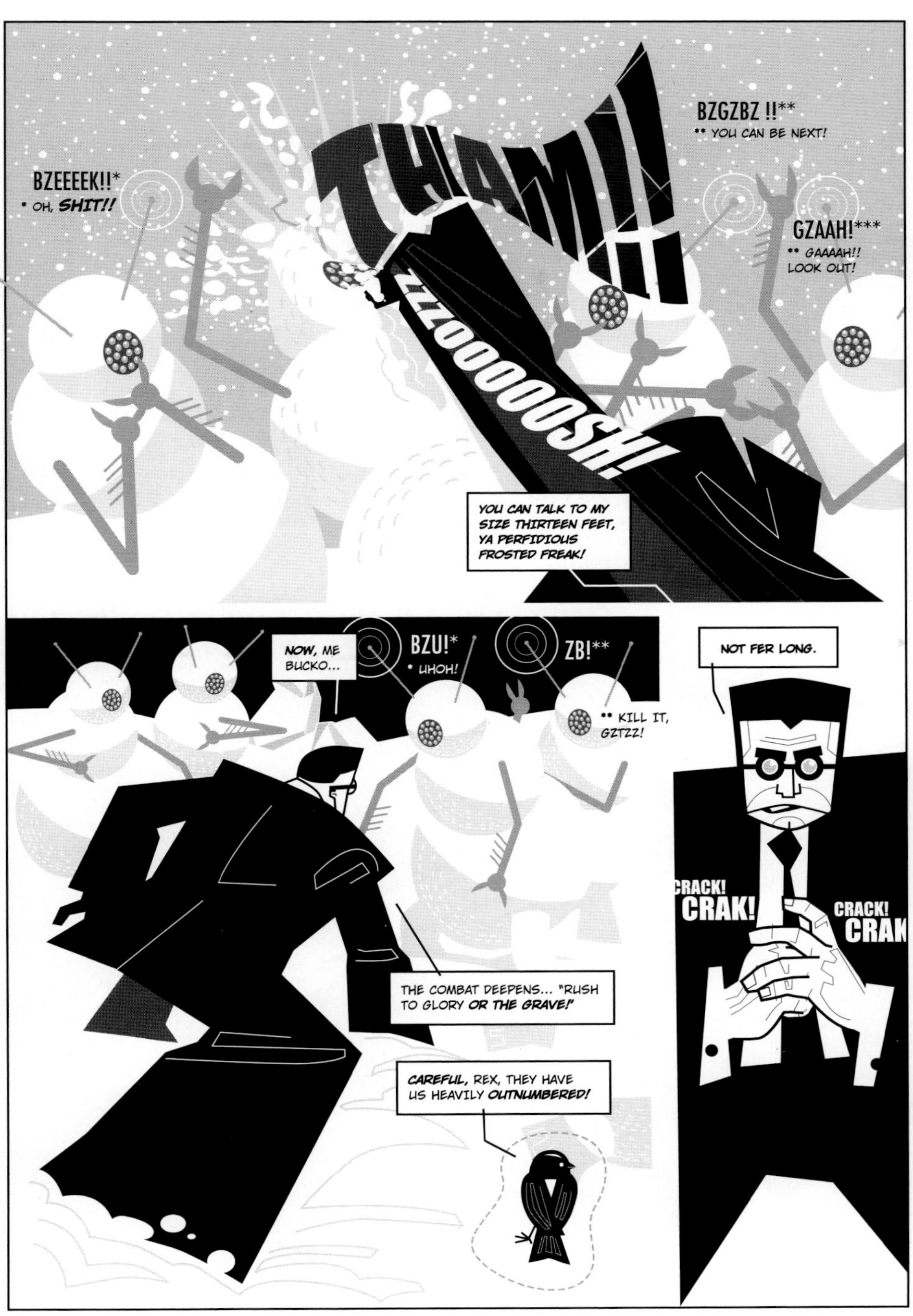
BZEEEEK!!*
* OH, SHIT!!
THWAM!!
BZGZBZ !!**
** YOU CAN BE NEXT!
GZAAH!***
** GAAAAH!! LOOK OUT!
ZZZOOOOOOSH!
YOU CAN TALK TO MY SIZE THIRTEEN FEET, YA PERFIDIOUS FROSTED FREAK!
NOW, ME BUCKO...
BZU!*
* UHOH!
ZB!**
** KILL IT, GZTZZ!
NOT FER LONG.
CRACK! CRAK!
CRACK! CRAK
THE COMBAT DEEPENS... "RUSH TO GLORY OR THE GRAVE!"
CAREFUL, REX, THEY HAVE US HEAVILY OUTNUMBERED!

* FOOLS! I WILL KILL THIS ALIEN BEAST! IT SHALL FALL BEFORE ME!
GZT!*
WOOOSH!
TAKE THAT, YA LUMBERIN' ICE CREAM CONE!
GOTTA KEEP MOVING, KEEP THESE ICE EGGS OFF BALANCE! SIMON'S RIGHT! THERE ARE A LOT OF THEM!
POW!
BZZZORT!**
** BWAARGHFF!
BUT THEY AREN'T WELL CO-ORDINATED, OR -- WHOOPS!
ALMOST DIDN'T SEE THAT ONE IN TIME! I'M WAY TOO EXPOSED OUT HERE ON THIS ICE SHEET. THEY CAN HIT ME FROM ALL SIDES. GOTTA PULL BACK! GET 'EM ALL WHERE I CAN SEE 'EM!
THOOOSH!
WATCH MY BACK, SIMON!
BZOORK!*
* — BZOAAAGH!
THOCK!

OKAY... THEY'RE BEHIND YOU!... IF YOU'D LET ME BRING A GUN, MAYBE I COULD DO SOMETHING ABOUT IT!
JUST NEED SOME WARNING TIME, LIL' BUDDY; THEIR GRIP PACKS A REAL ELECTRIC WHALLOP!
I'M GONNA MAKE A BREAK UP THE GLACIER. COME ON!
?!?
?!?
THUNK!
THAP!
OUTTA MY WAY, SNOW CONE!
UP THE GLACIER? WHAT FOR?
NARROWER! THEY WON'T BE ABLE TO ATTACK ALL AT ONCE THERE.
AH! I'LL GO SCOUT AHEAD!
TOOF!

ALL CLEAR! COME ON!
COMIN'!
UP HERE, REX. THIS SHOULD BE A GOOD SPOT. WE CAN SEE THE ENTIRE VALLEY FROM HERE.
GREAT. HUFF! TH' DEEP SNOW IS WEARIN' ME OUT. HOW FAR BEHIND ME ARE THEY?
HEH. DON'T WORRY. THEY WADDLE ALONG LIKE A BUNCH OF OBESE TURTLES. YOU CAN RUN CIRCLES AROUND 'EM, EVEN IN DEEP SNOW.
BZzzZTZ!*
GZRBZZzzT!**
UZzzGzZT!***
* LOOK! THE COWARDLY ALIEN FLEES FROM US IN TERROR! AFTER IT!
** WE ARE TOO MUCH FOR THE BEAST!
*** IT IS AFRAID TO FACE US!
**** DON'T LET IT GET AWAY!
IF THESE FELLAS ARE VAGLOX'S GOONS, WE SHOULDN'T HAVE TOO MUCH TROUBLE GETTIN' THE BOOK BACK BACK FROM HIM!
I SUSPECT THEY AREN'T! VAGLOX IS A CHANDELIER ON LEGS, A DIAMOND. DESE ICE EGG FELLAS AREN'T EVEN THE SAME FORM OF LIFE!
I THINK HE'D PICK MORE EFFECTIVE ALIEN MERCENARIES, IF HE WAS GONNA IMPORT 'EM, DON'T YOU?
WHO THE HADES ARE THESE GUYS THEN?
MILITIA? OUTLAWS? SPACE BANDITS?
DUNNO. BUT WE MIGHT NOT NEED TO FIGHT 'EM AT ALL, SINCE THEY'RE AS SLOW AS SEAWEED. WE CAN JUST WALK AROUND.
WHOA. LOOK! THEY'RE SPEEDING UP!

WHAT THE?
SKITCH!
BY GOD! THEIR INTERNAL STRUCTURE MUST BE EXTREMELY ADAPTIVE. THEY'VE TURNED THEIR TRUNK, OR A SECTION OF IT, INTO A GYROSCOPE, AND BY DRAWING UPON THE STATIC ELECTRICITY OF THE PLANET ITSELF, THEY'RE SHOOTIN' ACROSS ITS ICY SURFACE LIKE IT WAS A GIANT OMNIDIRECTIONAL RAILWAY SYSTEM!
WELL.
A PLANAR RESTRICTED MULTIDIRECTIONAL STREETCAR SYSTEM, AT LEAST. WOW.
THIS IS FASCINATIN'! TO DO THAT, THEIR CELLS MUST BE ABLE TO COORDINATE INTELLIGENTLY, ACROSS FRACTURES AND HIGH SPEEDS.
SCREEEEEEEEEEEE!!
THESE CRITTERS HAVE CERTAINLY GOTTEN INTERESTING.
BAH. I SEEN BETTER.
FLUMPF!
YEAH.
I SUPPOSE....
HEY, LET ME HAVE YOUR GUN. I CAN PICK OFF A FEW OF THEM BEFORE THEY GET UP HERE. QUICK!! NO TIME TO THINK!
HAW! FORGET IT. YOU'RE A MENACE WITH A FIREARM.
NICE TRY, THO.
HOW LONG ARE YOU GOING TO HOLD THAT LITTLE MISHAP AT THE KHYBER PASS AGAINST ME, ANYWAY?

IT ISN'T JUST--
YOU KNOW I'M WILLING TO TAKE A COURSE IN THE PROPER HANDLING OF FIREARMS...
AND ULTIMATELY IT WOULD BE TO YOUR BENEFIT IF I COULD CONTRIBUTE MORE TO THESE RETRIEVAL MISSIONS.
WHAT IF YOU WERE CAPTURED, OR WOUNDED, AND NEEDED A FORCE-BACKED EXTRACTION? WHAT IF YOU'RE KNOCKED OUT AND BESIEGED BY A SWARM OF MAN EATING MOLLUSCS?
WHAT THEN, HMM?
WELL...
HOW WILL I BE ABLE TO SAVE YOU IF I'M UNARMED AND HELP-LESS BEFORE THE FORCES OF EVIL, WHILE YOU SIT IN DIRE PERIL, MENACED BY EVIL, MALIGNANT SPACE MOLLUSCS?
IN SUCH A SITUATION, AS YOUR FRIEND AND FELLOW TRAVELLER, IT WOULD BE INCUMBENT UPON ME TO OFFER YOU AID! YET AS THINGS STAND, THAT WOULD BE IMPOSSIBLE!
AS A SMALL BIRD, I NEED SOME SORT OF FORCE MULTIPLIER TO FEND OFF SPACE MOLLUSCS. IN FACT, UNARMED, AM I NOT LITTLE MORE THAN A POTENTIAL, IF HIGHLY VALUABLE, HOSTAGE FOR MENACING ALIENS?
AND ON TOP OF ALL THAT, ISN'T IT TACTICALLY SOUND TO HAVE BACK-UP IN POTENTIALLY VOLATILE SITUATIONS?
YOUR OWN LIBRARIAN COMMANDO TRAINING HAS SURELY INFORMED YOU OF THE MERITS OF ARMED BACK-UP!
WELL, DAMN. YOU'RE RIGHT. I SHOULDA BROUGHT HYPATIA.
HYPATIA!? FORGET HYPATIA! WHAT ABOUT ME? I'M HERE, AFTER ALL. WHAT ABOUT MY RIGHT TO BEAR ARMS?
DAT DOESN'T APPLY TO BIRDS.
THAT'S JUST OUTRIGHT ANTI-BIRD PREJUDICE!
'SIDES...
I DON'T WANNA USE LETHAL FORCE AGAINST THESE ELECTRIC TRIPLE SCOOPS UNLESS I HAVE TO. IF MY SUSPICION PROVES CORRECT, WE MAY BE ABLE TO CO-OPT THEM INTO HELPIN US GET THE 'PRINCIPIA MATH-EMATICA' BOOK BACK.
IF I COULD JUST FIGURE OUTTA WAY TA TALK TO 'EM. I'M SURE I'M FOR-GETTING SOMETHING! IF ONLY I COULD REMEMBER WHAT!
TOO LATE! THEY'RE HERE!

MEANWHILE, BACK AT MIDDLETON PUBLIC LIBRARY....
SO... ARE YOU... THE ORIGINAL?
CIRCE? YES, I AM. WHY DO YOU ASK?
I DON'T KNOW... IT'S JUST ODD TO SEE YOU HERE. IN A LIBRARY. I HEARD YOU WERE... WELL... A REAL TROUBLEMAKER.
YOU KNOW...
EVIL.
MUMBLE MUMBLE GRUMBLE MUMBLE GAWD DAMN PEOPLE!
IN
OH, WE ALL MELLOW WITH AGE, DEAR.
I'M OVER 2000 YEARS OLD. MY TROUBLE-MAKING DAYS ARE LONG BEHIND ME. WREAKING HAVOC AND SEDUCING ADVENTURING HEROES IS FOR YOUNG PEOPLE. THESE DAYS I LIKE TO CURL UP WITH A GOOD BOOK AND A HOT CUP OF TEA.
DO YOU EVER MISS IT?
BEING A VILLAINESS, I MEAN? BEING FREE FROM MORAL CONSTRAINTS?
NOT REALLY.
DESTROYING LIVES, SEEKING POWER... IT ISN'T VERY FULFILLING.
AS FOR THE SEDUCTION....
AFTER THE FIRST FEW MILLENNIA, THE SEX GETS A LITTLE BORING. THERE ARE ONLY SO MANY VARIATIONS. THE EMOTIONS AROUND THE SEX HAVE ALWAYS BEEN THE REAL SPICE. STIMULATING JEALOUSY, SPIKING ENVY, AND AROUSING AGGRESSION AND ANGER IN A SUITOR CAN MAKE THINGS TERRIBLY EXCITING AND LIFT ONE'S EGO....
!?!
DELICIOUSLY DESTRUCTIVE, ADDICTIVE, AND SALACIOUS, BUT OVER TIME, IN THE LONG RUN, NAUSEATING. THINK OF BEING STUCK ON A HUNDRED YEAR LONG ROLLER-COASTER RIDE.
IT'S JUST NOT A HEALTHY WAY TO LIVE.
BAD FOR ONE'S SENSE OF BALANCE.
EGO TRIPS OF EVIL ARE ONLY ENTICING IN THE ABSTRACT.... IF YOU REACH MY AGE, YOU'LL HAVE SEEN PLENTY OF HORRIBLE THINGS.

THINGS NO ONE SHOULD EVER HAVE TO WITNESS, MUCH LESS ENDURE. UN-MENTIONABLE BUTCHERY AND INHUMANITY DOWN THROUGH THE AGES... OF SUCH UN-FATHOMABLE, GROTESQUE IMMENSITY THAT THE MEMORY GNAWS AT MY SANITY.
AS A VILLAINESS, THAT'S WHAT I WAS CONTRIBUTING TO. IF I WASN'T, I WOULDN'T BE A VILLAINESS. YOU SEE?
AND I DIDN'T WANT TO POSE AS A 'BAD ASS' JUST TO BE CHIC ANYMORE, EITHER. I DID THAT UNTIL, OH, THE EARLY SIXTEEN HUNDREDS. THE DRESS-ING IN BLACK, THE REPUTATION AS A CARNAL, SINNING HEDONIST, THE ORGIES, THE FEAR, THE WHOLE BIT. ALL THE VILLAGERS BEING AFRAID I'D TURN THEM INTO TOADS, LOOKING DOWN WHEN I PASSED, CRINGING, OH, THE RESPECT I GOT...!!
SIGH.
YOU GROW OUT OF IT.
IF THERE'S ONE THING I'VE LEARNED, IT'S THAT EVIL HAS A LOT TO DO WITH AN UN-HINGED EGO. NOW THAT I'M COMFORTABLE WITH WHO I AM, THER'S LITTLE NEED FOR GRATUITOUS SHIT-DISTURBING.
I'LL LEAVE ALL THAT FOR THE IMMATURE.
I HAVE BETTER THINGS TO DO NOW. SUCH AS...
-- BAKING.
WOULD YOU LIKE A COOKIE? I MADE THEM THIS MORNING.

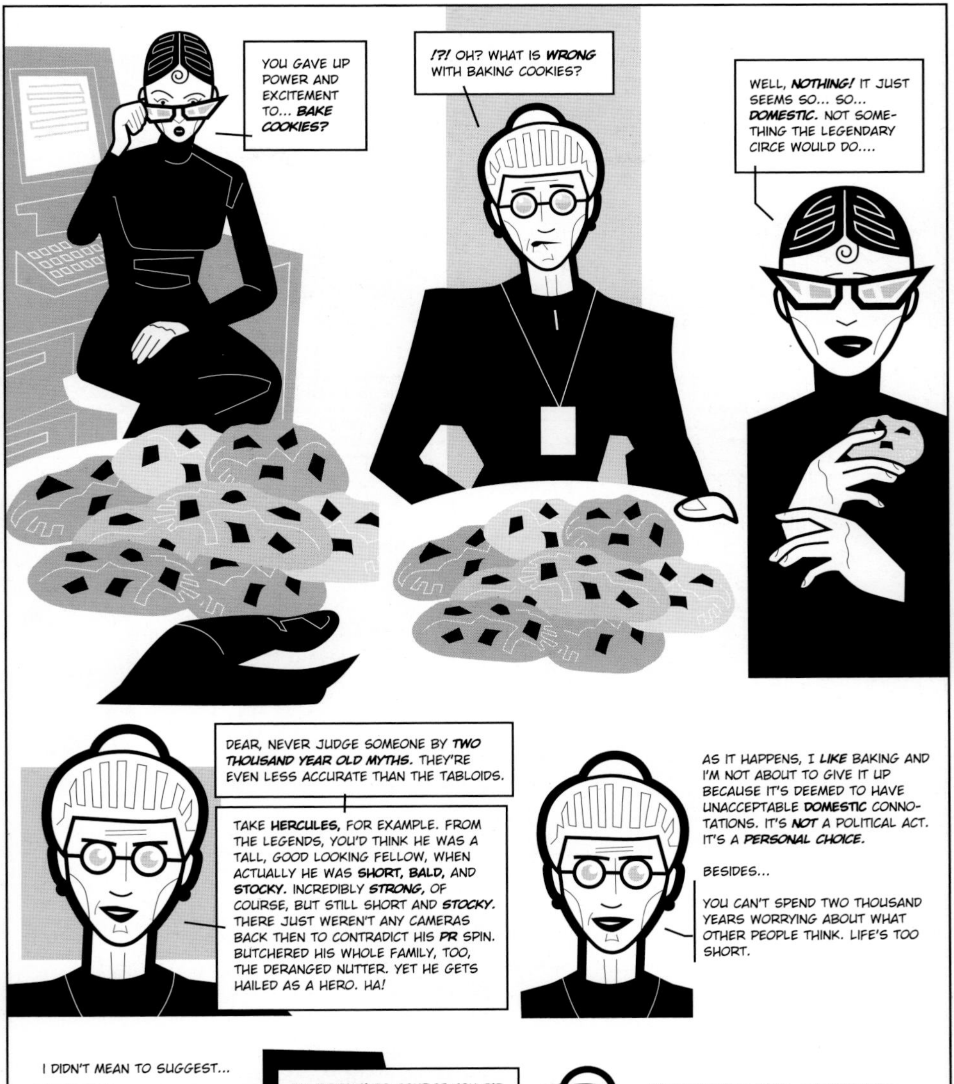

YOU GAVE UP POWER AND EXCITEMENT TO... **BAKE COOKIES?**

!?! OH? WHAT IS **WRONG** WITH BAKING COOKIES?

WELL, **NOTHING!** IT JUST SEEMS SO... SO... **DOMESTIC.** NOT SOME-THING THE LEGENDARY CIRCE WOULD DO....

HMM.
CRUNCH
CRUNCH
CRUNCH
CRUNCH
MMM! THAT'S A DAMN FINE COOKIE.
THANK YOU. THE CHILDREN HERE LOVE THEM.
YOU KNOW, REX TOLD ME THAT YOU'D BEEN BANNED FROM GOING ON MISSIONS FOR TURNING PATRONS INTO PIGS...
OH!
TRUE, I'M AFRAID. MIND YOU, THEY WERE BEING LOUD, BOORISH, AND OBNOXIOUS IN THE LIBRARY. I'D SAY THEY WERE ALREADY SWINE, LONG BEFORE I DID ANYTHING. SUCH A FUSS OVER NOTHING....
IF I'D LOST MY TEMPER, I COULD HAVE DONE MUCH WORSE. HAVE ANOTHER COOKIE, DEAR.
WELL MAYBE JUST ONE....
THANK GOD! LIBRARIANS!
HELP!

THE MONTGOMERY READING ROOM!
THEY CAME FROM OUT OF NOWHERE! VANDALS! THEY JUST STARTED TRASHING THE PLACE!
I BARELY ESCAPED!
THE OTHERS ARE GONERS! GET OUT WHILE YOU STILL CAN! BEFORE IT'S TOO LATE! RUN, I TELL YOU!
RUN FOR YOUR LIVES! AAAAH!
HEY! WAIT!
JEEZ. TALK ABOUT AN OVER-REACTION.

CIRCE, CAN YOU BELIEVE THAT...
HERE.
CHIK-SNIK!
JUST A SECOND...
TAKE THE TWELVE GAUGE, DEAR.
I'LL GO SORT THESE WIPPERSNAP-PERS OUT. WATCH THE INFORMATION DESK. IF THEY GET BY ME, DON'T LET THEM GET INTO THE SOUTH WING OF THE LIBRARY.
!?! WHAT? AGAINST VANDALS? ISN'T THIS ALL A BIT EXTREME? THE NEIGHBOURHOOD ISN'T THAT BAD, IS IT? SHOULDN'T WE JUST CALL THE POLICE? OR GIVE THEM A STERN TALKING-TO?

GOODNESS, NO. DIDN'T REX TELL YOU? MIDDLETON IS ATOP THE MOST POWERFUL LEY POINT ON THE PLANET. WE GET FAR, FAR MORE POTENT PSYCHIC MANIFESTATIONS THAN ANYWHERE ELSE. WELL. EXCEPT PERHAPS AREA 51 AND STONEHENGE. THE POLICE JUST AREN'T EQUIPPED TO HANDLE THE SORT OF ECLECTIC THREAT WE FACE AT THIS BRANCH. IT'S WHY REX AND THE ADMINISTRATOR ARE HERE. IT'S WHY I'M HERE. AND IT'S WHY YOU'RE HERE.
SO HERE. TAKE THE SHOTGUN.
OKAY. BUT IF THIS, WHATEVER THIS IS, IS AS DANGEROUS AS YOU SAY, SHOULDN'T YOU TAKE A WEAPON?
PSHAW! NONSENSE. THAT WOULD BE LIKE ARMING A NUCLEAR MISSILE WITH A PEA SHOOTER.
I'M MUCH MORE DANGEROUS THAN THAT.
SAVE THE REST OF THE COOKIES FOR THE CHILDREN'S READING GROUP...
WAIT! SHOULDN'T I BACK YOU UP? ARTICLE 1, SUBSECTION A OF THE COMBAT GUIDELINES SPECIFICALLY STATES--
NONSENSE!
CAN'T ABANDON THE INFORMATION DESK, HYPATIA. WHAT IF SOMEONE WANTED TO TAKE OUT A BOOK? REMEMBER YOUR PRIORITIES!
FINE.

SHORTLY....
<BRING ME BOOKS ON THE SECRETS OF BOAT BUILDING!>
OH HADES. IT'S WORSE THAN I EXPECTED!
IT'S GAISERIC--KING OF THE VANDALS!
<A WENCH!>
<GET HER!>
NEXT ISSUE: BATTLE ON BENZINE!

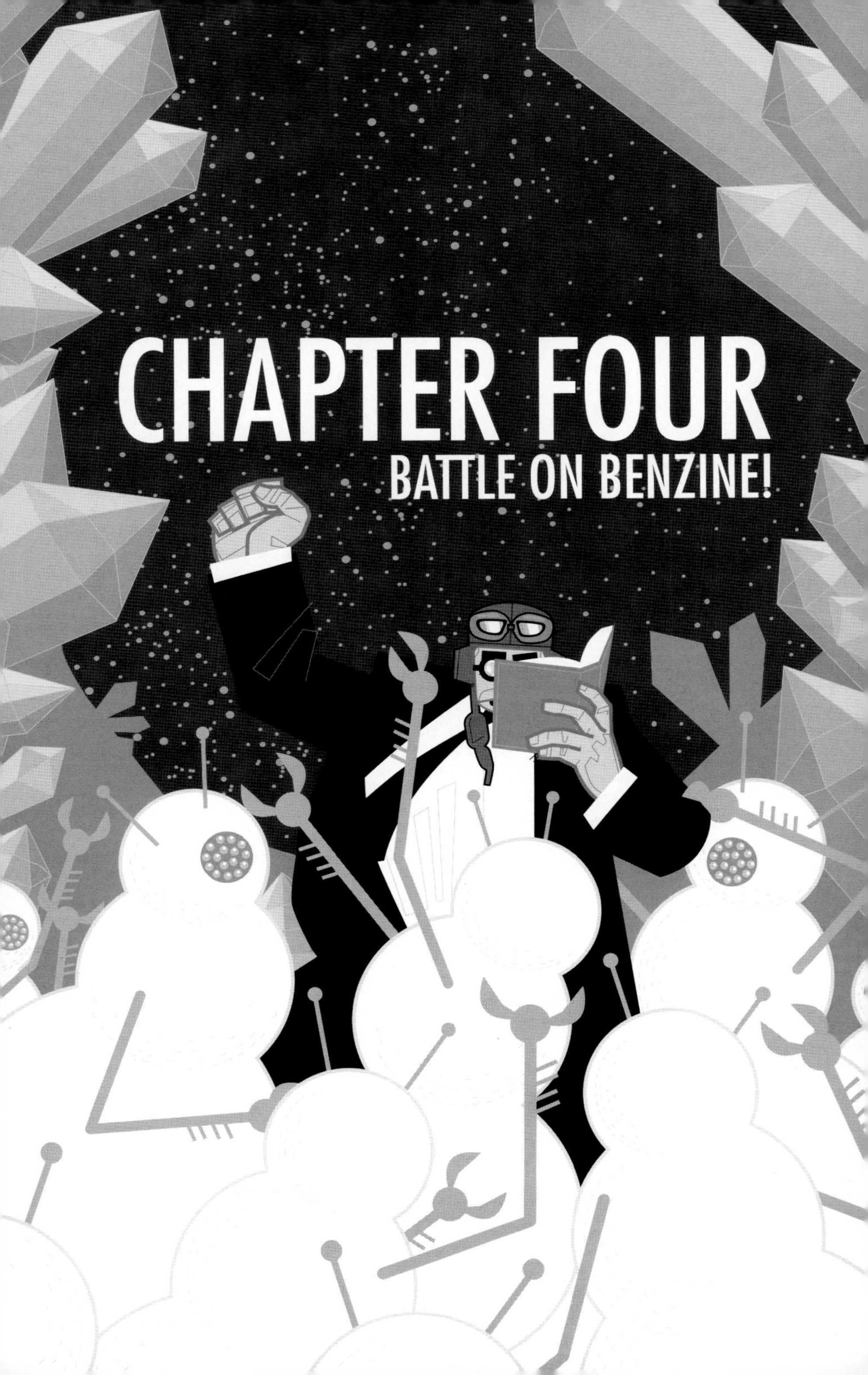
CHAPTER FOUR
BATTLE ON BENZINE!

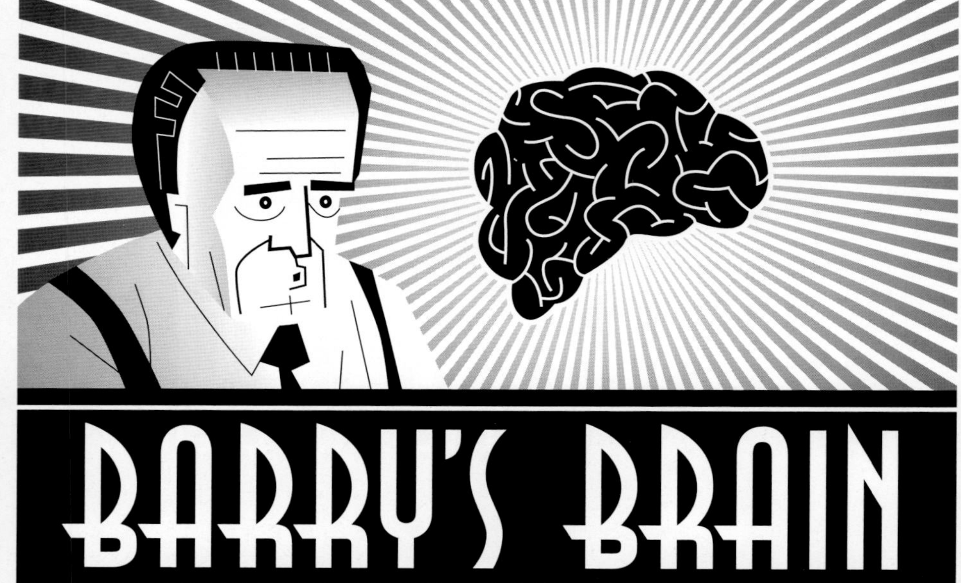

Welcome to the fabulous fourth issue! Rex Libris continues to go strong. It's controversial, graphic, and full of words. Yes, we got a discount on those. Not everything has worked out quite as we planned, however. Incredible, you say? Incredible but true, dear readers! The riches we had anticipated have yet to materialize. Believe it! In fact, the comix biz is beginning to look as if it is far less profitable than the latest Arachnid Lad movie made me think it was. But fear not! We've put forth four lavishly produced issues of the fighting librarian and there's still no sign of Hermeneutic Press going into bankruptcy. I keep burying them. The signs, that is. What the bank doesn't know won't hurt them, after all. Besides, we just got a new loan from Financial Hoard Bank to launch several new and exciting series!

That's right! Hermeneutic Press is branching out and we're flooding the market with Visicomboic masterpieces! I'm not going to disclose all the new titles, but one I'm particularly excited about is Last Hero Standing Comix! We throw a dozen old, defunct Megaheroes™ (some other pernicious brands have apparently claimed copyright over the term 's****hero,' which leaves us stuck with all the Megaheroes) and Megavillains™ into an Underground Secret Lair™ and watch them conspire and compete against each other until only one remains! They'll perform all sorts of exciting, unusual tasks and reward challenges each issue, such as navigating deadly obstacle courses, fighting giant robots, and standing atop a stump! (Who can stand longer: Megaman or that evil fiend, Immovableman? We'll finally know the answer!) Eventually, only one will remain, and they'll receive their own comic book series! Innovation? We've got it in spades!

There's an old marketing maxim that states that four out of every five new products fails. That's why we're introducing four other comic series. One is bound to succeed. And one will be concerned with bondage. We're cutting edge here! Expect the unexpected, that's our motto. Obviously, we're following the whole in-for-a-penny, in-for-a-dollar philosophy. I'm not sure if that was Nietzsche or Byron. No matter. Admittedly, it might not work out. But wily ol' B. Barry Horst has a plan for just that eventuality! It has been said that there is no money in writing (Pity I didn't read that before I got into publishing): the real money is in religion. So that's our next goal: to found a new faith. We'll call it Juamism. That or we'll go with the Automobilology. We'll follow the Great Cab, help our followers Tune Up, have Emission Tests for the Psychic Pollutants that are causing our Internal Engines trouble, or are causing Traffic (social stagnation/difficulty), and so on. It'll be one of those Hot Chicks Only kind of religions. There are a few like that in Quebec. If you're going to lead a cult, I mean religion, you might as well have all the perks!

Till next time,

B. Barry Horst

B. Barry Horst

WELCOME ONCE AGAIN, FAITHFUL READERS, TO THE TUMULTUOUS TALE OF LIBRARIAN REX LIBRIS AND HIS UNENDING BATTLE AGAINST THE FORCES OF EVIL. BORN IN ANCIENT GREECE (OR WAS IT ROME?), HE HAS WORKED TO PRESERVE KNOWLEDGE AND WISDOM FOR THOUSANDS OF YEARS AGAINST ALL FORMS OF PERFIDY, FROM BOOK BASHING BOOGEYMEN TO MOANING UNDEAD LEGIONS WHO IGNORE THE 'QUIET PLEASE' SIGN. NOT EVEN SUPERPOWERED, DELINQUENT ALIEN CHILDREN CAN ABSCOND WITH BOOKS WITHOUT SIGNING THEM OUT WHILE REX IS ON THE JOB! FOR THE FIRST TIME THE SECRET WORLD OF LIBRARIANS AND THEIR DAILY STRUGGLE TO PROTECT CIVILIZATION AND THE KNOWLEDGE IT IS FOUNDED UPON IS REVEALED! FOR THIS IS THE WORLD OF...

REX • LIBRIS

P!
A!
I!
N!
IT'S A NOUN! ONE: AN UNPLEASANT SENSATION N' -- *AW, WHAT THE HELL AM I DOIN'?*
THAK
I MEANT FIGURATIVELY, REX, FIGURATIVELY!
YEAH, YEAH.
SHEESH.
BONK!
THWOPK!
DIS IS LIKE FIGHTIN' BOWLING PINS!
PLOP!
CRUNCH!
CRUNCH!
GET THAT GUY! THE ONE ON THE RIGHT! HE'S GONNA LUNGE AT YOU! *QUICK!!*

KPOW!
NOT IF I BEAT HIM TO IT!
WELL DONE, LIBRIS!
CRUNCH!
CRUNCH!
*QUICKLY! ATTACK THE DEFORMED POD BEING FROM BEHIND!
BGGZZT!*
HEY!
THAT ONE GAVE YOU A NASTY LOOK! KICK HIS ASS--
--WAIT! REX! LOOK OUT! THEY'RE SURROUNDING YOU AGAIN!
I HAVE IT UNDER CONTROL, SIMON!
--I'LL COVER YOUR BACK! I CAN WIELD YOUR GUN WITH PIN POINT ACCURACY USING MY TELEKINETIC POWERS!
SIMON, STOP!
DON'T WORRY, I KNOW WHAT I'M DOING!
SHWIF!

FWIP!
CHIK SNIK!
I'M A WARRIOR AT HEART!

EAT LEAD SCUMSLUSHIES!
YAAAAAAAAAAAAAAAAAAAAAAAHHH!!!!
BLAM!
BLAM!
BLAM!
BLAM!
BLAM!
BLAM!
BLAM!

BLAM!
BLAM!
SHTHAK!
BLAM!
YAAAAAAHHH!!!!

BLAM!
BLAM!
PCHOK!
BZGRT!!
BLAM!
YAAAAAAHHH!!!!

BLAM!
GAAH!!
HEWGH! SHPAT!
BLAM!
YAAAAAAHHH!!!!

YAAAAAAHHH!!!!
GIVE ME THAT THING!
CLICK
CLICK
CLICK
IT'S JUST LIKE THE GORGE OF TUNGHEE TAREEKEE ALL OVER AGAIN -- MINUS THE GHILZYES!
WHAT A RUSH!!
SIMON, I OUGHTA--
FOR BACK IN 1842....
AZ BARAE KHODA!
YOU... YOU SHOT ME, OLD BOY.
PAK!
PAK!
POW!
ZIP!
ZING!
ZING!
YOU JUMPED INTO MY LINE OF FIRE!
BULLOCKS! I HAVEN'T MOVED A MUSCLE!
IT WAS JUST A RICOCHET! IT BARELY GRAZED YOU!
POW!
BANG!
RICOCHET? YOU PUT THREE BULLETS INTO MY BELLY AT POINT BLANK RANGE, YOU BUMBLING BUDGIE!
OH STOP BEING SUCH A BABY!

PAK! PAK! PAK! PAK! PAK! PAK! PAK! PAK!
WHATEVER HAPPENED TO THE STIFF UPPER LIP, EH? YOU ARE AN OFFICER IN HER MAJESTY'S SERVICE! SHOW SOME SPINE!
I'M NO OFFICER! YOU KNOW DAMN WELL I GOT THIS UNIFORM AT A COSTUME SHOP IN DELHI!
AND THANKS TO **YOU** AND THAT NINCOMPOOP ELPHINSTONE, WE'LL BE LUCKY TO GET BACK TO INDIA ALIVE! I JUST HOPE THE COPY OF ***'SHAH NAMEH'*** WE BOUGHT IN KABUL GETS BACK TO MIDDLETON IN ONE PIECE! NOT TO MENTION ***'KATTAK'S 101 GREAT RECIPES WITH GHEE*'.***
EYES TO THE FRONT MULVANEY!
AYE, LEAROYD!
PAK! PAK! PAK! PAK!
SA, SA, SA--AAHH!
PAK!
"I WENT THROUGH HELL GETTIN' THAT BOOK! TOOK A YEAR TO LOCATE THE HIDDEN RUINS OF THE LOST CITY OF JEWELS. THEN I HAD TA EVADE IT'S MALEFIC SPIRIT DENIZENS, CRAWL THROUGH THE TUNNEL OF FIRE, PENETRATE THE TOMB OF HAE-JENG, BEAT THE HORRIFIC JINN BEAST IBLEE, AND GET OUT ALIVE, BEFORE THE PLACE BLEW UP."
THESE DELICIOUS RECIPES DESERVE TO BE SHARED!
*GHEE: AFGHANI BUTTER SAUCE EQUIVALENT OF CHEEZ WHIZ -- BARRY
BY THE BY, HAVE YOU SEEN DOCTOR BRYDON? I SEEM TO BE BLEEDING RATHER... **PROFUSELY.**
GENERAL ELPHINSTONE CALLED A MEETING TO DISCUSS OUR CURRENT PREDICAMENT. I THINK THE DOCTOR IS WITH 'EM.
ZING! POW!
POW!
A MEETING? ***NOW?***
I'LL GO AND GET HIM IF YOU LIKE.
RRAAAHH1!
NEVERMIND!
MÊN TÊRA JÊNIN!

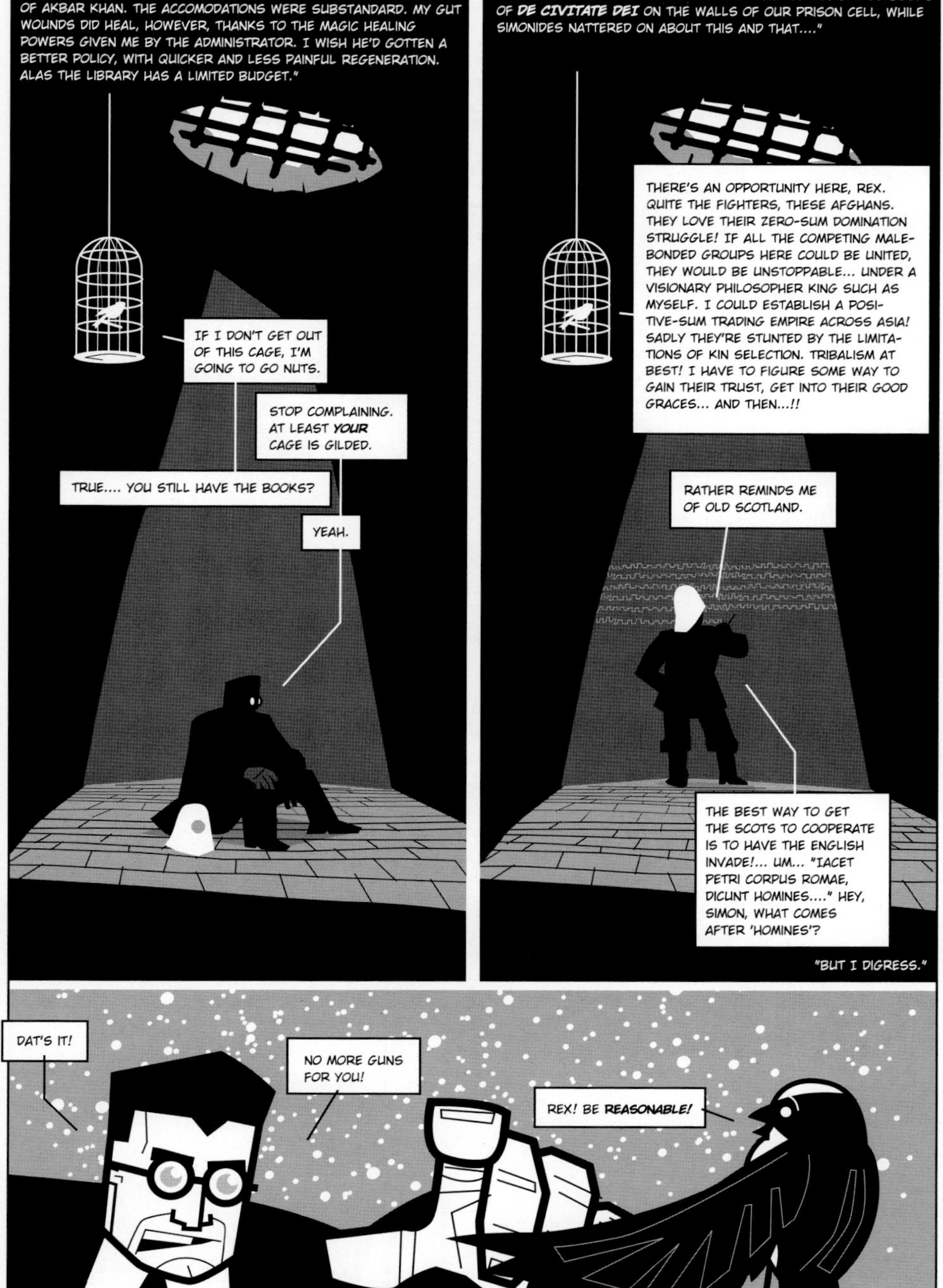
"WE WERE CAPTURED AND SPENT SIX HELLISH MONTHS AS GUESTS OF AKBAR KHAN. THE ACCOMODATIONS WERE SUBSTANDARD. MY GUT WOUNDS DID HEAL, HOWEVER, THANKS TO THE MAGIC HEALING POWERS GIVEN ME BY THE ADMINISTRATOR. I WISH HE'D GOTTEN A BETTER POLICY, WITH QUICKER AND LESS PAINFUL REGENERATION. ALAS THE LIBRARY HAS A LIMITED BUDGET."
IF I DON'T GET OUT OF THIS CAGE, I'M GOING TO GO NUTS.
STOP COMPLAINING. AT LEAST ***YOUR*** CAGE IS GILDED.
TRUE.... YOU STILL HAVE THE BOOKS?
YEAH.
"I KEPT MY SANITY BY SCRATCHING OUT THE TEXT OF ALL 22 BOOKS OF ***DE CIVITATE DEI*** ON THE WALLS OF OUR PRISON CELL, WHILE SIMONIDES NATTERED ON ABOUT THIS AND THAT...."
THERE'S AN OPPORTUNITY HERE, REX. QUITE THE FIGHTERS, THESE AFGHANS. THEY LOVE THEIR ZERO-SUM DOMINATION STRUGGLE! IF ALL THE COMPETING MALE-BONDED GROUPS HERE COULD BE UNITED, THEY WOULD BE UNSTOPPABLE... UNDER A VISIONARY PHILOSOPHER KING SUCH AS MYSELF. I COULD ESTABLISH A POSITIVE-SUM TRADING EMPIRE ACROSS ASIA! SADLY THEY'RE STUNTED BY THE LIMITATIONS OF KIN SELECTION. TRIBALISM AT BEST! I HAVE TO FIGURE SOME WAY TO GAIN THEIR TRUST, GET INTO THEIR GOOD GRACES... AND THEN...!!
RATHER REMINDS ME OF OLD SCOTLAND.
THE BEST WAY TO GET THE SCOTS TO COOPERATE IS TO HAVE THE ENGLISH INVADE!... UM... "IACET PETRI CORPUS ROMAE, DICUNT HOMINES...." HEY, SIMON, WHAT COMES AFTER 'HOMINES'?
"BUT I DIGRESS."
DAT'S IT!
NO MORE GUNS FOR YOU!
REX! BE **REASONABLE!**

SIMON, YOU'VE SAVED MY LIFE IN THE PAST, BUT SO HELP ME...
...SOMETIMES I THINK THE PRICE OF YOUR FRIENDSHIP IS JUST TOO DAMN HIGH!
I TOOK OUT AT LEAST SIX OF THEM! I SAVED YOUR ASS!
'SIDES...
IT'S NOT LIKE YOU CAN NEGOTIATE YOUR WAY OUT OF THIS! THEY EITHER CAN'T UNDERSTAND YOU OR THEY CAN'T HEAR YOU!
CAN'T HEAR ME....? OF COURSE! I SHOULD HAVE REALIZED!
MY HAT!
IT HAS A RADIO TRANSMITTER! USIN' IT, I SHOULD BE ABLE TO TALK TO 'EM.
EH?
THERE'S NO SOUND IN SPACE! THE MAGICAL PROTECTION POLICY THOTH GOT US ALLOWS US TO HEAR, BUT IT DOESN'T EXTEND TO THEM.
IT'S TOO LATE FOR TALK!
KILL THEM BEFORE THEY REGROUP!
QUIET, YOU!
<GREETINGS, SNOWFLAKE-BASED LIFEFORMS! CAN YOU HEAR ME? I COME IN PEACE!>

<IT SPEAKS GALACTIKESE!>
<BY THE COMETS!>
IT'S WORKING, SIMON! THEY CAN HEAR ME!
<I MEAN YOU NO HARM! I'M A **LIBRARIAN!** I COME IN PEACE!>
FIGURATIVELY SPEAKING.
<YOU CRUSH OUR DEAR LEADER INTO POWDER, BEAT DOZENS OF US SENSELESS, FIRE PROJECTILES INTO OUR SENSORY BULBS, AND **NOW** YOU CLAIM TO COME IN PEACE?>
<YOU SPEAK RUBBISH!!>
<**WHOA!** HOLD ON THERE!>
<CRUSHING YOUR LEADER WAS AN **ACCIDENT!**>
<THIS FIGHT HAS ALL BEEN A TERRIBLE MISUNDERSTAND-ING!>

<BROTHERS! **KILL** THIS ALIEN! AVENGE OUR DEAR DEPARTED LEADER!>
<WAIT... ARE WE DOING ALL THIS FIGHTING FOR **THAT** ASSHOLE?>
<YEAH! I **HATED** OUR DEAR LEADER.>
<HE WAS A SELFISH BASTARD!>
<WHAT!? THE LEADER HAS BEEN REBUKED! >
<VERY WELL!>
<WE MUST PERFORM THE ***BZZT BZZT: THE BATTLE TO THE DEATH*** TO DETERMINE THE NEXT LEADER OF OUR PEOPLE. WE BEGIN!
<WAIT! STOP!>
<WHAT?>
<YOU ***DARE*** INTERRUPT THE ***BZZT BZZT?***>

<I DO!>
<THERE'S AN EASIER WAY TO PICK A NEW LEADER:>
<DEMOCRATICALLY!>

<EXPLAIN.>

<IT'S EASY!>

<INSTEAD OF FIGHTING YOU DECIDE WITH A VOTE! IT'S A GREAT INNOVATION! HARNESSES THE MASS MIND, THE COLLECTIVE CONSCIENCE, THE UNDERLYING WISDOM OF THE COMMUNITY! IT ALLOWS A GROUP TO DECIDE UPON ITS FUTURE, AS A WHOLE!>

<YEAH...LIKE A MOB.>
<SSH! JUST CAN YOUR FLOCCINAUCINIHILIPILIFICATION OF DEMOCRACY, FOR A MINUTE, SIMON!>

<IT IS A STRANGE CONCEPT, ALIEN PRUNE BULB. AND YET... WE HAVE BEEN PERFORMING BZZT BZZT FOR AS LONG AS MY SPECIES HAS EXISTED! NONE OF US HERE EVER WIN. WE SHALL TRY YOUR NEW WAY!>

<EXCELLENT! YOU WON'T REGRET THIS!>
<SO: WHO WANTS TO BE LEADER?>

<I DO, I DO!>
<NO, ME!>
<ME! ME!>
<I WANT TO BE LEADER!>
<YOU'RE AN IDIOT, GRZT! I MUST RULE!>
<ME!>
<ME! ME!>

<NO NO NO. NOT **EVERYONE** CAN BE A CANDIDATE!>
<WHY NOT!?>
<YEAH! THIS 'DEMOCRACY' BLOWS!>
CLUMPF!
CLUMPF!
CLUMPF!
<HMM.>
<AWRIGHT! LISTEN UP! WE'LL USE MULTIPLE BALLOTS, WINNOW DOWN THE POOL OF CANDIDATES GRADUALLY, TILL WE HAVE YOUR NEXT LEADER. OKAY?>
<VERY WELL!>
<DIS IS GONNA TAKE A LITTLE WHILE. BUT IT'LL BE WORTH IT IN THE END...>
<....WE'LL DO THIS WITHOUT **ANY** BLOODSHED OR KILLING.>
<NO NEED FOR NASTY **AGON-ISTICS!**>
<RIGHT!>
<YOU! WHO DO YOU WANT TO NOMINATE FOR LEADER?>
<UHH...>
<ME!>

MEANWHILE, BACK AT THE MIDDLETON PUBLIC LIBRARY, CIRCE IS TRYING TO DEFUSE A CONFRONTATION FRAUGHT WITH PSYCHO-SEXUAL CONNOTATIONS....
<I SHALL HANDLE THE UPSTART WENCH! NO ONE DICTATES TO THE WARRIORS OF KING GAISERIC AND LIVES!>
<YOU BOYS SETTLE DOWN.>
<JUST **SHUSH**-- OR YOU'LL HAVE TO LEAVE!>
<PREPARE TO DIE, OLD WOMAN!>
<AMMATAS! GET THE TORCHES LIT! WE SHALL BURN THIS PAGAN TEMPLE TO THE GROUND!>

SWIIIIIIIIIIIIIIISSSSSSSSSSSSSSSSSSSSSSSSSSSSSSSSSSSSSSSSSSSSSSSSSHT!
<OH MY GOODNESS!>
<WHAT IS THIS!?>
<THE HAG MOVES WITH THE SPEED OF AN ANTELOPE!>
<SUCH ANGER!>
KLANKT!
<YOU OUGHT TO READ ***THE CONTEMPLATIVE LIFE***, OR ***THE CONSOLATION OF PHILOSOPHY*** BY BOETHIUS-- ***EEEK!***>
<***DAMN YOU,*** HERETIC SCUM! ***STAY STILL!***>
THAM!
FWOOSH!
<WATCH YOUR LANGUAGE, YOUNG MAN!>
AAAH!

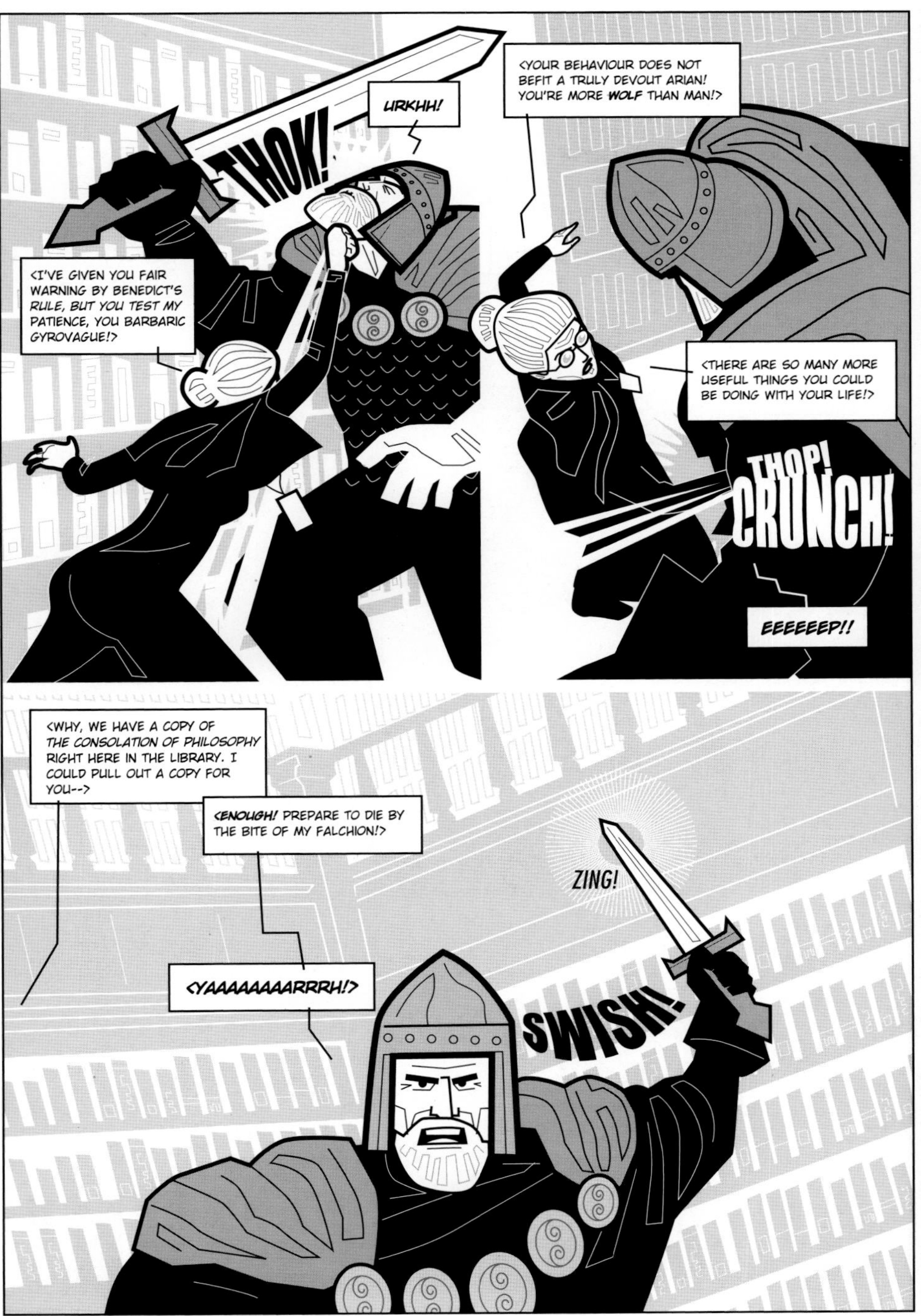
<I'VE GIVEN YOU FAIR WARNING BY BENEDICT'S RULE, BUT YOU TEST MY PATIENCE, YOU BARBARIC GYROVAGUE!>
THOK!
URKHH!
<YOUR BEHAVIOUR DOES NOT BEFIT A TRULY DEVOUT ARIAN! YOU'RE MORE WOLF THAN MAN!>
<THERE ARE SO MANY MORE USEFUL THINGS YOU COULD BE DOING WITH YOUR LIFE!>
THOP!
CRUNCH!
EEEEEEP!!
<WHY, WE HAVE A COPY OF THE CONSOLATION OF PHILOSOPHY RIGHT HERE IN THE LIBRARY. I COULD PULL OUT A COPY FOR YOU-->
<ENOUGH! PREPARE TO DIE BY THE BITE OF MY FALCHION!>
ZING!
<YAAAAAAAARRRH!>
SWISH!

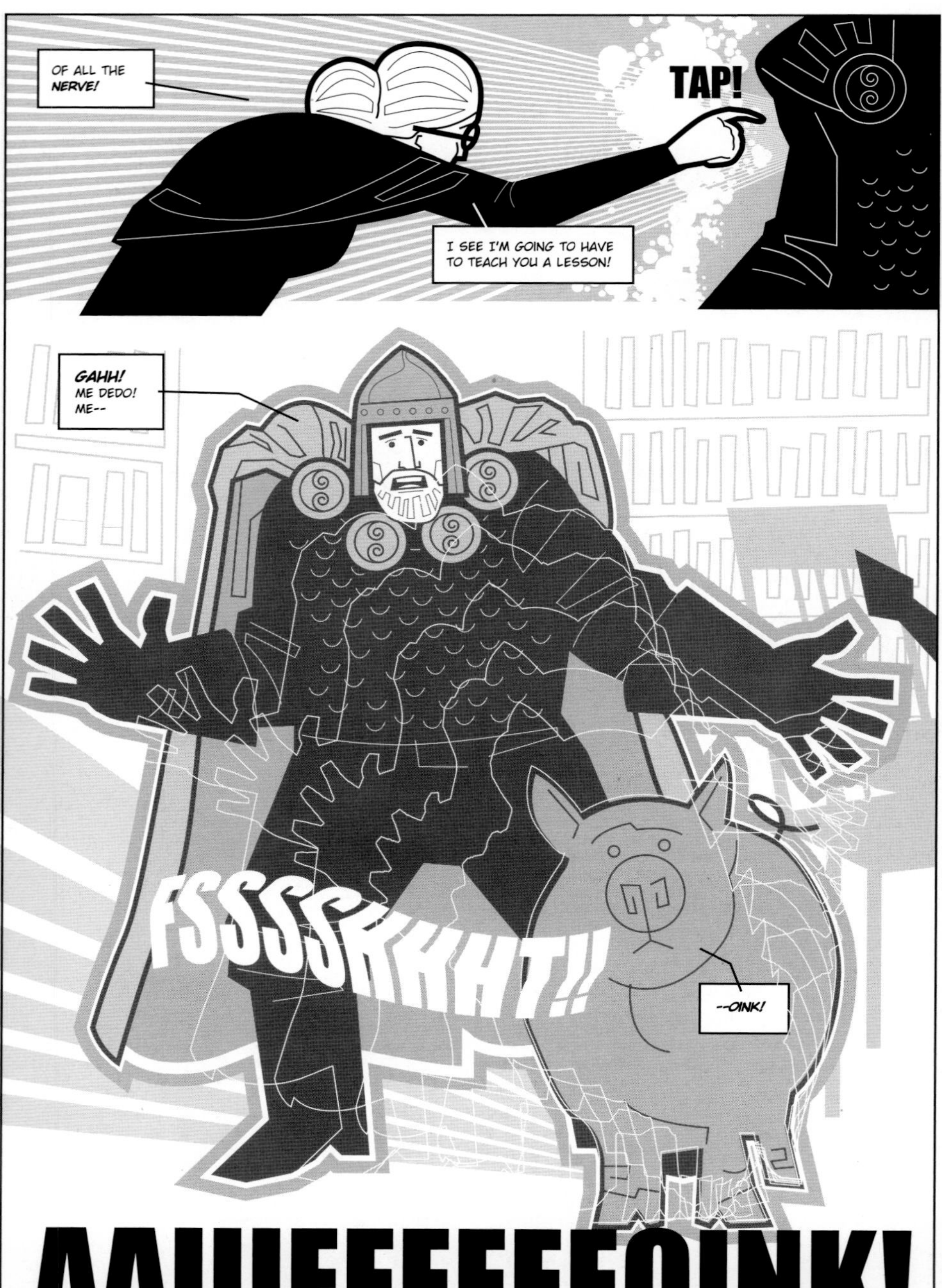
OF ALL THE NERVE!
TAP!
I SEE I'M GOING TO HAVE TO TEACH YOU A LESSON!
GAHH! ME DEDO! ME--
FSSSSRHHT!!
--OINK!
AAIIIEEEEEEEOINK!

<SHE'S A WITCH!>
<BURN HER!>
<BURN!!>
<BURN THE WITCH!!>
<BURN!!>
<AMMATAS! THE TORCHES!>
SKNEF!
SKIFF!
SKNEF!
SKIFF!
SKNEF!
SKIFF!
SKNEF!
<DON'T RUSH ME, DAMNIT!>
<THAT'S ENOUGH! EITHER YOU BOYS SIT DOWN AND READ QUIETLY, OR I'LL TURN THE WHOLE LOT OF YOU INTO PIGS! I'LL GIVE YOU TILL THE COUNT OF THREE!...>
<...ONE!...>
OINK!

<TWO!>
<THREE!>
CITY OF GOD
SAINT AUGUSTINE
GIBBONS
THE CONQUEST OF HAPPINESS
<MUCH BETTER.>
<YOU BOYS ARE WELCOME TO STAY AND READ QUIETLY UNTIL YOU DISSIPATE...>
<BUT NO TRYING TO BURN DOWN THE LIBRARY AFTER I LEAVE!>

WHILE BACK AT THE FRONT DESK....
SIGH.
THEY REALLY OUGHT TO HAVE CLERKS TO DO THIS DREARY DESK DUTY. I SHOULD BE IN THERE, WHERE THE ACTION IS!
HMM. IT'S GOTTEN AWFULLY QUIET. I HOPE CIRCE IS ALL RIGHT!
I'M SURE SHE WOULDN'T MIND IF I LEFT THE DESK FOR A SECOND OR TWO... JUST TO MAKE SURE SHE'S OKAY...
...MAYBE FIND A LITTLE EXCITEMENT!

WELL, THAT GAISERIC! JUST AS I REMEMBER HIM: THE ETERNAL INSTIGATOR!
I'VE GOTTEN THE LOT SETTLED DOWN. THEY'LL READ QUIETLY UNTIL THEY JUST FADE AWAY.
SQUEEEEE!
OF COURSE! ALL THE PSYCHIC EMANATIONS IN THE LIBRARY CAN READ. ONE OF THE PERKS OF BEING A FICTIONAL CHARACTER.
THEY CAN **READ?**
THEY SHOULD FADE AWAY PEACEFULLY BEFORE THE READING GROUP ARRIVES--
OH.
HYPATIA, DID YOU EAT **ALL** THE COOKIES?

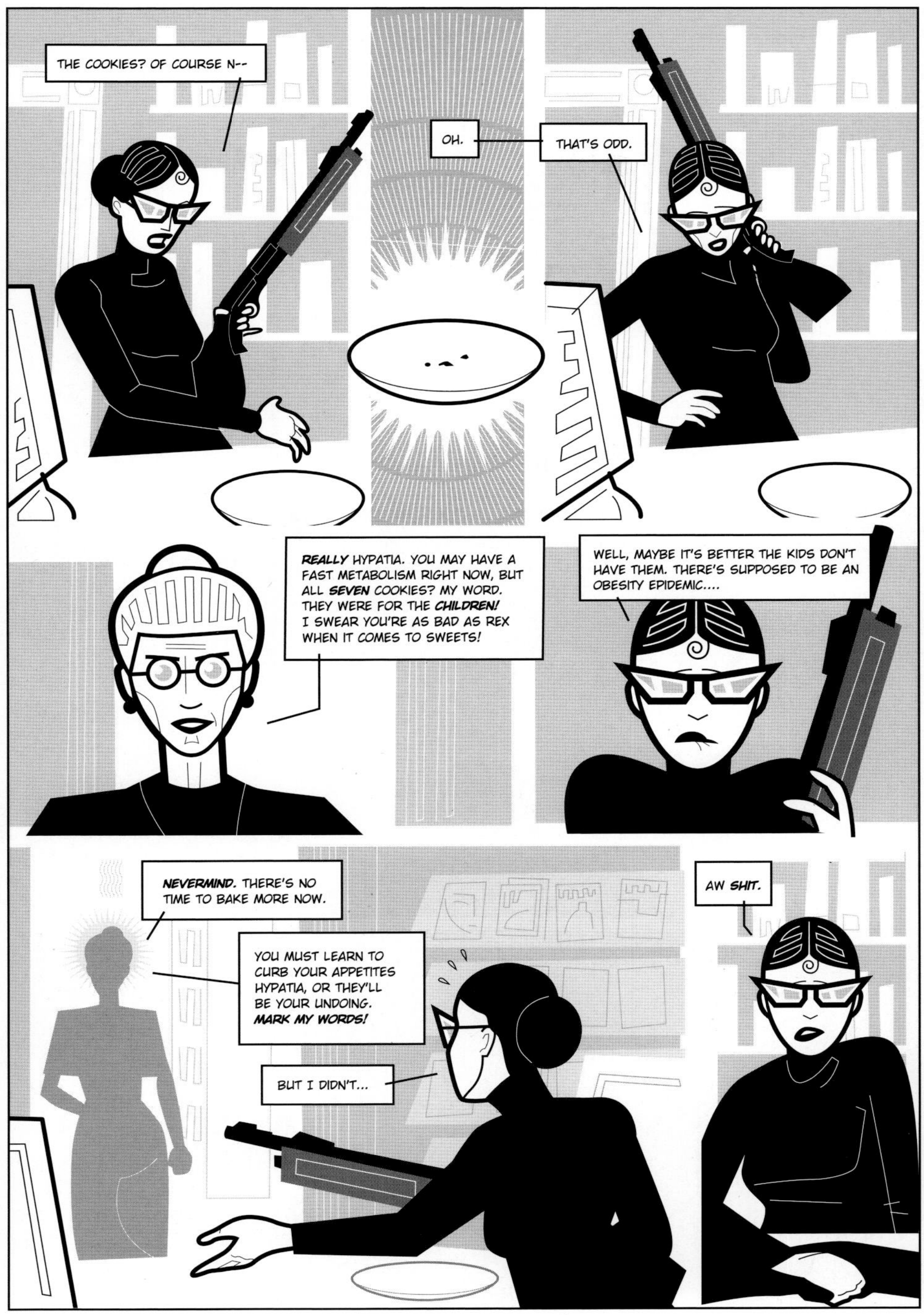
THE COOKIES? OF COURSE N--
OH.
THAT'S ODD.
REALLY HYPATIA. YOU MAY HAVE A FAST METABOLISM RIGHT NOW, BUT ALL SEVEN COOKIES? MY WORD. THEY WERE FOR THE CHILDREN! I SWEAR YOU'RE AS BAD AS REX WHEN IT COMES TO SWEETS!
WELL, MAYBE IT'S BETTER THE KIDS DON'T HAVE THEM. THERE'S SUPPOSED TO BE AN OBESITY EPIDEMIC....
NEVERMIND. THERE'S NO TIME TO BAKE MORE NOW.
YOU MUST LEARN TO CURB YOUR APPETITES HYPATIA, OR THEY'LL BE YOUR UNDOING. MARK MY WORDS!
BUT I DIDN'T...
AW SHIT.

MEANWHILE, BACK ON BENZINE V...
AWRIGHT, AWRIGHT! I SHOULDA FIGURED ***THAT*** WOULDN'T WORK.
<YOU GUYS EVER THOUGHT ABOUT BECOMING A SOCIAL ANARCHY, AND DOIN' AWAY WITH THE WHOLE LEADERSHIP ISSUE ENTIRELY?>
<NO.>
<HMM. YOU FELLAS ARE ESCAPED SERFS, AREN'T YOU?>
<YES! WE ESCAPED FROM THE TYRANNICAL OPPRESSION OF THE EVIL WARLORD VAGLOX!>
<OUR PEOPLE ONCE RULED THIS PLANET. THEN THE STRONTIANS CAME. THEY SMASHED OUR CITIES AND HERDED US INTO SERVITUDE. NOW OUR PEOPEL DIE BY THE THOUSAND IN HIS METHANE MINES. OUR GREAT PROGENITOR FRZZZTI ESCAPED; FLED TO FIND US A NEW WORLD TO LIVE ON. TO START ANEW.>
<WHOA. HOLD ON THERE. WHAT HAPPENED TO THIS 'PROGENITOR'?>
<THE LEGEND IS TRAGIC. HE IS SAID TO HAVE FOUND US A NEW PLANET. HIS LAST REPORT STATED THAT THE SURFACE TEMPERATURE OF THE PLANET WAS RISING OMINOUSLY, AND THAT HE HAD BEEN BLINDED BY SOME WILD BEAST THAT HAD STUCK A CARROT IN HIS EYE. WE... WE NEVER HEARD FROM THE PROGENITOR AGAIN.>
<WE ARE THE KANIKTSHAK, AND THIS IS PLANET KANOOT. OR WAS, UNTIL VAGLOX RENAMED IT.>
YES! THESE SNOW BEINGS ARE PERFECT FOR MY PURPOSES! THEY ARE FRESH SOIL, A COMPLETE TABULA RASA, READY TO ACCEPT THE ***SPERMATIKOS LOGOS OF SIMONIDES!***

"I CAN USE THEM TO ESTABLISH A TRUE UTOPIA, WITH ME AS ITS PHILOSOPHER KING! CREATE AN EMPIRE WHERE THE PHILOSOPHIC NATURE CAN FLOURISH! THEN, CONQUER THE GALAXY AND IMPLEMENT A PAX SIMONIDES. BRING **ALL** UNDER MY BENEVOLENT RULE, AND SPREAD WEALTH, TRUTH AND JUSTICE TO THE FARTHEST CORNERS OF UNIVERSE. MY VERY OWN COSMIC LEVIATHAN!"
EAT THE DUST OF MY FORTUNE ARCHYTAS, YOU TOAD-SPOTTED SOT! **HAHA!**
NEVER BEFORE HAVE I HAD SUCH A PERFECT OPPORTUNITY! I MUST ACT QUICKLY, BEFORE REX CAN TURN OFF HIS RADIO MICROPHONE!
HERE ME, SNOW BEINGS!
YOU SEEK LEADERSHIP! I AM SIMONIDES -- **SPACE PHILOSOPHER!** AND I ASK YOU: WHO IS MORE QUALIFIED TO LEAD THAN ONE LEARNED IN REASON, SUCH AS I? I KNOW THE FLAVOUR OF TRUTH! I HAVE THE WISDOM OF AGE AND THE AGES! I AM A LEADER BY BOTH ART AND NATURE, VERSED IN THE WAYS OF THE UNIVERSE, AND I FEEL YOUR PAIN!
NO SPECIES SHOULD SUFFER THE INDIGNITY OF SLAVERY! IT IS A FATE **WORSE** THAN DEATH! I CAN HELP YOU ASCEND TO YOUR RIGHTFUL PLACE IN THE UNIVERSE AND FULFILL YOUR **TRUE,** NOBLE FUNCTION!
FOR IF YOU CHOSE **ME** AS YOUR LEADER, I SHALL ENSURE YOU ARE **NEVER** SLAVES AGAIN! I'LL TRAIN YOU **ALL** IN MIND AND BODY TO BE THE **GUARDIANS** OF THE GALAXY! TEACH YOU GRAVITAS! COURAGE! **HONOUR!**
AND WE SHALL **CRUSH** THE PETTY TYRANT VAGLOX AND **RECLAIM** THIS PLANET!

<WOW! THAT SOUNDS AWESOME!>
<IT IS YOUR DECISION! ALL IN FAVOUR OF MY LEADERSHIP RAISE YOUR ARM AND SAY 'AYE'!>
<AYE!>
OH CRAP.
<JUST HOLD ON A MINUTE HERE, KANOOTEANS!>
<ONE MINUTE WHILE I CONSULT MY 'COLLEAGUE.'>
WE HAD A DEAL YA DAMN BIRD! NO MORE CONQUERING!
I WAS ELECTED!
THERE'S A DIFFERENCE!
YOU'RE LEADING THESE POOR PEOPLE DOWN THE GARDEN PATH!
ADEIMANTUS WAS RIGHT! YOU'RE BOTH DANGEROUS AND USELESS!
WHAT!? YOU WOUND ME DEEPLY! I'M DOING THIS FOR THE SAKE OF THE GREATER GOOD! THESE ALIENS ARE TOO PRIMITIVE TO FORM A DEMOCRACY. I CAN HELP GUIDE THEM TOWARDS ENLIGHTENMENT. ISN'T THAT WHAT YOU'D WANT? THEY NEED OUR HELP, REX!
MAYBE...
I CAN ORGANIZE THEM TO HELP OVERTHROW VAGLOX, AND END SLAVERY ON THIS PLANET, AND HELP RETRIEVE THE BOOK YOU'RE LOOKING FOR.
TWO BIRDS WITH ONE STONE, EH? WELL... OKAY, SO LONG AS YOU AREN'T HARBOURING PLANS FOR INTER-GALACTIC CONQUEST....
FURTHEST THING FROM MY MIND!

HONEST!
YEAH. **RIGHT.** I CAN'T WAIT UNTIL YOU'VE TRAINED THESE GUYS. WE'VE WASTED TOO MUCH TIME AS IT IS.
<HEY FELLAS! WHICH WAY TO THE LAIR OF VAGLOX?>
<YOU CAN SEE IT FROM THE TOP OF THIS RIDGE.>
<THERE! BEYOND THE SEA OF CRUSHED ICE: THE **STRONGHOLD,** CAPITAL OF THE STRONTIAN EMPIRE OF WARLORD VAGLOX!>
<IT IS A HATED, EVIL PLACE!>
<IT'S ALSO GOTTA BE TWENTY OR THIRTY CLICKS AWAY! MY GEOMETRY IS RUSTIER THAN I THOUGHT...>
<DO NOT DESPAIR, PRUNE BULB. WE HAVE TRANSPORT NEARBY. JUST DOWN THE ICE SHEET. WE CAN BE AT THE CAPITAL IN AN HOUR, IF SIMON SO WISHES.>
<WHY, THAT'S EXACTLY WHAT SIMON WISHES, AIN'T IT?>
<ER... YES! THAT'S RIGHT. LET US SCOUT OUT THE CITY!>
CLUMPF!
CLUMPF!
CLUMPF!
<TELL YER BOYS TO BRING ALONG SOME OF THOSE POP GUNS OF THEIRS, JUST IN CASE WE RUN INTO TROUBLE.>

A FEW MINUTES LATER, AT THE BASE OF THE GLACIER....
<BEHOLD, THE MIGHTY BERYL BEASTS!>
<CRYSTALLINE MAMMOTHS! I'D LIKE TO SEE THE PEG-MATITE THAT THING CAME FROM!>
CLUMPF!
CLUMPF!
NOT EXACTLY COMFORTABLE...
<FORWARD, TO THE CASTLE OF THE ENEMY!>
...BUT I'LL BET THERE'S ENOUGH PSYCHIC ENERGY IN THIS THING TO POWER A THOUSAND THOUSAND TELEPORTS!
THUMP!
BRZZZGGZZT!!
H-H-HOL-L-LY C-C-CR-A-AA-A-A-PP, IT RI-I-D-E-E-S LI-I-I KE A B-R-R-ON-N-N-CO-OH-OH!
THUMP!
THUMP!
THUMP!
THUMP!
THUMP!

THRUM THRUM THRUM THRUM THRUM THRUM
BZT!
<THERE'S A SHIP UP THERE--!!>
<PAY IT NO HEED, LEADER SIMONIDES>
THUMP! THUMP!
<THEY'RE LOOKING FOR ZARGITE RAIDERS. VAGLOX IS AT WAR WITH THEIR AUTARCH, GURTZ. THE PATROL CRAFT DON'T LOOK TOO CLOSE AT BERYL BEASTS. WE ONLY HAVE TO WORRY ABOUT GROUND PATROLS, AND THEY ARE FEW AND FAR BETWEEN....>
<AH.>
THUMP! THUMP!
<SO-O-O TELL ME ABOW-OWOWT THE CITEE-EE OF VAGLAW-AW-AWX!...>
<IT IS AN ADAMANTIUM STRUCTURE BUILT OVER A DEEP FISSURE...>
THUMP! THUMP!
AN HOUR LATER, REX AND THE REBELS ARRIVE AT THE OUTSKIRTS OF WARLORD VAGLOX'S CITY....
<WHAT ARE ALL THOSE SLATS?>
<DISCHARGE VENTS FOR THE MOLTEN REFUSE FROM THE WAR FACTORIES. THEY EXPEL IT WHEN THE CRYSTAL GROWTHS AND SNOW GET TOO HIGH ON THE WALLS.>
<HOW LARGE ARE DUCTS...?>
<LARGE, BUT IMPENETRABLE. WE WOULD MELT BEFORE WE GOT TEN PSEUDOPODS INSIDE!>
<EXCELLENT! I THINK I'VE JUST FOUND MY POINT OF INGRESS!>
THUMP! THUMP!

<HOLD ON, REX. IF YOU GO IN, HOW WILL I TALK TO MY PEOPLE? I NEED YOUR RADIO MICRO-PHONE.>
<NO CAN DO, LITTLE BUDDY. I NEED IT TA REASON WITH WARLORD VAGLOX.>
<THERE IS NO REASONING WITH THAT CRAZY CRYSTAL!>
<YOU WON'T NEED YOUR MICRO-PHONE IN THE CITY. VAGLOX HAD PSYCHIC TRANSLATOR UNITS IN-STALLED. HE DIDN'T WANT HIS SECRET POLICE MONITORS TO MISS ANY POTENTIALLY SUBVERSIVE COMMENTS.>
YOU FEEL DAT?
VIBRATIONS IN THE GROUND?
NO, A BUZZIN'. MAKIN' MY HAIR STAND ON END. I'D SWEAR WE'RE ATOP AN INCREDIBLY POWERFUL TELLURIC ENERGY HUB....
THUNK! THUNK! THUNK!
I THINK WE HAVE A BIGGER PROBLEM RIGHT NOW!
THUNK!
THUNK!
THUNK!
<THEY'VE FOUND US!>
<EGADS!>
<WE'VE ONLY GOT ONE CHANCE, OR WE'RE ALL DEAD!>
TO BE CONCLUDED NEXT ISSUE!

CHAPTER FIVE
TEA WITH VAGLOX

BARRY'S BRAIN

The ancient Spartans used to flog children for each use of an unnecessary word. Obviously, everyone here at Hermeneutic Press would be beaten to death if we were to live under their rigid rule. No matter! We'll leave that particular scenario to the fantasies of our detractors. Sparta was a proto-totalitarian hell hole anyway (Damn good enemies to be known by; Hermeneutic Press is proud to be at odds with their dead civilization). Let the words and the information flow freely, I say! Let prolixity run amok, rampage down the streets, and wax eloquent! Let the river of verbal diarrhea flow like the mighty Yangtze! Let it overflow the banks and spread out unto the floodplains! In this way we shall fertilize the world of comics and give rise to a new creative golden age of innovation, verbal inebriation, and turgidity! No other brand is so fearless in the face of huge hordes of words. Dictionaries brim with them, an almost endless stream of named memes which threaten to drown us in their great numbers. We shall co-opt them in the name of the comic book medium, like no other before us, and harness their eco-friendly powers for the good of all humanity! Remember, if anyone can bring hyperbole into reality, we're the ones to do it. It will be just one more great triumph for the pioneering medium of Visicomboics! Why do we do all this silliness? This insouciant madness? Why, to have fun, by God!

We have already taken steps in this direction with the employment of the greatly under-used word **floccinaucinihilipilification** in issue four. We have every reason to believe that this is the first time in the history of the comics that the word floccinaucinihilipilification has ever been employed. And who brought it to you first? **Hermeneutic Press!** Not only that, we have now included this fabulous word in our introduction twice, increasing it's exposure by 200%! This is just the beginning. With a little effort, it is conceivable that we could replace every commonly used word in this comic with a more obscure equivalent. We could resuscitate such words as **arenaceous, fissiparous, barbate, duopilomundopothic**, and **tramontane.** The elites will have no choice but to notice comics by the time we are done!

They say brevity is the soul of wit. Make no mistake: here at Hermeneutic we are doing **dirty things** to wit's soul. And as everyone knows, **dirt sells!**

Prolixity!

B. Barry Horst

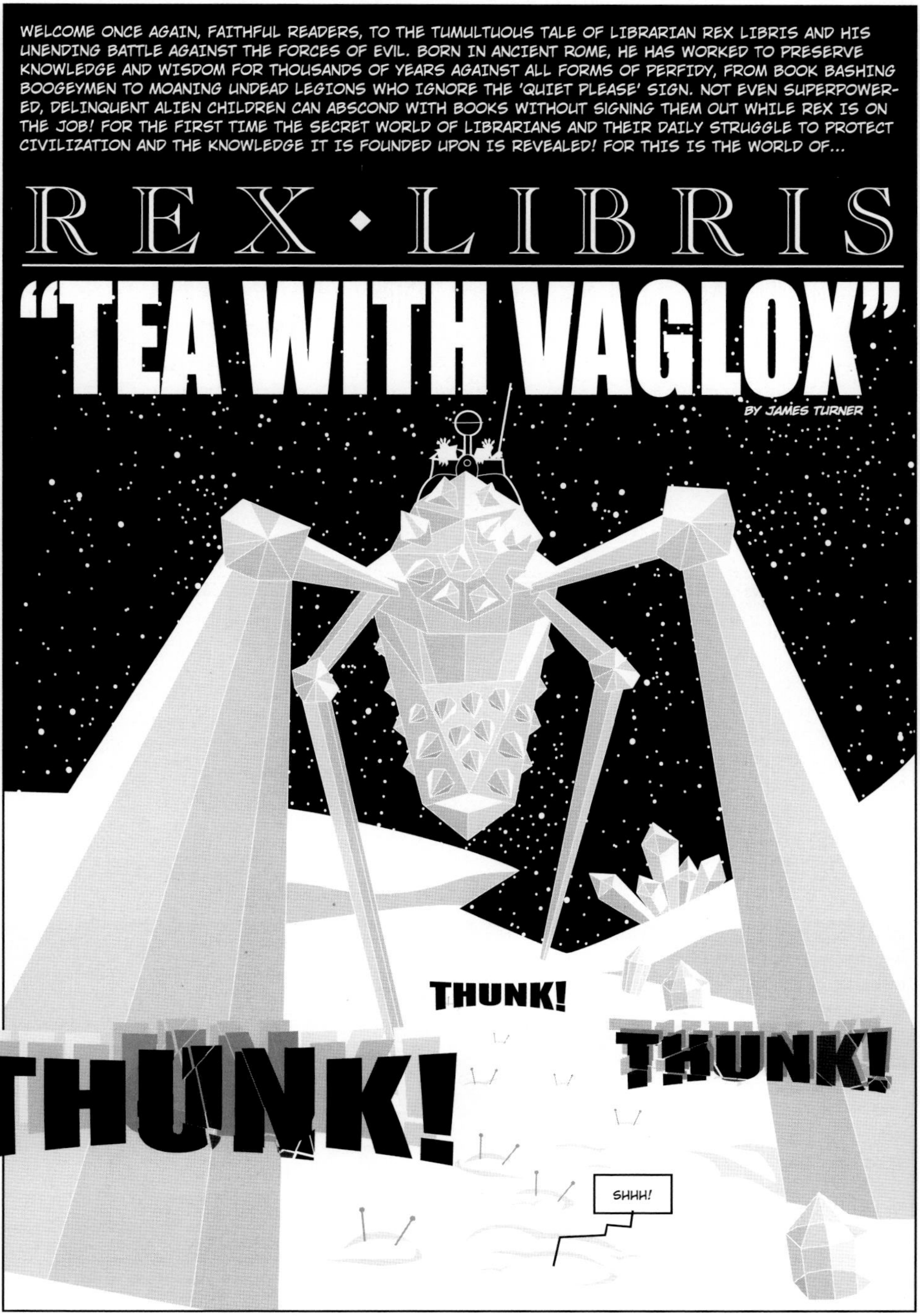

WELCOME ONCE AGAIN, FAITHFUL READERS, TO THE TUMULTUOUS TALE OF LIBRARIAN REX LIBRIS AND HIS UNENDING BATTLE AGAINST THE FORCES OF EVIL. BORN IN ANCIENT ROME, HE HAS WORKED TO PRESERVE KNOWLEDGE AND WISDOM FOR THOUSANDS OF YEARS AGAINST ALL FORMS OF PERFIDY, FROM BOOK BASHING BOOGEYMEN TO MOANING UNDEAD LEGIONS WHO IGNORE THE 'QUIET PLEASE' SIGN. NOT EVEN SUPERPOWERED, DELINQUENT ALIEN CHILDREN CAN ABSCOND WITH BOOKS WITHOUT SIGNING THEM OUT WHILE REX IS ON THE JOB! FOR THE FIRST TIME THE SECRET WORLD OF LIBRARIANS AND THEIR DAILY STRUGGLE TO PROTECT CIVILIZATION AND THE KNOWLEDGE IT IS FOUNDED UPON IS REVEALED! FOR THIS IS THE WORLD OF...

REX · LIBRIS

"TEA WITH VAGLOX"

BY JAMES TURNER

THUNK!
THUNK!
THUNK!
SHHH!

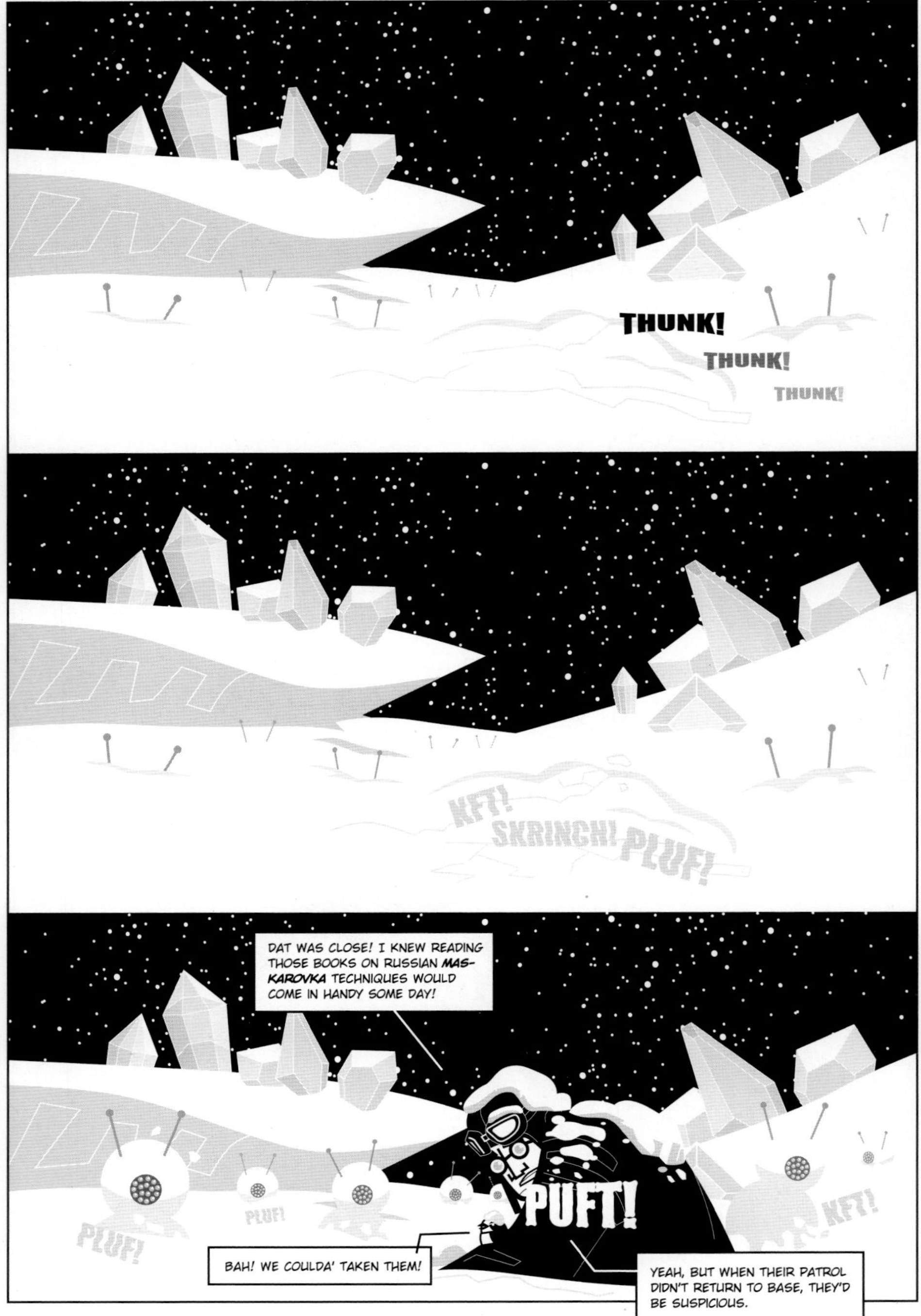
THUNK!
THUNK!
THUNK!
KFT!
SKRINCH!
PLUF!
DAT WAS CLOSE! I KNEW READING THOSE BOOKS ON RUSSIAN *MAS-KAROVKA* TECHNIQUES WOULD COME IN HANDY SOME DAY!
PLUF!
PLUF!
PUFT!
KFT!
BAH! WE COULDA' TAKEN THEM!
YEAH, BUT WHEN THEIR PATROL DIDN'T RETURN TO BASE, THEY'D BE SUSPICIOUS.

RIGHT NOW THERE'S SOMETHING I GOTTA CHECK OUT. THE T-COUNTER IS READING UNPRECENDENTED LEVELS OF ENERGY COMING FROM NEAR HERE.
SPIFF!
SPIFF!
SPIFF!
THERE! THAT HOAR-FROSTED CRYSTAL CLUSTER!
TICK
TICK
TICK
TICK
TICK
THIS CRYSTAL OUTCROP MUST HAVE BEEN HERE FOR THOUSANDS OF YEARS! AND RIGHT ATOP AN INCREDIBLY POWERFUL LEY POINT!
CLUMF!
CLUMF!
I WAS RIGHT! THESE DOUBLE TERMINATED CRYSTAL SHARDS HAVE ENOUGH TELLURIC ENERGY IN THEM TO TELEPORT BOTH OF US FROM ONE END OF THE GALAXY AND BACK AGAIN!
MY CRYSTALS. THE PLANET RIGHTFULLY BELONGS TO THE KANIKTSHAK, AND I'M THEIR DULY ELECTED SUPREME LEADER!
SCRUNCH!

WHY YOU CHEEKY, MIMSY JUBJUB! ALRIGHT, WHADDAYA WANT FOR THE CRYSTALS?
...NOTHING MUCH. I'M A VERY REASONABLE BIRD. JUST YOUR MATHEMATICAL FORMULAS FOR TELEPORTATION...
...AND FOR CIRCE TO TURN ME BACK INTO A MAN.
...AND TEN YEARS SUPPLY OF FOOD.
...AND ALL THE ADVANCED WEAPONRY YOU HAVE BACK AT THE LIBRARY.
FERGET IT. YOU KNOW I CAN'T GIVE YOU DAT STUFF. YOU DON'T HAVE OWNERSHIP OVER THE PLANET YET ANYWAY, AND YOU'RE NOT GONNA WITHOUT MY HELP. I'LL LETCHA HAVE ALL THE BIRD SEED YOU WANT AND KEEP YOU ON THE LIBRARY IMMORTALITY POLICY. DAT'S IT.
COME ON, REX! THIS IS MY BIG CHANCE! MY SPACE EMPIRE WILL BE TOTALLY PG-RATED, I SWEAR!
TAKE IT OR LEAVE IT, LITTLE BUDDY.
ALRIGHT, ALRIGHT! I'LL TAKE IT.
BUT THIS IS AN INAUSPICIOUS BEGINNING FOR THE FUTURE RULER OF THE GALAXY!
WHATEVER. GIMME A SEC HERE, I JUST WANT TA GATHER UP THESE CRYSTAL SHARDS AND FICTIONALIZE 'EM INTO MY BLACK BOOK FER STORAGE....
TINK!
THERE WE GO.
ZRAK!
POIT!

RIGHT! LET'S GET BACK TO YOUR MINIONS, PLAN THE BOOK RETRIEVAL RAID AND THE INCIDENTAL DOWNFALL OF DIS WARLORD VAGLOX--
OH BELGIUM.
THWOK!!
UNNFFH!
HMMMMMMMMMMMMMMM!
DEATH TO ALL WHO OPPOSE THE STRONTIAN TITANATE!
WAIT! WAIT! I'M FROM THE GALACTIC LOTTERY CORPORATION!
HMMMMMMMMMMMMMMM!
!?! THE GALACTIC--

POW!
BAM!
KBLAM!
KRACK!
KPOW!
KTHANG!
KTHOW!
SUCKERS.
REX-- OVER THE CREST...!
I SEE IT! ANOTHER CRYSTALLINE CREEP OF VAGLOX'S CRAVEN COMITATUS!
CLUMF!
CLUMF!
CLUMF!
<WE ARE UNDER ATTACK! I MUST WARN TITAN VAGLOX!>
HMMMMMMMMMMM!

QUIET, YOU!
KPOW!
UNGH!!
POK!
BZZZM BZZZM BZZZZM BZZZZM BZZZM
OH MY GOD! REX! LOOK TO YOUR LEFT! LOOK TO YOUR LEFT!
WHAT? WHERE ARE THEY-- !?!
OH MY.
FWIP!
VA-VA-VOOOM! THIS IS WHAT BEING A GALACTIC TYRANT IS ALL ABOUT, REX: IMPRESSING THE SPACE BABES!
BUT... BUT THIS ISN'T POSSIBLE. PULCHRITUDINOUS SPACE AMAZONS COULDN'T EXIST IN THIS ENVIRON-MENT....
DAMMIT, BARRY!
BARRY!!

ER... YES, REX?
DAMMIT, BARRY! YA CAN'T GO AND PUT SPACE AMAZONS ON BENZINE V! THEY'D FREEZE! THEY DON'T HAVE MAGICAL PROTECTION FOR ADVERSE ENVIRONMENTS!
THEY ONLY INHABIT TEMPERATE TO TROPICAL CLIMATE ZONES DUE TO THEIR DEADLY ALLERGIC REACTION TO COPIOUS AMOUNTS OF CLOTHING! EVERY XENOBIOLOGIST KNOWS THAT!
REX! REX! RELAX. I WAS JUST TRYING TO SPICE UP THE BACK-GROUNDS. ADD SIZZLE.
I KNOW REALISM CONCERNS YOU. IF YOU'D TOLD ME THEY CAN'T SURVIVE ON BENZINE V I NEVER WOULD HAVE ADDED THEM IN THE FIRST PLACE! I'M JUST TRYING TO DO WHAT'S BEST FOR YOUR BOOK.
YEAH, I GUESS....
IT'S JUST SUCH A WELL KNOWN FACT OF XENOBIOLOGY. I DON'T WANT TA LOSE ALL CREDIBILITY WITH THE SCIENTIFIC CROWD!

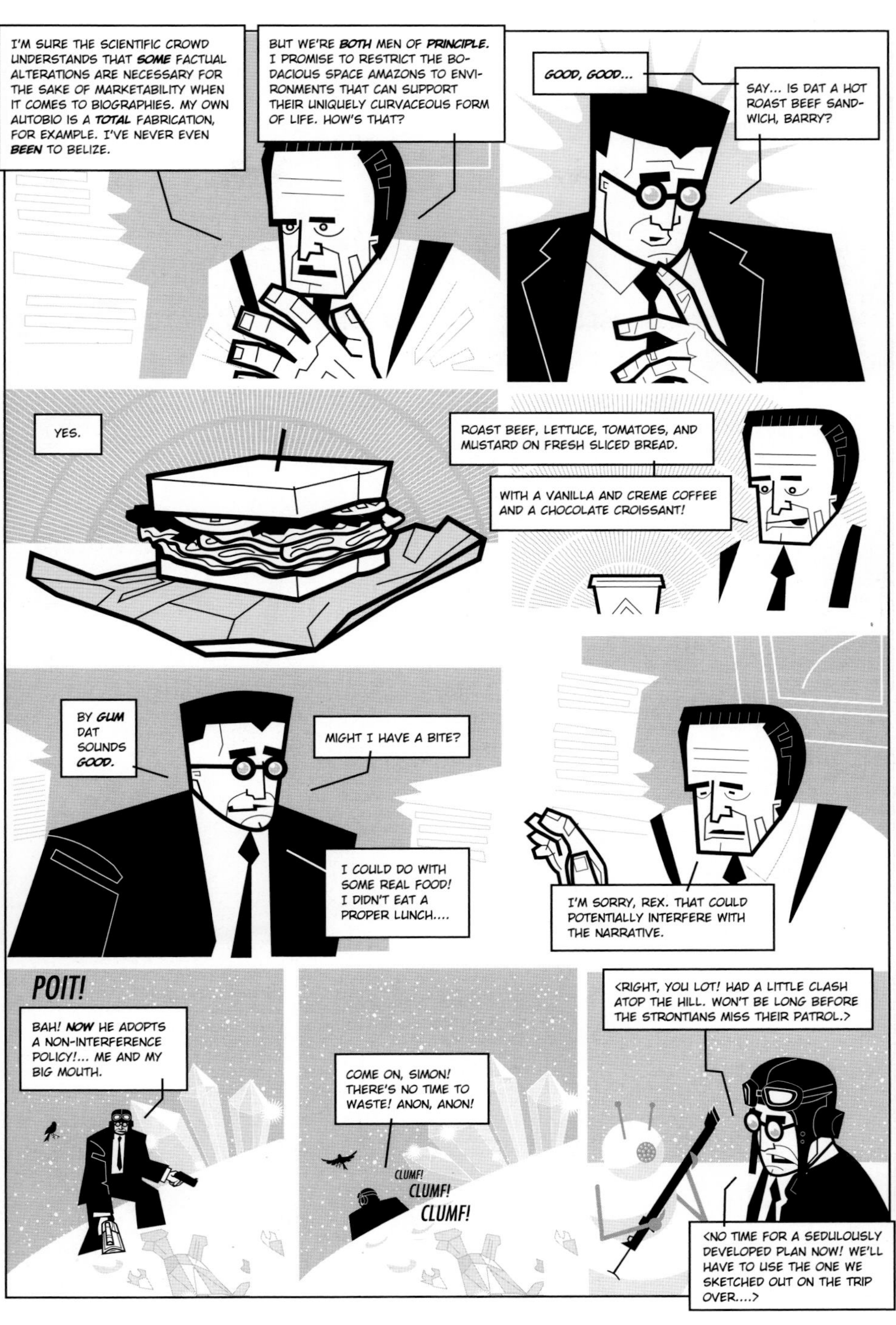
I'M SURE THE SCIENTIFIC CROWD UNDERSTANDS THAT **SOME** FACTUAL ALTERATIONS ARE NECESSARY FOR THE SAKE OF MARKETABILITY WHEN IT COMES TO BIOGRAPHIES. MY OWN AUTOBIO IS A **TOTAL** FABRICATION, FOR EXAMPLE. I'VE NEVER EVEN **BEEN** TO BELIZE.
BUT WE'RE **BOTH** MEN OF **PRINCIPLE.** I PROMISE TO RESTRICT THE BODACIOUS SPACE AMAZONS TO ENVIRONMENTS THAT CAN SUPPORT THEIR UNIQUELY CURVACEOUS FORM OF LIFE. HOW'S THAT?
GOOD, GOOD...
SAY... IS DAT A HOT ROAST BEEF SANDWICH, BARRY?
YES.
ROAST BEEF, LETTUCE, TOMATOES, AND MUSTARD ON FRESH SLICED BREAD.
WITH A VANILLA AND CREME COFFEE AND A CHOCOLATE CROISSANT!
BY ***GUM*** DAT SOUNDS ***GOOD.***
MIGHT I HAVE A BITE?
I COULD DO WITH SOME REAL FOOD! I DIDN'T EAT A PROPER LUNCH....
I'M SORRY, REX. THAT COULD POTENTIALLY INTERFERE WITH THE NARRATIVE.
POIT!
BAH! **NOW** HE ADOPTS A NON-INTERFERENCE POLICY!... ME AND MY BIG MOUTH.
COME ON, SIMON! THERE'S NO TIME TO WASTE! ANON, ANON!
CLUMF!
CLUMF!
CLUMF!
<RIGHT, YOU LOT! HAD A LITTLE CLASH ATOP THE HILL. WON'T BE LONG BEFORE THE STRONTIANS MISS THEIR PATROL.>
<NO TIME FOR A SEDULOUSLY DEVELOPED PLAN NOW! WE'LL HAVE TO USE THE ONE WE SKETCHED OUT ON THE TRIP OVER....>

<I ONLY WISH I HAD A MORE PRECISE LAYOUT OF THE STRONTIAN STRONG-HOLD THAN THE VAGUE DESCRIPTION OF BRZTZOT!>
<GAH! WHAT THE...?>
THAK! THAK! THAK!
<STAND STILL!>
<I AM TRYING TO INSERT AN INFORM-ATION CRYSTAL INTO YOUR SENSORY POD. IT WILL INSTANTLY DOWNLOAD OUR KNOWLEDGE INTO YOUR BRAIN!>
<REMARKABLE!>
<INSTANTANEOUS INFORMATION ABSORPTION! WHAT KINDA RECALL DO YOU HAVE, BRZTZOT?>
<COMPLETE! BUT WE ONLY HAVE WHAT KNOWLEDGE WE CAN ASSEMBLE OUR-SELVES. EDUCATION IS FORBIDDEN FOR SLAVES!>
<WHY THAT NO GOOD FLAGITIOUS SCALAWAG VAGLOX!>
<DENYIN' FREEDOM OF OPPORTUNITY JUST PISSES ME OFF!>
<BUT I GOT ME AN IDEA THAT'LL CHANGE EVERY-THING.>
<I PICKED UP AN EQUIPMENT BOOK BEFORE WE LEFT.>
<IT'S FILLED WITH ALL KINDS OF USEFUL STUFF--GADGETS, WEAPONS, BOOKS, YOU NAME IT!>
<ALL TRANSFERRED INTA A CONCEPTUAL QUANTUM DIMENSION FER EASY TRANSPORT!>

*NOTE: THIS WWI ARMY MANUAL WAS RENAMED AFTER COMPLAINTS THE TITLE WAS TOO VIOLENT. AN ESTIMATED 704,205 BRITISH MEN DIED AT THE FRONT BEFORE THE WAR WAS OVER. – BARRY

...AN' PRESTO: AN INSTANT-MILITARY-GENIUS-NINJA PILL!
SIMON WITH AN ARMY OF SUPER NINJAS...
BETTER ADD A FEW **OTHER** BOOKS....
ZAP!
ZAP!
ZAP!
CLUMF!
CLUMF!
CLUMF!
CLUMF!
<OKAY, ALL SET! DIS LITTLE CRYSTAL HAS EVERYTHING YA NEED TA KNOW TO START A REVOLUTION!>
<EXCELLENT!>
<SIMON, I'LL LEAVE BRZTZOT MY CAP AND R/T SET SO YA CAN TALK TO YER TRIPLE-SCOOP FRIENDS.>
<GRACIAS!>
THAP!
GOOD LUCK, REX!
FREE MY MINIONS!
HEH. YEAH. WHATEVER.
PLOPF!
GIMME AN HOUR TO SHUT DOWN THE SECURITY SYSTEMS.

FORTUNATELY THOSE SUB-ORBITAL BATTLEPLATFORMS ARE ALL ORIENTED SPACE-WARD!
CLUMF!
CLUMF!
CLUMF!
I CAN'T WAIT TA SHOW MR. THOTH THE MEGAPOW-ERED CRYSTALS I FOUND!
TUNK!
TUNK!
TUNK!
TUNK!
TUNK!
BZRACK!
TUNK!
TUNK!
GAH! ELECTRIFIED PLATING! HIGH INTENSITY, VARIABLE ELECTRICAL PULSES!
ENOUGH TA DISRUPT A KANIKTSHAK!
BUT NOT ME! ALWAYS HELPS TA HAVE INSU-LATED FOOTWEAR!
SCHWIP!
TUNK!

BIT OF A BREEZE IN HERE... DEY MUST BE VENTIN' TRACE ATMOSPHERE.
NO MATTER! MY BIOPOLY-TRONIC MASKING FIELD WILL KEEP THEIR SENSORS FROM DETECTING ME!
THE INCREDIBLE HEAT IN DESE WALLS WOULD CONDUCT UP MY BOOTS AND FRY ME IF IT WEREN'T FOR THE LIBRARY'S MAGICAL OUTER SPACE PROTECTION POLICY!
GLUNK!
GLUNK!
IF BRZTZOT'S DIRECTIONS ARE RIGHT, DIS VENT INTERSECTS WITH A MAINTENANCE SHAFT DAT LEADS RIGHT TA THE PRIMARY COMPUTER CABLE NEXUS!
GLUNK!
GLUNK!
YES! THESE CABLES GO DOWN TA THE ARMOURED COMPUTER CORE SEVERAL MILES BENEATH DA CITY. ALL I GOTTA DO IS DISABLE THE CABLE HUB. THAT'LL CUT OFF THE CENTRAL COMPUTER FROM ALL OF ITS PERIPHERALS.
GLUNK! GLUNK!
SCHGLUP!
INCLUDING THE SECURITY SYSTEMS!
BEEP! BEEP!
JUST ONE MORE STOP, ATOP DA EAST METHANE HOLDING TANK REPAIR ACCESSWAY....
GLUNK! GLUNK! GLUNK! GLUNK! GLUNK!
BEEP! BEEP!
35:00
DONE!
NOW IT'S ON TO THE THRONE ROOM OF VAGLOX!

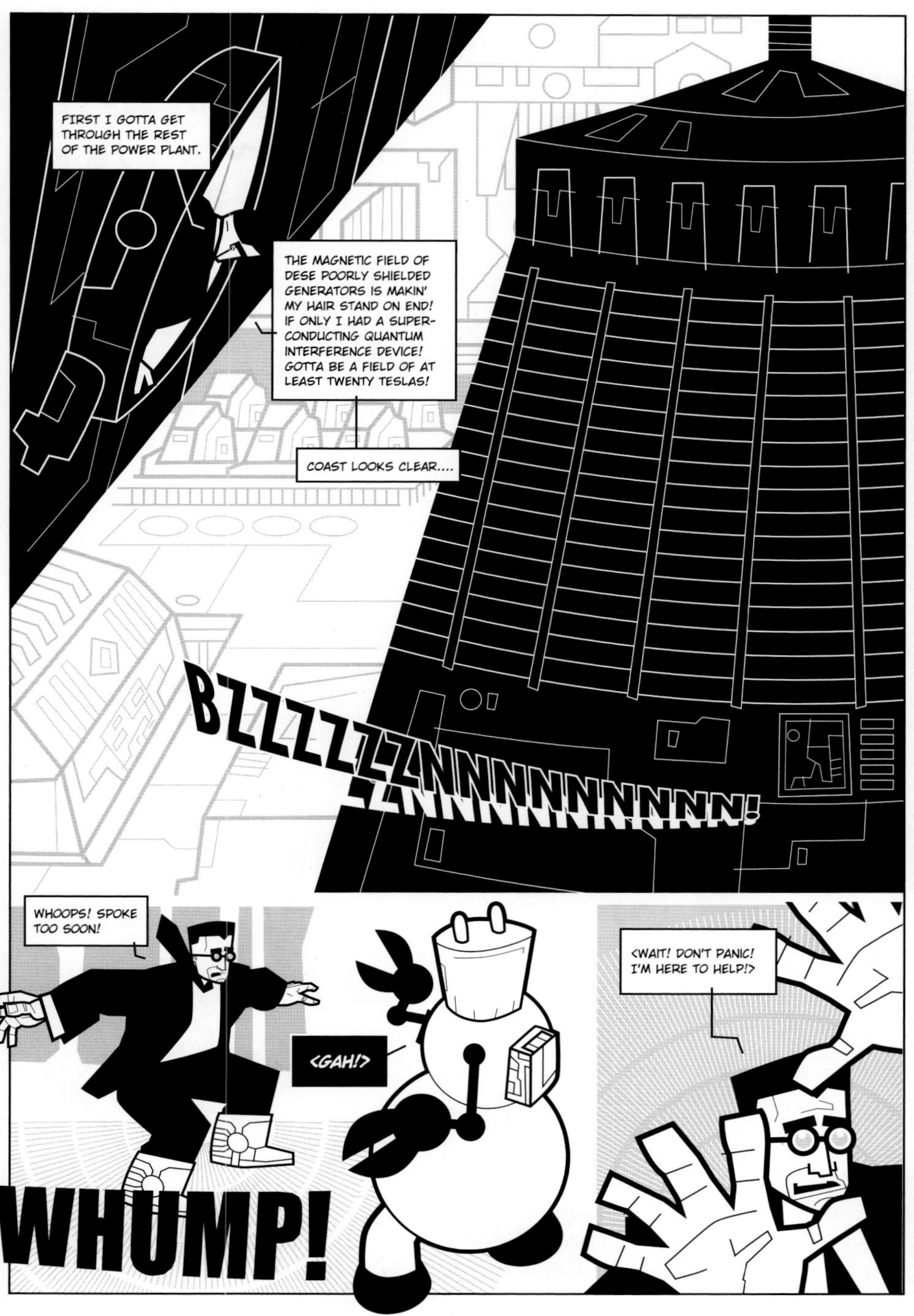
FIRST I GOTTA GET THROUGH THE REST OF THE POWER PLANT.
THE MAGNETIC FIELD OF DESE POORLY SHIELDED GENERATORS IS MAKIN' MY HAIR STAND ON END! IF ONLY I HAD A SUPER-CONDUCTING QUANTUM INTERFERENCE DEVICE! GOTTA BE A FIELD OF AT LEAST TWENTY TESLAS!
COAST LOOKS CLEAR....
BZZZZZZZNNNNNNNNNNNN!
WHOOPS! SPOKE TOO SOON!
<GAH!>
WHUMP!
<WAIT! DON'T PANIC! I'M HERE TO HELP!>

!?!?!
<GUARD!>
<INTRUDER!>
OH SHIT.
SHHHHH!!
<ALIEN INTRUDER!!>
HSST!!
<KEEP IT DOWN!!!>
<ALARM! ALARM!>
WHAM!
<UNGH!>

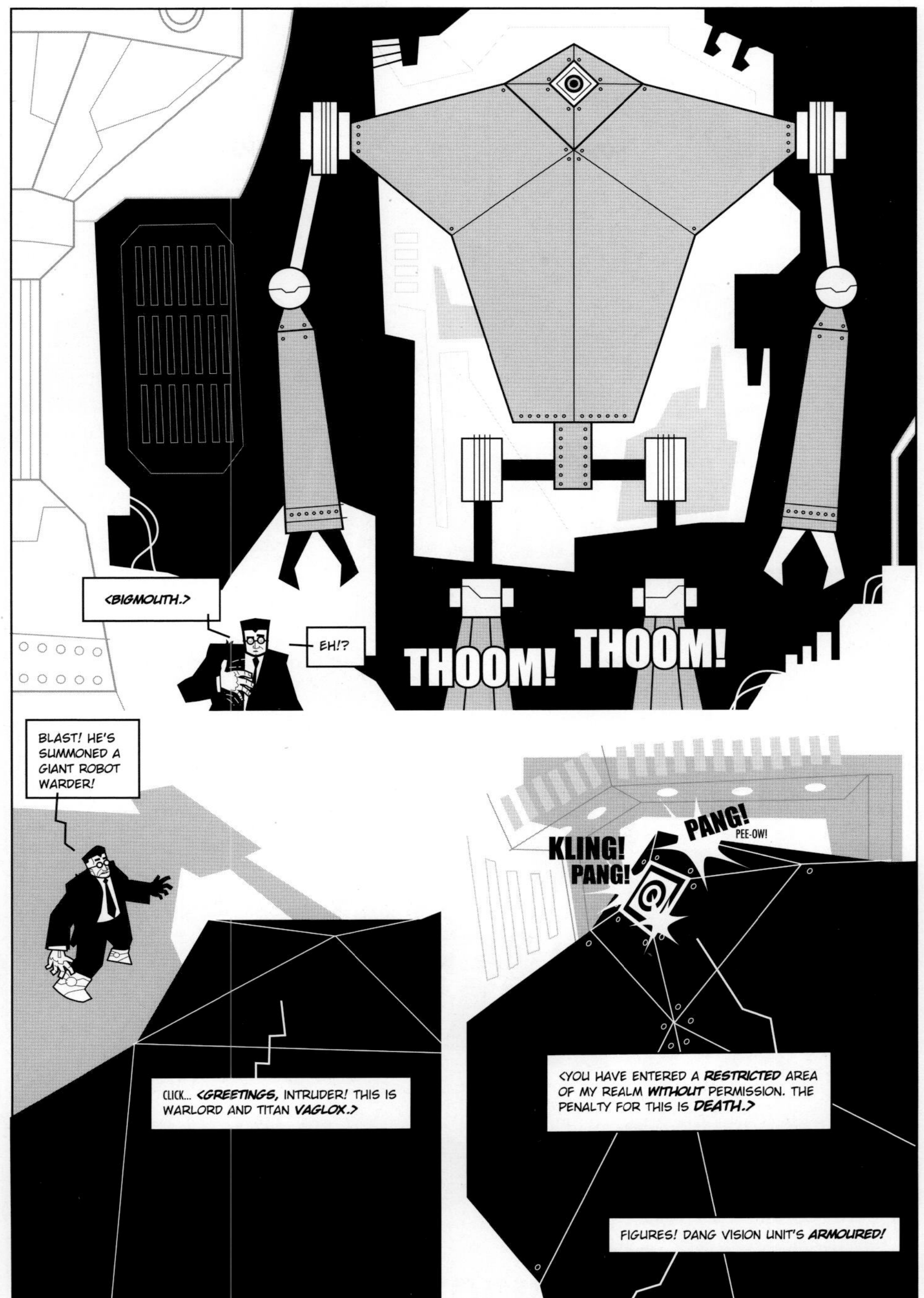
<BIGMOUTH.>
EH!?
THOOM!
THOOM!
BLAST! HE'S SUMMONED A GIANT ROBOT WARDER!
CLICK... <GREETINGS, INTRUDER! THIS IS WARLORD AND TITAN VAGLOX.>
KLING!
PANG!
PANG!
PEE-OW!
<YOU HAVE ENTERED A RESTRICTED AREA OF MY REALM WITHOUT PERMISSION. THE PENALTY FOR THIS IS DEATH.>
FIGURES! DANG VISION UNIT'S ARMOURED!

<IGNORANCE OF MY LAW IS NO EXCUSE. YET, AS I AM A ***MERCIFUL*** TITAN....>
GAH!
FWOOOOOOSHH!!
KATHOOM!
<...I SHALL ENDEAVOUR TO ENSURE THAT YOUR DEMISE IS AS QUICK AND PAINLESS AS POSSIBLE, IN KEEPING WITH THE ENLIGHTENED VALUES I HOLD DEAR. MAY YOUR SOUL TRANSMIGRATE SUCCESS-FULLY....> CLICK
TOO POWERFUL!
DIS ROBOT ISN'T GONNA TAKE A STEP BACK 'CAUSE OF ME!
DOESN'T ANYBODY TEACH THEIR DEATH MACHINES THE THREE LAWS OF ROBOTICS ANYMORE!?
KATHAIN!
<PLEASE REMAIN STATIONARY.>
GOTTA HEAD INTA THE MACHINERY--
THOOM!
THOOM!
THOOM!

THE MACHINERY MAY CONFUSE ITS SENSORS!
GLUNK!
GLUNK!
GLUNK!
GLUNK!
BZZZZTT!
DISTINTEGRATOR BEAMS!
IT'S VARYING ITS ATTACK! QUICK ACTING, ADAPTIVE HEURISTIC PROGRAMMIN' IN ACTION!
BUT THEESE GENERATORS GIMME AN IDEA!
ZRAK!
BZZZZZZZZZMMM!
UNGH! IT'S FASTER THAN I THOUGHT!
FWOOOOOOSHH!!
KTHAM!
GLUNK!
GLUNK!
GLUNK!
GLUNK!

BZZZZZZZZZMMM!
YA DON'T HAVE VERY SENSITIVE PEIZO ELECTRIC POLYMERS, DO YA?
GLUNK! GLUNK!
BZZZZZZZZZMMM!
BZZZZZZZZZMMM!
BZZZZTTT!
ZRAK
GLUNK!
GAH!
BZZZZZZZZZMMM!
BZZZZZZZZZMMM!
BZZZZZZZZZMMM!
!?!
BZZZZTTT!
ZRAK!
FIRST RULE O' COMBAT: ZIG WHEN THEY THINK YER GONNA ZAG!
SCHTHUP!
00:01
3... 2... 1...!!
BAW!!
BOOMBOS!
GLUNK! GLUNK! GLUNK!
EH!?
BLAST! NOT A SCRATCH ON HIM!
DAMN MACHINED DEUSEXIUM ARMOUR PLATING MAKES HIM VIRTUALLY INVULNERABLE!

BZZZTT!
BZZZZZZZZMMM!
SCHZAK!
THE GENERATORS ARE MY ONLY CHANCE NOW!
ITS TARGETING COMPUTER IS A FRACTION OF A SECOND SLOWER THAN MY REACTION TIMES! BUT SOON IT'LL HAVE ENOUGH DATA TO ANTICIPATE MY MOVES!
ZAK!
ZRAK!!
C'MON GENERATORS!
GZZZZZZZZZZZZZZZZZTT
GLUNK!
GLUNK!
GLUNK!
TICK-ZZZZZZZZZSK!
K-POP!
KREEEEEEEEEEEEEEEEEEEEEAAAA
THA CLANG!!
YEAH! FOX ONE, LION ZERO!

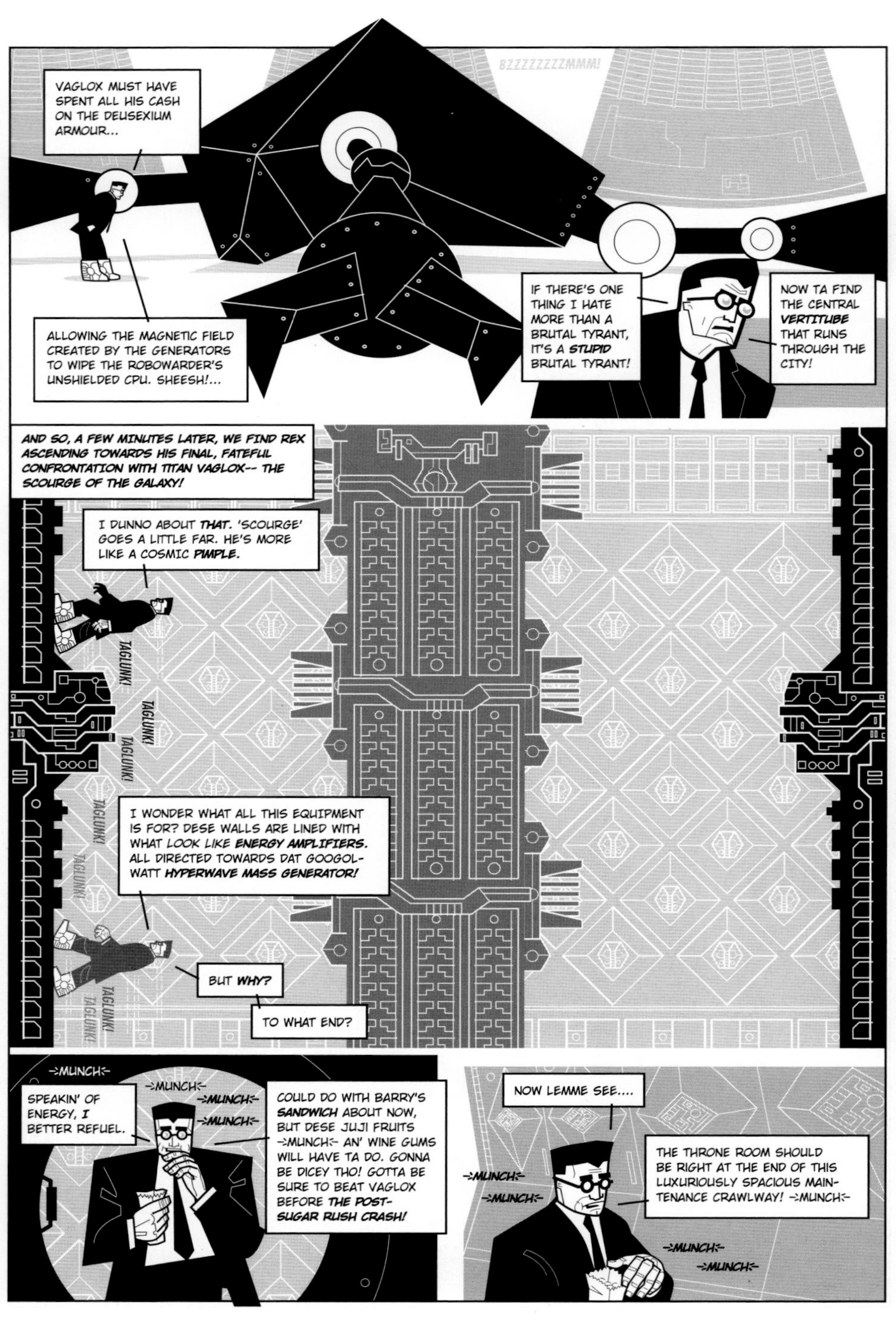
BZZZZZZZZMMM!
VAGLOX MUST HAVE SPENT ALL HIS CASH ON THE DEUSEXIUM ARMOUR...
ALLOWING THE MAGNETIC FIELD CREATED BY THE GENERATORS TO WIPE THE ROBOWARDER'S UNSHIELDED CPU. SHEESH!...
IF THERE'S ONE THING I HATE MORE THAN A BRUTAL TYRANT, IT'S A STUPID BRUTAL TYRANT!
NOW TA FIND THE CENTRAL VERTITUBE THAT RUNS THROUGH THE CITY!
AND SO, A FEW MINUTES LATER, WE FIND REX ASCENDING TOWARDS HIS FINAL, FATEFUL CONFRONTATION WITH TITAN VAGLOX-- THE SCOURGE OF THE GALAXY!
I DUNNO ABOUT THAT. 'SCOURGE' GOES A LITTLE FAR. HE'S MORE LIKE A COSMIC PIMPLE.
TAGLUNK!
TAGLUNK!
TAGLUNK!
TAGLUNK!
TAGLUNK!
I WONDER WHAT ALL THIS EQUIPMENT IS FOR? DESE WALLS ARE LINED WITH WHAT LOOK LIKE ENERGY AMPLIFIERS. ALL DIRECTED TOWARDS DAT GOOGOL-WATT HYPERWAVE MASS GENERATOR!
BUT WHY?
TO WHAT END?
TAGLUNK!
TAGLUNK!
-MUNCH-
SPEAKIN' OF ENERGY, I BETTER REFUEL.
-MUNCH-
-MUNCH-
-MUNCH-
COULD DO WITH BARRY'S SANDWICH ABOUT NOW, BUT DESE JUJI FRUITS -MUNCH- AN' WINE GUMS WILL HAVE TA DO. GONNA BE DICEY THO! GOTTA BE SURE TO BEAT VAGLOX BEFORE THE POST-SUGAR RUSH CRASH!
NOW LEMME SEE....
THE THRONE ROOM SHOULD BE RIGHT AT THE END OF THIS LUXURIOUSLY SPACIOUS MAIN-TENANCE CRAWLWAY! -MUNCH-
-MUNCH-
-MUNCH-
-MUNCH-
-MUNCH-

ALL TOO--
<LOOK! THERE!>
<THE VIBRATION DETECTOR WAS RIGHT!>
<THE INTRUDER WAS IN THE MAINTENANCE TUBES!>
BGZZT!
BGZZT!
<KILL IT!>
<DIE, ALIEN OBSCENITY!>
ZAK!
<OI! DAT TICKLES!>
ZAK!
ZAK
ZAK
ZAK!
<GRAKK!>
<FROZEN SUNS! NO EFFECT! THE BEAST STILL STANDS!>
<WE'RE DOOMED!>
<THE ALIEN IS IMMUNE TO OUR ELECTRODISRUPTION WEAPONS! SUMMON THE SCIENCE SLAVES!>
<TOO LATE! RUN! FLEE!>
<IT IS INVINCIBLE!>
<TOO BAD YA DIDN'T DO YER RESEARCH, BOYS, CAUSE I DID!>

BAW!
PERFECT TIME FOR AN E.M. PULSE BOMB!
IT'LL KEEP THESE CRYSTALLOIDS UNCONSCIOUS FOR HOURS!
<GRAKK! THIS... CREATURE EVADED NINETY BILLION CREDITS WORTH OF ORBITAL DEFENSES, MY SURFACE PATROLS, PENETRATED MY ARMOURED CITADEL, WENT UNDETECTED BY THE LIFE FORM SENSOR NET, DESTROYED MY ROBOWARDER COLOSSUS, VANQUISHED MY ELITE GUARDS LIKE THEY WERE INERT ICICLES, AND NOW APPROACHES MY THRONE ROOM WITH WILFULL INSOLENCE! WHO IS THIS BEING!?!>
<VAGLOX!>
<IT IS HERE!>
<MUST ACT CALM!>
<WELCOME, ALIEN, TO MY PALACE...>

I AM TITAN VAGLOX, SUPREME RULER OF THE STRONTIAN TITANATE, BRINGER OF JUSTICE, CREATOR OF ORDER, LIGHT OF THE GALAXY, DELIVERER OF DESTRUCTION, VORTEX OF-->

<YEAH, YEAH YEAH. I GET YER POINT. YER THE BIG CHEESE, DA SANGUINARY COXCOMB, THE PRATTLING PROLIX, THE TOP TYRANT. SPEED IT UP, WILL YA?>
<SUCH IMPUDENCE!>
<WHO ARE YOU, ALIEN, AND WHY ARE YOU HERE?>

<I'M REX LIBRIS, PUBLIC LIBRARIAN. WE TALKED EARLIER VIA QUANTUM ELECTROMAGNETOPHONE. IT'S ABOUT DAT BOOK YA HAVEN'T RETURNED.>
<CURSED SPACE GOATS! THE LIBRARIAN!!>
<AH YES. LET US DISCUSS THE MATTER LIKE CIVILIZED BEINGS...>
<HE DOESN'T FOOL ME! HE IS AFTER NO BOOK. HE SEEKS TO SUPPLANT ME! TO SEIZE MY THRONE!>

<SOUNDS GOOD...>
NOW FER A BIT OF MISDIRECTION... PLAY ON HIS INSECURITIES. FAN HIS FEARS!
<...AFTER ALL, IT WAS REAL EASY TA FIGHT MY WAY IN HERE.>

<YA GOT A MIGHTY NICE PALACE, VAGGIE-- CAN I CALL YA VAGGIE?-- REAL SPACIOUS. A FELLA COULD GET... COMFORTABLE IN A PLACE LIKE THIS. SO MUCH BETTER THAN LIVIN' BENEATH A LITTLE LIBRARY. YEAH... THIS PAD IS REAL NICE.>

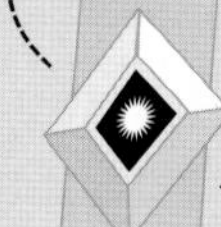
<DAMMIT! I KNEW IT! IT'S ONE FREAKIN' USURPER AFTER THE OTHER!>
<UH... NOT THAT NICE. THE ROOF LEAKS ATMOSPHERE WHEN THE ROOM IS PRESSURIZED.... NO INSULATION AT ALL.>

<BUT YER A TYRANT! A WARLORD! I CAN SEE WHY YOU'D LIKE THE JOB. SUCH WEALTH! SUCH POSSESSIONS! SUCH POWER! SUCH PROCREATIVE POSSIBILITIES!>
<THERE IS WHERE YOU ARE WRONG, LIBRARIAN. BEING A TYRANT IS TERRIBLE!>

<I AM IN AN INESCAPABLE PRISON OF POWER, UNABLE TO ENJOY THE SIMPLE PLEASURES OF LIFE! THE MOTIVES OF ALL WHO ARE CLOSE TO ME ARE SUSPECT, THEIR SYCOPHANTIC ACCOLADES EMPTY!>

<I CANNOT SLEEP SOUNDLY, FOR FEAR OF A STEALTHY BLOW OUT OF THE DARK.>

<I TAKE NO PLEASURE DIPPING BENEATH THE CRUST OF THE PEGMATITE POOLS FOR WORRY OF BEING POISONED BY MY UNDERLINGS!>
YES! HE'S SCARED!

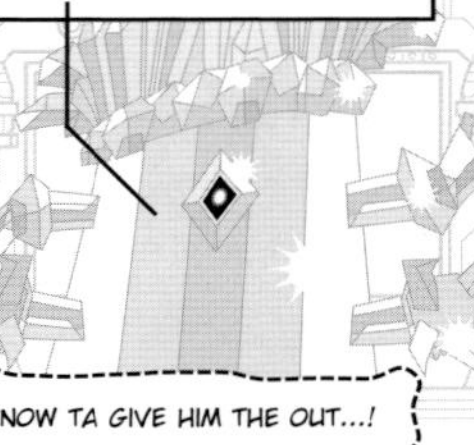
<NO, LIBRARIAN, DO NOT ENVY ME. IT IS ALL I CAN DO TO NOT THROW MYSELF INTO THE DISINTEGRATOR, SO ***MISERABLE*** IS MY EXISTENCE.>
NOW TA GIVE HIM THE OUT...!

<GEE, DAT'S TOO BAD, ***VAGGIE BABY.*** JUST HAND OVER TH' BOOK YA BORROWED, ***THE PRINCIPIA MATHEMATICA,*** AND THE LATE FEE, AND I'LL GET OUTTA YER FACE ROYAL FACE PRONTO.>
<LETCHA GET BACK TA GALACTIC CONQUEST OR ***WHATEVER.*** YA GROK ME?>

<OH, I... AH... ***RETURNED*** IT.>

<DAT ***SO?*** MY TRACKER SAYS TH' BOOK IS IN ***THIS*** BUILDING, NOT TWENTY METERS AWAY FROM WHERE WE STAND....>

<OH!>
<RIGHT! ***THAT*** BOOK. I THOUGHT YOU MEANT ***NEWTON'S*** PRINCIPIA MATHEMATICA....>

<BOLLOCKS!>
<YOU KNEW ***EXACTLY*** WHAT I MEANT, ***MISTER.>***

IT'S NOT THE ***FINE,*** IS IT? CRIPES, YOU HAVE THE RESOURCES OF AN ENTIRE ***SPACE EMPIRE*** TO DRAW UPON! ***SURELY*** YOU CAN AFFORD THE SEVEN BUCKS!

IF YA PAID, YER REPUTATION AS AN HONOURABLE RULER WOULD ***GROW!***
<HONOUR N' TRUST WOULD ALLOW YA TO ***TRADE*** INSTEAD OF PILLAGE!>

<HELL, ***EMANCIPATE*** YER HELOTS, MAXIMIZE THE POTENTIAL OF YOUR PEOPLE WITH ***EDUCATION AND FREEDOM,*** AND SEE ***PROS-PERITY*** GROW AND CREDIT ACCRUE TO YOUR REPUTATION ***AND*** YER STATE COFFERS.>
<I CAN RECOMMEND A SLEW OF WRITERS TO YA: ***JOHN STUART MILL, AMARTYA SEN, FAREED ZAKARIA, GURGOLZORG THE ELDER OF PLANET DEMOSPERO FIVE...*** I'M TELLIN YA-->

<--SCIENCE AND DEMOCRACY MAKE THE ***PERFECT*** COUPLE! START AN EXPANDIN' CIRCLE OF ***TRUST.*** YA DON'T HAVE TO SLEEP IN ***FEAR!*** THERE'S ***ANOTHER WAY,*** VAGLO!>
<IT DOESN'T HAVE TO ***BE*** A ***ZERO SUM GAME!*** TRUST ***OVER*** FEAR, BABY! ***TRUST*** OVER FEAR!>

<HMM.>

<TEA?>

<TEA?>

<TO ACCOMPANY OUR DISCUSSION. I UNDERSTAND IT IS A PART OF PROPER ETIQUETTE, FOR YOUR SPECIES, TO OFFER LIQUID REFRESHMENTS.>

<THE CUP HAS A VAPOUR FIELD GENERATOR TO KEEP IT FROM BOILING OFF INTO SPACE, AND A FUSION POWERED HEATER TO KEEP IT FROM FREEZING SOLID.>

SCHWIP!

<IT USES THE HYDROGEN IN THE WATER FOR POWER SO BEST TO DRINK IT QUICKLY.>

<GEE...>

<THANKS. HAVE SOME SUGAR LEFT OVER FROM ***THE INFINITE CUP*** WITH ME... AN A LIL' STIR SPOON...>

<NO!!>

TINK

TINK

SSSSSSSS!!!

<WHAT DA--!?! YA POISONED THE ***TEA!?*** OF ALL THE CRUMMY, ***LOW*** THINGS TA DO...>

SSSS!

<BAH!>

<I WAS HOPING TO DISPOSE OF YOU QUIETLY, YOU INSOLENT ***BOOK-SHELVING USURPER!>***

<NEVER! IT IS A MATTER OF PRINCIPAL: TITANS DO NOT TAKE ORDERS FROM ***HELOTS!*** THE VERY IDEA IS OUTRAGEOUS! FOR YOUR PRESUMPTION, YOUR OBSCENE ***IMPERTINENCE,*** I SHALL WRING THE LIFE OUT OF YOU, AND THEN I SHALL BLAST YOUR PITIFUL LITTLE PLANET INTO ***ATOMS!>***

<FOOL! ISN'T IT OBVIOUS?>

<THAT BOOK WILL BE THE JEWEL OF MY PERSONAL LIBRARY! IT WILL MAKE ME THE ***ENVY*** OF ALL THE LOCAL SYSTEM WARLORDS! DESTROYING YOUR PLANET WILL MAKE IT ***UNIQUE,*** AND INCREASE ITS VALUE A ***THOUSAND*** TIMES! BESIDES...>

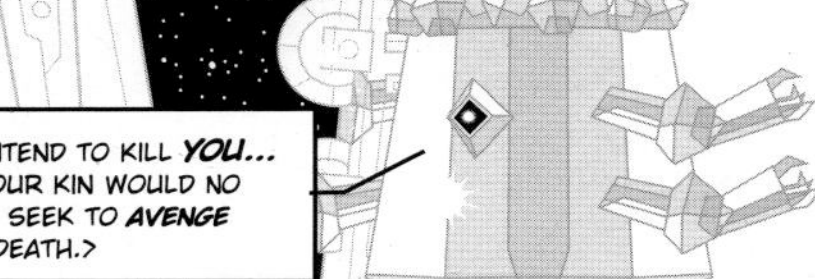

<WOW. CONCUPISCENT DESTRUCTION!>

<I THINK YER A LITTLE TOO CAUGHT UP IN SOCIAL HIERARCHY. C'MON! GET A LITTLE PERSPECTIVE! MIGHT DOES NOT MAKE RIGHT, BUCKO!>

<OF COURSE IT DOES. MIGHT MAKES ANYTHING IT WANTS. THAT'S WHY IT'S MIGHT.>

<YEAH. WELL. LITTLE POINT IN ARGUING MORALS WITH A RUTHLESS, PSYCHOPATHIC, PLANET BUSTING LUNATIC....>
<...I GUESS THE GODS HAVE DECIDED YER TIME IS UP....>

<YOU MUST HAVE SEEN THE MACHINERY ON YOUR WAY IN.>
<THE DEVICE WILL PROJECT AN ARTIFICIAL BLACK HOLE INTO THE CENTRE OF YOUR PLANET THROUGH A QUANTUM GATE. IT ONLY LASTS FOR A SPLIT SECOND, BUT IN THAT SECOND, YOUR PLANET AND THE SURROUNDING SOLAR SYSTEM WILL BE SUCKED INTO A SINGULARITY. THE BLACK HOLE THEN DISSIPATES, THE SINGULARITY EXPLODES, AND EVENTUALLY THE RELEASED MATTER COALESCES INTO A NEW SOLAR SYSTEM....>

<DAT'S MONSTROUS!>

<NOTHING IS GOOD OR BAD, LIBRARIAN -- ONLY YOUR THINKING MAKES IT SO! BESIDES! I PREFER TO THINK OF THIS AS 'CREATIVE DESTRUCTION.' LIKE NATURE. OR CAPITALISM.>
<WHOA! THAT'S A RATHER... UNCHARITABLE DESCRIPTION. YOU'D DESTROY A CIVILIZATION AND REPLACE IT WITH AN EMPTY SHELL! WHERE IS THE CREATIVE PART?>

<WHY, SOME DAY LIFE MAY EVOLVE AGAIN IN YOUR REBORN SOLAR SYSTEM. LIFE IS EPHEMERAL, BOOK SHELVER.>

<FEH! DIS IS NO LONGER TIME FER ME TA BE MAGNANIMOUS! IF YA WON'T GO FOR THE CARROT....

<...THEN YER GOIN' DOWN, YA CRAZY CRYSTALLINE KYLON!>
BLAM!
BLAM!
BLAM!
BLAM!
FWIP!

TKLAOW!
SPEOW!
<HAHAHA! OUR CRYSTALLINE STRUCTURE METALLIZES AS WE AGE! THAT PUNY WEAPON CANNOT AFFECT ME NOW!>
BLAM! BLAM!
CLANG! CLANG! CLANG!
<CRAP! WHY DO I EVEN CARRY THIS THING?>
FLICK!
<I CAN STILL USE YOUR OWN WEAPON AGAINST YOU-->
<ARGH!!>
HIS REFLEXES... IMPROBABLY FAST!
WOK!
FWAAAAAAP!
LIKE LIGHTNING!
I NEED SOME DISTANCE! GOTTA GET OUTTA RANGE OF THOSE DIAMOND-HARD FISTS OF HIS!
THOK!
<OOF!!>
<HA! YOU ARE JUST FEEBLE FLESH WRAPPED AROUND BRITTLE BONES!!>
DAT'S ONE WAY TO DO IT!
SKIIIIIIIIIIIIIIISSSSSSSSHHH!!!

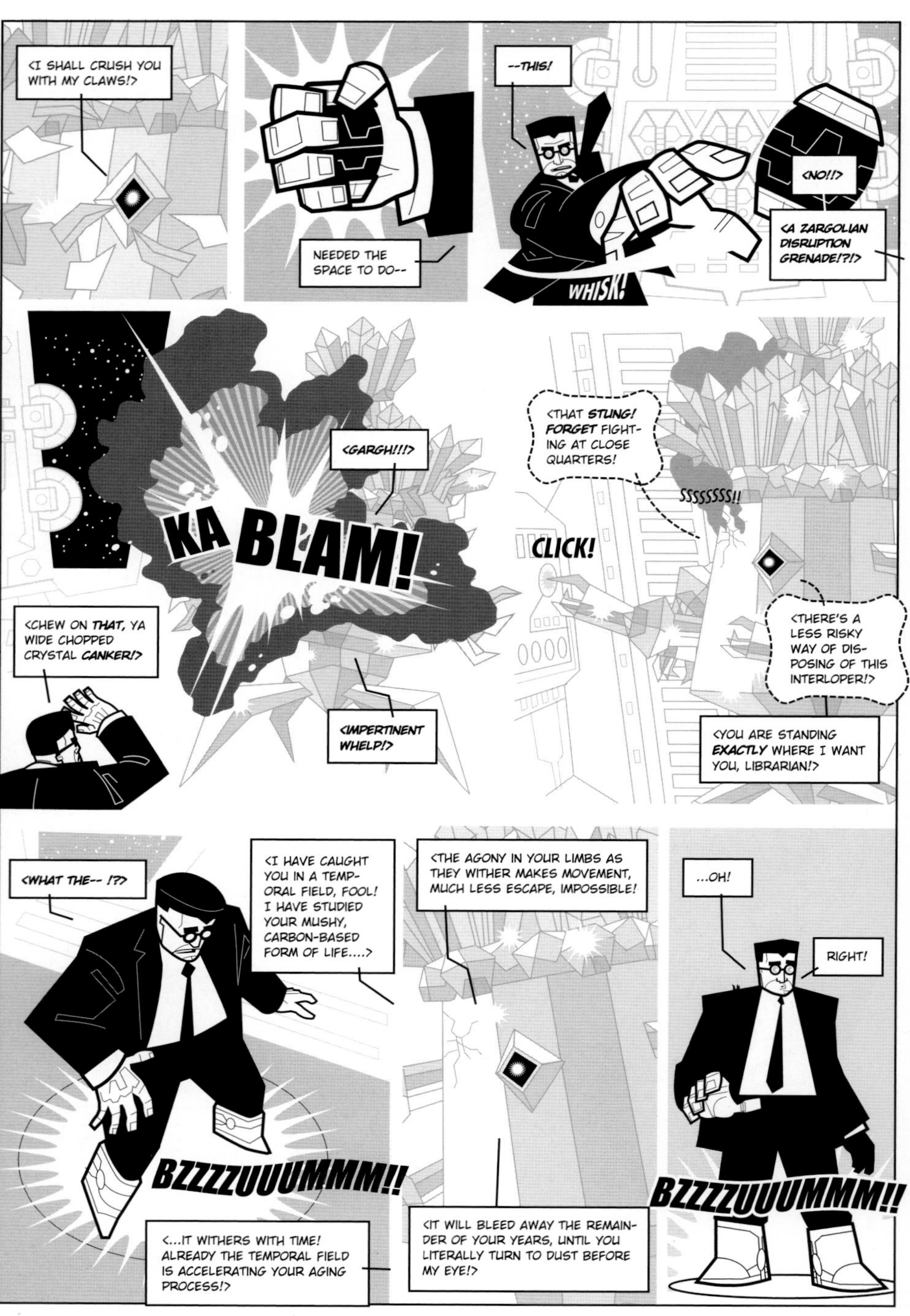
<I SHALL CRUSH YOU WITH MY CLAWS!>
NEEDED THE SPACE TO DO--
--THIS!
WHISK!
<NO!!>
<A ZARGOLIAN DISRUPTION GRENADE!?!>
KA BLAM!
<GARGH!!!>
<CHEW ON THAT, YA WIDE CHOPPED CRYSTAL CANKER!>
<IMPERTINENT WHELP!>
<THAT STUNG! FORGET FIGHTING AT CLOSE QUARTERS!
SSSSSSSS!!
CLICK!
<THERE'S A LESS RISKY WAY OF DISPOSING OF THIS INTERLOPER!>
<YOU ARE STANDING EXACTLY WHERE I WANT YOU, LIBRARIAN!>
<WHAT THE-- !?>
<I HAVE CAUGHT YOU IN A TEMPORAL FIELD, FOOL! I HAVE STUDIED YOUR MUSHY, CARBON-BASED FORM OF LIFE....>
BZZZZUUUMMM!!
<...IT WITHERS WITH TIME! ALREADY THE TEMPORAL FIELD IS ACCELERATING YOUR AGING PROCESS!>
<THE AGONY IN YOUR LIMBS AS THEY WITHER MAKES MOVEMENT, MUCH LESS ESCAPE, IMPOSSIBLE!
<IT WILL BLEED AWAY THE REMAINDER OF YOUR YEARS, UNTIL YOU LITERALLY TURN TO DUST BEFORE MY EYE!>
...OH!
RIGHT!
BZZZZUUUMMM!!

UNGH!
OOOO!
AAAAH!
AARRGH!
<DIE, LIBRARIAN, DIE!! HAHA!
<...I'M MELTING! MELLLLTING!!...>
PAGE 52....
<THE PAIN!>
HEH HEH!
ZAP!
ZAP!
BZZZZZZZZUUUUUUUUUUUUUUUUUMMMMMMMMMMUUUUZZZZZZZZUUUUUUUUUUMMMMMMMMUUUUUUZZUUUUUM!
<YOUR AGONY IS JUST THE APPETIZER OF MY FEAST! SOON YOUR PLANET WILL JOIN YOU IN OBLIVIO-->
BOOM!
BABOOM!
<WHAT!?!>
THANKS TA BARRY'S AMAZON INTERRUPTION, SPACE IS GETTIN' TIGHT! I'VE BARELY ROOM TA FINISH THE CHAPTER!
<MY GARRISON-- DESTROYED IN A MASSIVE METHANE EXPLOSION!?! SECURITY SYSTEMS OFF-LINE!? SNOWHELOTS INVADING!?!>
<THIS IS YOUR DOING, YOU MEDDLING BIBLIOMANIAC!-->
<TELL IT TO MY ROCKET LAUNCHER.>
CLICK
<ARRGH!!>
BAKRAKOOM!
FWOOOOOOOOSHSSSSSSSH!!
<NOW...>
<...LET'S SEE....>
CLICK
CLICK
CLICK
CLICK
<YEAH!>
<YOUR GOONS ARE BEATEN, VAGLOX! THE JIG IS UP!>
<VAGLOX?>
<WELL I'LL BE. HE'S BUGGERED OFF.>

AFTER PULLING THE PLUG ON THE GRAVITIC WEAPON, REX HEADS DOWNSTAIRS TO CHECK ON THE REVOLUTION....
HEYA SIMON! VAGLOX IS FINISHED! HOW'D THINGS GO DOWN HERE?
GOOD! I HAVE A FEW STORIES TO TELL YOU--
NO TIME! HAVE TO TELEPORT BACK AND WRAP THE ISSUE UP! I GUESS YER IN CHARGE HERE NOW. DON'T SCREW IT UP!
DON'T WORRY, REX! IF ST. AUGUSTINE CAN TURN A NEW LEAF, SO CAN I! IT'LL BE AN ENLIGHTENED PARADISE!
YEAH, YEAH! I'LL BE BACK SOON WITH SOME BIRD FOOD. DON'T LET ME FIND YA WEAR-IN' ANY MYRTLE CROWN!
CIAO!
SHORTLY, BACK AT MIDDLETON PUBLIC LIBRARY....
MR. LIBRIS! YOU'RE BACK! THERE WAS AN INCIDENT WHILE YOU WERE GONE: VANDALS ATTACKED--
OH? HOW'S GAISERIC?
GONE! I MEAN, CIRCE SETTLED THEM DOWN-- THEY WERE ROWDY AT FIRST, BUT THEN THERE WERE THESE... HORRIBLE SCREAMS, AND WHEN WE WENT BACK, THE VANDALS WERE GONE, JUST BITS OF ARMOUR LEFT, AND BIG CHUNKS BITTEN OUT OF THE TABLES. WE FOUND A TOOTH THERE!
FASCINATIN'! CAN'T TALK! IN A HURRY. BACK LATER!
HEYA BOSS! I'M BACK!
OI, YOU HAVEN'T BEEN DRINKIN' AGAIN, HAVE YA?
NO.
REPORT, AGENT OF--HIC--THOTH!
MISSION WENT GREAT, BOSS!
WE OVERTHREW THE DICTATOR, FREED THE SNOW PEOPLE HE'D ENSLAVED... SIMON'S STAYIN' ON TA ESTABLISH A NEW, ENLIGHTENED SOCIETY-- HE BETTER! AND I PICKED UP A LOAD OF DESE PUPPIES: SUPER POWERFUL CRYSTALS! LIKE NONE WE'VE SEEN BEFORE, BOSS! GOT ENOUGH TELLURIC JUICE TA SEND A MAN ACROSS THE GALAXY-- AND BACK AGAIN! THINK OF IT!!
WHERE'S THE BOOK?
"THE BOOK?"
'THE PRINCIPIA MATHEMATICA.'
I'LL BE RIGHT BACK.
THE END (OF BOOK ONE)
NEXT ISSUE: BOOK OF MONSTERS!

The Ordo Bibliotheca

An inside look at the secret organization that works to safeguard the future of human civilization.

It has long been supposed that the librarian is a quiet and docile member of society whose function is to do little more than reshelve books. Librarians are often depicted as old maids, as if the library were a repository for unmarried women. This, of course, is exactly what they want you to think. These stereotypes are constructs of an intense and long standing disinformation campaign designed to hide the true activities of public librarians internationally. The veil of secrecy that has surrounded the Ordo Bibliotheca, the secrect International Order of Librarians, has been so complete and well maintained that it has, unlike the cover stories of the Templars and the Masons, remained completely unpenetrated by conspiracy theorists. Recently, however, new information has come to light which reveal both the depth of librarian influence on the development of human civilization, and show conclusively that the superficial docility of the librarian is but a mask that enables them to operate freely, behind the scenes, in our society.

The 'old maid' image (which most often consists of the combination of conservative attire and glasses, with hair worn in a tight bun) has been an especially effective means of disguise for concealing the formidable, sultry side of femme fatale librarian agents who employ a variety of methods, from lethal martial arts to feminine wiles, to protect knowledge, retrieve books, and add to the library collection. The practical nature of this disguise, and its brilliant simplicity, are typical of the Ordo Bibliotheca: efficient and, as necessary, ruthless. Among the most practical ever devised, the disguise does not impede movement and can easily and quickly be discarded, simply by unbuttoning a shirt, removing a hair pin, and wearing contact lenses. A femme fatale librarian, therefore, can switch modes so quickly, and metamorphize so completely, that they are virtually impossible for conventional secret agents to follow. Female librarian operatives are perceived as being less threatening than male agents, yet this too is part of the brilliant camouflage deployed by the Ordo Bibliotheca. Since at least the Sixth Century all librarians have received extensive combat training and are lethal with even the common toothpick.

To the conventional mind, this all sounds incredible, even unbelievable. Yet such skepticism simply serves the interests of the Ordo cover operation. The time has come for the shroud to be pulled back, and for the history of the Ordo Bibliotheca to be exposed to the light of day, so that all may understand the vital importance libraries have played in the development of human civilization. This material is undeniably explosive, and may very well change forever your view of the world and how it works.

First, librarians have been subtly guiding human civilization for almost two thousand years. By emphasizing, or deemphasizing, strains of knowledge, they are able to influence the development of our societies. They approach human knowledge as if it were a great Bonsai tree, and they cull and encourage it into the desired shape.

Second, librarians are all part of a secret society called the Ordo Bibliotheca, known in some circles as the Litterati Sodalicium. Its existence has been successfully concealed from the public since its inception in 242 BC in Ptolemaic Egypt. Founded by Callimachus, the chief librarian at Alexandria, and funded by Ptolemy Philadelphus, the society quickly expanded throughout the Middle East, to Rhodes (237 AD), Athens (235 AD) and in 230 AD, Pergamum. All were major Telluric energy hubs. The order outlived the fall of the Ptolemaic Empire, and continued to spread throughout Europe and the East under the Romans, working tirelessly to advance human knowledge and minimize the unspeakable, yet waning, influence of the mad Old Ones and their Chthonian minons.

During the Dark Ages, during which many libraries were burned by Christian fanatics, hundreds in the order fled to Persia, where under native Persian Avicenna (Also known as Sahib Al-Masahif, and the first Archmagus of the order, from 1015-1037 AD), they worked to establish an extensive series of libraries throughout the Islamic world, and to suppress the malefic influence of the Djinn of Melkemut. All that remained in Europe were a few isolated strongholds of knowledge, such as Vivarium in Southern Italy, where Rex was chief librarian for several years (and the leader of the book retrieval commando team that was instrumental in eliminating the brain-eating, book-burning zombie mercenaries that plagued Southern Italy throughout the Eleventh Century). As stability slowly returned to Europe, so did the Ordo Bibliotheca. Rex moved to Paris in the Twelfth Century to participate in the expansion of the Sarbonne Library, and later helped establish the University of Salamanca in Spain in the Fourteenth.

There can be little doubt that without the timely intervention of Ordo Bibliotheca, much of the knowledge of the ancients would have been lost. What little civilization remained was kept alive at heavily defended monasteries guarded by the Ordo Bibliotheca and its combat trained librarians. In addition to infiltrating the church, the order also worked to co-opt, influence, and enlighten the emerging royal families of Europe, as well as protect civilization from destructive supernatural phenomenon, such as the Ghaslichubi and the corpulent Unhs.

Richard Bentley (and future Archmagus and Procurator Bibliothecarum, 1695-1699), a senior Bibliophile in the order, was sent by the Grand Librarian in 1692 as a liaison to the British Royal Family, establishing a library branch in the Palace of Saint James in 1694. Bestowed the title of Keeper of the Royal Library, he expelled the Gundar Beast of Zoogh (1675-1694) and helped steer the British crown in the direction of responsible government. The influence of the librarian order culminated with the establishment of the Royal Library George III, and it is from there that the Ordo Bibliotheca would coordinate the promotion of the Enlightenment.

In North America, the establishment of an open, democratic society was championed by Benjamin Franklin (Archmagi Americanus 1770-1790), and as such the Ordo Bibliotheca was deeply involved in the creation of the United States.

In 1799 an elite team of librarians was embedded with Napoleon's expedition to Egypt, tasked with preventing the fruition of an ancient prophecy of doom by the malicious Egyptian god Seth. When French troops digging trenches unearthed the entrance to a long lost tomb, sealed since 190 BC, the librarian team intervened, and beat back the unspeakable, dessicated horrors that emerged from within, and saved the world from certain destruction. In a feat of great daring, team leader Rex Libris ventured into the nightmarish depths of this hieroglyph lined hell to retrieve the black basalt slab that became known as the Rosetta Stone. Jean Francois Champollion, assisted by several librarians, deciphered the stone in 1822, leading to the foundation of the field of Egyptology.

In 1828, librarian Rex Libris foiled a plot in Modena, Italy, by a clandestine secret order to expose the Ordo Bibliotheca by having Antonio Panizzi, a deep cover librarian, arrested on trumped up charges of being involved with Masonic mysticism. Rex rescued Panizzi and smuggled him to England, where in 1837 Panizzi became Keeper of Printed Books and the new Archmagus of the Ordo Bibliotheca. Panizzi is seen as the second greatest Archmagus, right after Melvil Dewey.

Reactionary forces, in the form of secret orders such as the malevolent Illuminati, the Legion of the Librinatrix, and the Ordo Magi Malignus (not to mention the Dark Teliki-iki-iki Beast Cult of the Urug'blech'gu' from Southern Mongolia in 1927) have impeded, hampered, and thwarted many librarian driven efforts, and caused a good deal of consternation and difficulty, not to mention setbacks, over the years, but by the mid to late Twentieth Century, Franklin's vision of a prosperous, democratic, and tolerant Union had been realized.

With the innovation of the teleportation crystal in 1921 by Litteratus Magi Rex Libris, a whole new era in lending opened up: interstellar book loans became possible. By 1960, over ten thousand volumes of extraterrestrial origin had been collected and stored at the Middleton Book Repository, a ceramic encased bunker deep beneath the Middleton Public Library. It remains one of the most important reference collections of xenognomic material, and is often used by the Pentagon during alien invasions. Middleton library staff, led by Head Librarian Rex Libris, used information from the interstellar collection to repel an attack by the malevolent Sl'uklu'uhk (hideous, giant space molluscs from beyond Pluto) in 1967, although little information on this event has ever been released to the public.

Crystals, of course, have long been used by librarians to explore the Oneirimundus (dreamworld), and to facilitate entry into the world of literature itself. It can takes surprisingly little Telluric current to enter a fictional quantum dimension, but a great deal to move anything from fiction into reality.

A great deal of information about the International Order of Librarians remains hidden from the general public, which may not, indeed, be ready yet to know the true history of this venerable institution. At this point, however, it is indisputable that the Ordo Bibliotheca, despite it's secretive beginnings, is both benevolent and a force for good. As always, it stands for reason tempered by empathy, and empathy tempered by reason-- circumstances permitting. The current Archmagus of the Ordo Bibliotheca is unknown, but one can be sure that they are working behind the scenes for the sake of all humanity, and their efforts to disseminate knowledge to the public can be seen, all over the world, at your local library branch.

THE YEAR IS 1918. THE LOCATION: 60 SQUADRON AIRBASE, IZEL LES HAMEAU, FILESCAMP FARM. 10 MILES BEHIND THE FRONT LINES....

REX · LIBRIS

vs. The Red Baron

ARE YOU SURE YOU'RE READY FOR THIS, REX?

SURE I'M SURE. HOW HARD CAN IT BE TO FLY ONE OF THESE THINGS, ANYWAY?

I DUNNO, REX. 1 IN 4 PILOTS CRASH ON THEIR FIRST FLIGHT....

H, DON'T WORRY, I'M TAKING THE MANUAL WITH IE. I GOT THE RFC HANDBOOK, TOO. SIDES, WE OTTA GET BACK TO MIDDLETON BY FOUR. I OTTA REORGANIZE THE FICTION DEPARTMENT EFORE THE BOSS GETS BACK.

LATER, HIGH ABOVE ALLIED LINES, A LONE RED TRIPLANE PROWLS. BARON MANFRED VON RICHTOFEN, COMMANDER OF JAGDESCHWADER I AND THE MOST DEADLY GERMAN PILOT ALIVE, IS ABOUT TO BECOME THE HUNTED!

*EDITOR NOTE: DUE TO REX'S POOR KNOWLEDGE OF GERMAN, THE RED BARON'S DIALOGUE HAS BEEN APPROXIMATED WITH THE AID OF A COPY OF 'SEE IT AND SAY IT IN GERMAN'

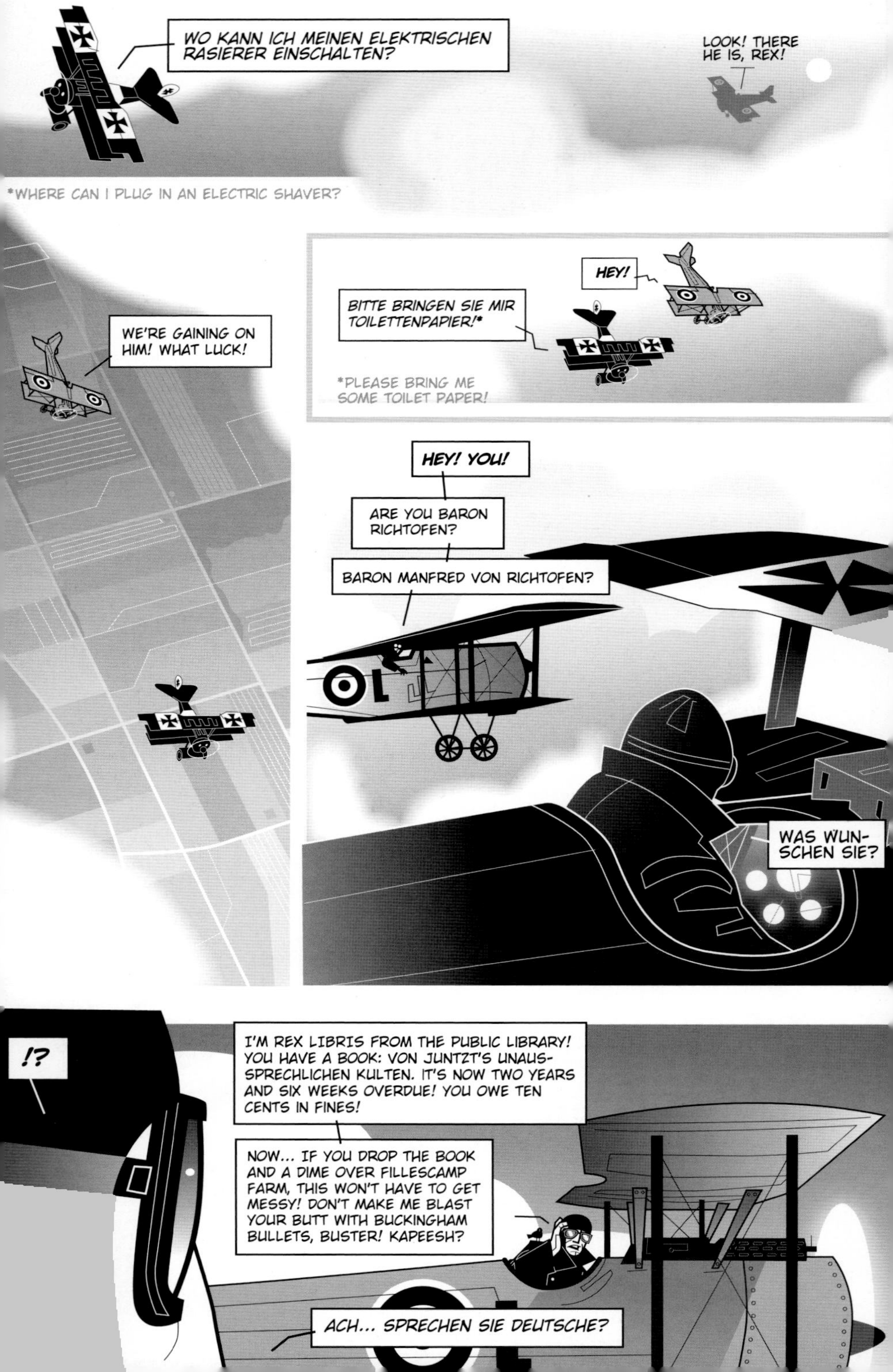

*WHERE CAN I PLUG IN AN ELECTRIC SHAVER?

WE'RE GAINING ON HIM! WHAT LUCK!

HEY!

BITTE BRINGEN SIE MIR TOILETTENPAPIER!*

*PLEASE BRING ME SOME TOILET PAPER!

HEY! YOU!

ARE YOU BARON RICHTOFEN?

BARON MANFRED VON RICHTOFEN?

WAS WUNSCHEN SIE?

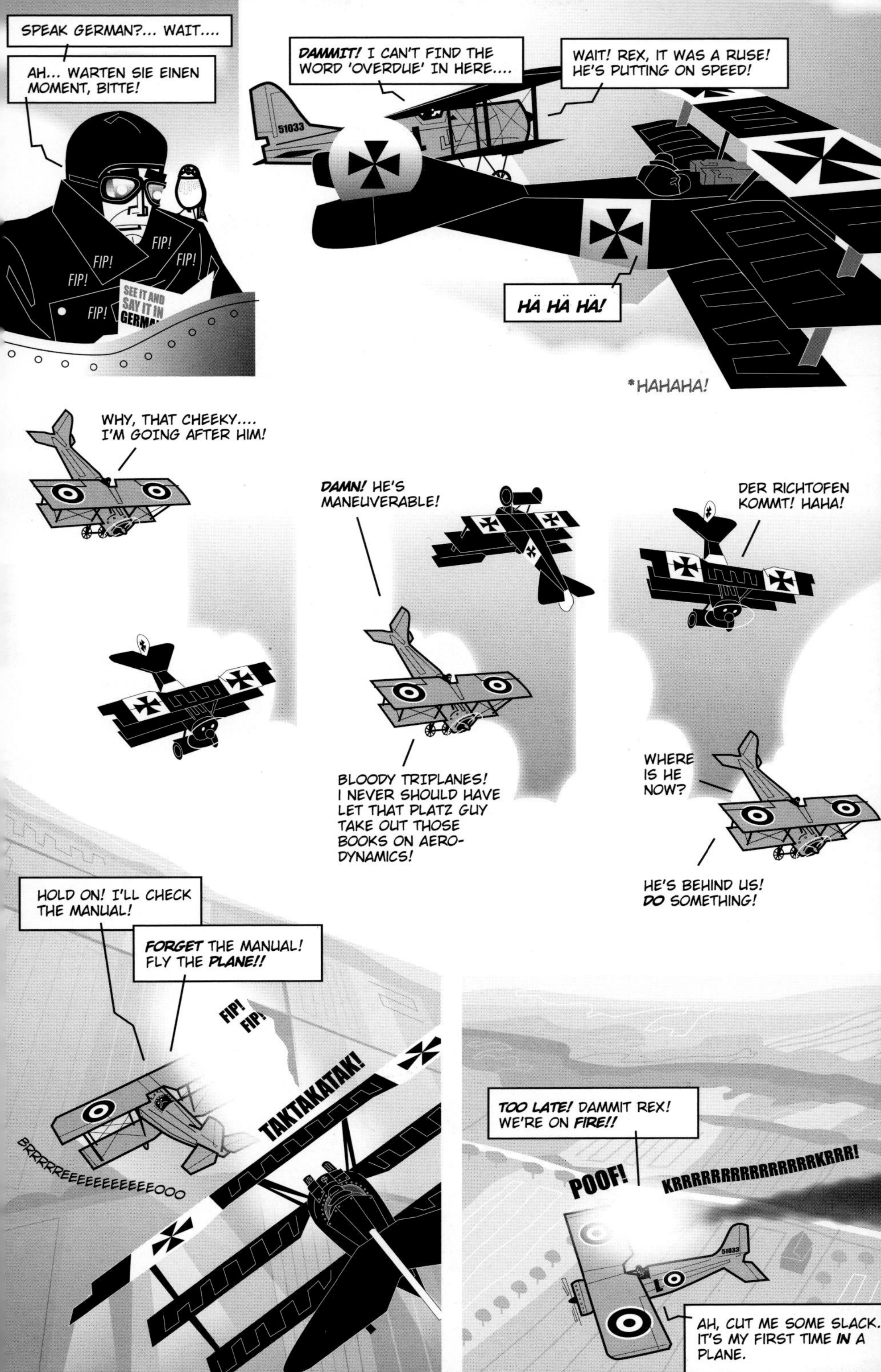
SPEAK GERMAN?... WAIT....
AH... WARTEN SIE EINEN MOMENT, BITTE!
FIP!
FIP!
FIP!
FIP!
FIP!
SEE IT AND SAY IT IN GERMAN
51033
DAMMIT! I CAN'T FIND THE WORD 'OVERDUE' IN HERE....
WAIT! REX, IT WAS A RUSE! HE'S PUTTING ON SPEED!
HÄ HÄ HÄ!
*HAHAHA!
WHY, THAT CHEEKY.... I'M GOING AFTER HIM!
DAMN! HE'S MANEUVERABLE!
DER RICHTOFEN KOMMT! HAHA!
BLOODY TRIPLANES! I NEVER SHOULD HAVE LET THAT PLATZ GUY TAKE OUT THOSE BOOKS ON AERO-DYNAMICS!
WHERE IS HE NOW?
HE'S BEHIND US! DO SOMETHING!
HOLD ON! I'LL CHECK THE MANUAL!
FORGET THE MANUAL! FLY THE PLANE!!
FIP! FIP!
TAKTAKATAK!
BRRRRREEEEEEEEEEEEOOO
TOO LATE! DAMMIT REX! WE'RE ON FIRE!!
POOF!
KRRRRRRRRRRRRRRRRKRRR!
51033
AH, CUT ME SOME SLACK. IT'S MY FIRST TIME IN A PLANE.

FLYING THIS RICKETY CRATE IS A LOT HARDER THAN IT LOOKS, YOU KNOW....
I TELL YA...
...THIS WHOLE MESS DOES BRING TO MIND THAT OLD SAYING, 'ONLY FOOLS RUSH IN.' I SHOULDA AT LEAST HAD A PRACTISE FLIGHT BEFORE TAKING ON THIS FELLOW....
WHATEVER! PONDER LATER! HERE COMES THE GROUND!

HANG ON!

YAAAAH!
KERASH

CURSE YOU, RED BARON! YOU'VE EXPOSED MY HEROIC HUBRIS!
BUT I'LL BE BACK, BUCKO! MARK MY WORDS: YOU HAVEN'T SEEN THE LAST OF REX LIBRIS, PUBLIC LIBRARIAN!

SIMON...
LET'S NOT TELL ANYONE ABOUT THIS, OKAY?
FIN

CHESTER BROWN

Chester William David Brown was born in 1960 and grew up in Chateauguay, Quebec. His latest graphic novel is Louis Riel: A Comic-Strip Biography. He currently lives in Toronto.
Favourite author: Colin Wilson **Favourite book:** Arf: The Life and Hard Times of Little Orphan Annie by Harold Gray

LOUIS FISHAUF

Louis Fishauf is an award-winning Toronto graphic designer, art director and illustrator.
Favourite authors: Clive Barker, Douglas Coupland, Dave Eggers, Philip Roth, Neil Gaiman, Tom Wolfe **Currently reading:** JPod by Douglas Coupland

JEFF JACKSON

Jeff Jackson divides his time between illustration and fine art. He currently has a show of Italian landscapes at Trattoria Zucca in Toronto. In the summer of 2007 he will travel to Italy to prepare for another exhibition of landscapes. For more info check out:
www.jeffjacksonart.com
Currently reading: Tenor of Love by Mary di Michele, Art and Architecture ROME by Brigitte Hintzen-Bohlen.

TYRONE MCARTHY

Tyrone McCarthy works as a freelance illustrator represented by Three in a Box. He has worked with such clients as The Wall Street Journal, Washington Times, Owl Magazine, and Today's Parent. He's also the creator of the indy comic Corduroy High. Tyrone graduated from Ontario College of Art and Design, majoring in Illustration. For more info check out: **www.CorduroyHigh.com**
Favourite book: Alice in Wonderland **Currently reading:** Fables: 1001 Nights of Snowfall

TOMIO NITTO

Tomio Nitto is an award-winning graphic artist whose illustrations have appeared in many publications including Esquire, Saturday Night, and the Washington Post Magazine. His work was also used in the movies The Fly and M Butterfly. His first children's book, "The Red Rock" was published in 2006
Favourite author: Shusaku Endo **Favourite book:** Chin-Moku

FIONA SMYTH

Toronto artist Fiona Smyth's comics have appeared in Exclaim, Vice, Twisted Sisters, Ben is Dead, Maow Maow, Legal Action Comics, Bust and Paper Rodeo. For more info check out **www.fionasmyth.com**. Hypatia Rules!!
Favourite author: Charles Bukowski **Favourite book:** Frank Herbert's Dune **Currently reading:** Japanese Tales edited and translated by Royall Tyler

RENE ZAMIC

Born in Thunder Bay (Port Arthur), Ontario, Rene studied at the Ontario College of Art and has been working in the commercial art field ever since. His work has appeared in The Boston Globe, PC Magazine, Rolling Stone, TV Guide, Marie Claire and The National Post. He works in a wide variety of media: air-brush, scratchboard, pen and ink, sculpted plaster models and computer-based electronic arts.
Favourite author: Arthur C. Clark **Currently reading:** Speer the Final Verdict by Joachim Fest

REX'S BOOK-RELATED ANECDOTES
This one's about Huey Long, who was a somewhat demagogic Louisiana governor and U-S senator back in the 1920s and 1930s.

One day in the early 30s, Long and a friend were walkin' along in New York when somethin' in a book-store window caught Long's eye.
© Chester Brown 2007

Hey, look what's on display here--
BOOKS

--"The Count of Monte Cristo".
BOOKS

I want to buy a copy.
BOOKS

This will just take a minute.

Would you like to read it? I'll buy you one too.
No thanks. I already read it when I was a kid.

Me too, but I re-read it every year. The guy in this book, he knew how to hate--

--and until you learn how to hate, you'll never get anywhere in this world.
Source: T. Harry William's HUEY LONG (1969, p. 34)

REX
FISHAUF

THE PAST
THE PRESENT
THE FUTURE
WHAT THE-
REX-LIBRIS
JACK
SON

HYPATIA
VERSUS
LAMIA
xFioNASMYTH07

COOL DOWN
OUT
OUT
OUT OF
THE ETHER
AN OBJECT>
SQUISHED AS
FLAT AS THE
PROVERBIAL
PANCAKE,
UNDER
UNBELIEVABLE
COMPRESSION OF
SIX DIMENSIONAL
G FORCES
THAT MADE
POSSIBLE THIS
TRANS-NEBULAIC
JOURNEY,
ENTERS KNOWN
SPACE.
STRETCHED
SENSORY
GATHERERS
PULLED THE
SAUCER-SHAPED
OUTLINE
TO THE
HORRIFYING
PURRSHAPE
KNOWN TO
SOME AS
THE
BATeAREDcAT.
CLEARANCE
FEELS SO
GOOD
PURR.
HUMM
BURR
SSS
BB
RR
RR
BB
RR
B
B
R
R
R
B...
PUTT-PUTT-PUTT-POP
GAUWK!
-R-RRETCH!
QUICK-ACTING DIMENSION EXCHANGER
KRICK
TOUCH-DOWN ON THE
PANET OF KNOWLEDGE

DAWN of CAT
!
BOOK RETURN
SHORT AND SWEET*
ONE MILLION YEARS LATE
CUTE. HE MUST HAVE TWO THUMBS.
THERE WILL BE NO LATE CHARGE.
JELLO! Ma PATRON, WOULD LIKE TO RETURN ZISS BOOK. HAD GREAT DISTANCE-COME. THANK YOUL. BYE, BYE.
GRRRrr.. HOLD IT! LOOKS LIKE 101AX-12B CATAGORY OVER-DAMAGE.. DAM! IS ITEM REPAIRABLE?
I-DON'T-TH-I-INK-SO.
SWISH BANG
QUIET
THRUST
BOW, WOW!
A.E. VAN VOGT
KLANG
2007

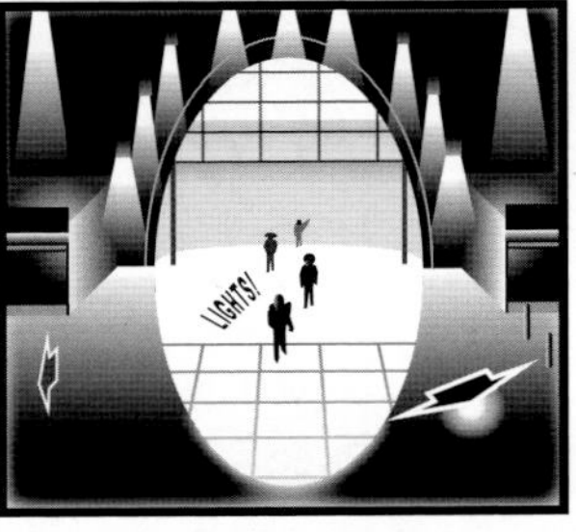

A RETURN TO **DAs BOOKWORLD,** *NOW* THAT WE HAVE THE LENDERS' CARD, WOULD BE **AOK BRIGHT**. DA STIPULATIONS WERE DRACONIAN. I FOR ONE HAVE A HANKER'N TO GET MY HEAD INTO SOME SERIOUS LITERATURE FOR A CHANGE - LIKE A COLLECTION OF OLD **'DOCTOR WHO'** EPISODES. GROUP DISCUSSION. I'D VOTE TO STAY A WHILE.

THE CREW THINKS! AN OBJECT OBSCURE HAS COME (UNKNOWN ENTERPRISE/ FATE OF THE UNIVERSE). ***..NOT*** THE DEVICE BELOW. IT'S A TENSION **PROP.**

THE DENIZENS... THEY SEEM SENSIBLE - READ A BOOK, EAT SOME PASTERY! - COOLIO. WHATS WITH WEIRD VAN VOGT- NEVER HEARD OF IT.. BAG OF HAMMERS. STRANGE ASSIGNMENT WITH NO LEAD TME - WHATS THE LINE PADRE? WHAT DO YOU KNOW? WE BACKBURN DELTOID FOR THIS PLANET WITH THE GARDEN OF KNOWLEDGE, AND NOTHING TO REWARD US, BUT A WALK IN THE SUN.

TIC TIC TIC TIC TIC TIC TIC TIC TIC TIC TICK

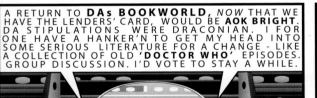

TIC TIC TIC TIC TIC TIC TIC TIC TIC TIC

SAY WHAT YOU MUST.

WHAT HAPPENED AND WHY THE RUSH TO LEAVE? MAYBE WE COULD'VE READ SOME **BOOKS.**

DID YOU ***SOCKIT*** WITH YOUR EXTRORDINARY TONGUE LAZER IMAGE ENHANCER? SMASH THE CREEP WITH BLASTS OF **FEAR** ENERGY?

NO. WE WENT IN LOADED FOR BEARS AND DIKK'N GET INTO THE FRONT DOOR. THEN, POOF.

POOF? WOW- VAPOURIXED? YAH! PERSONAL. LOOK IN THE EYES. **SEE** THE HURT.

. . .NO.. TAG CAME OUT WITH A PILE OF PAPERS, A LIBRARY CARD AND A RUB-ON TATOO. HONK'N ABOUT HALF-LIFE ON DELTOID AND ORBITING HERE LONGER.

IS IT TOO MUCH TO ASK THESE SIMPLE **DE'CRATIC** QUESTIONES, **PADRE?** **OOH!** DO WE HAVE ANY MORE DELICIOUS FRUIT BREAD FINGERS? THEY'RE SO GREAT WITH COFFEE.

I DON'T CARE *WHAT* **THE FANMAN** *SAYS*. PUT THAT IN PERSPECTIVE AND WE WOULD BE HERE A FORTNIGHT OR LONGER AND NO DOWN TIME ON DELTOID FOR **CHIRISAK!**

MUSINGS ON REX

Everyone likes a few extras with their trades, which is why I'm writing this illuminating little missive. Now if only I could think of something illuminating to write, it would work so much better.

Best to start with the basics. How did Rex come about?

It started back when I was working on Nil: A Land Beyond Belief (A wonderful little book that is still available for purchase – save a book from languishing in a large, impersonal warehouse. Give it a loving home!). Nil was a dark social satire, and after awhile of staring into the abyss and ridiculing it, I wanted to focus on something more positive. I wanted to work on the antidote. Something that celebrated life, that reveled in the marvel of the world around us, while at the same time indulging in an excess of imagination. Pure, hyperbolic fun. Rex was the result.

The project called for a different visual approach than I'd taken with Nil. While the characters in Nil (in the first draft) had no arms, the characters in Rex would have all the body parts we have come to know and love: heads, legs, feet, arms, hands, ears, etc. This leads to an obvious question: why, for God's sake, did the characters in Nil originally have free floating hands and no arms? The answer: because they had legs but no feet. Which is a wonderful example of my circular way of thinking. Anyway, in the end I made concessions to reality and added the missing limbs and feet. So while no one is going to confuse Rex with realism, the images are substantially more representational than in much of the rest of my work, which can be conveniently seen at my website: www.jtillustration.com. There you will find all sorts of silly things, including a make-a-robot section and an animated Nilscape.

The first drawings of Rex (at right) I did directly on the computer, and I've just gone with that look ever since. The whole book was done using a mouse, laying down one bezier point at a time. Style wise I wanted the comic to have a Jack Kirby feel, at least to some small extent, mixed in with my own approach – and a bit of Hergé (Tintin). I may be the only one who sees any of this.

What's in the future of Rex Libris? At some point I'd like to get guest authors to pop into the library and involve them in solving mysteries and brain twisting conundrums. Sort of like Scooby-Doo, but instead of rock bands, I'd want policy wonks and evolutionary biologists. Fareed Zakaria or Jared Diamond, for example. It'd be ridiculous and educational at the same time. How often do the two converge so perfectly? Combined with the occasional essay or short story at the back, it'd be sublime.

The book is obviously not for everyone. It revels in boundless, untrammeled silliness, of which I'm sure Graham Chapman's admonishing army officer would not approve.

I just can't seem to help myself.

I hope you enjoy(ed) the book!

cheers,
James Turner
February, 2007

My job can be tuff.
Real tuff. I'm talking like something outta Bukowski, or real nasty Elmore Leonard stuff, you know? Or Stephen King. We get a lot of freaks in dis library lemme tell yas! Hey! There's one now! Freeze you undead brain sucking scumbag! Put down the Nancy Drew Compedium nice n' slow! I don't want no trouble! I'll drop you real quick like!

The name's Libris. Rex Libris. Librarian. I watch over the book collection at the Middleton Library Branch. When people don't return a book, it's my job to get it back. And we got a neighbourhood of undead scum that likes to read our Nancy Drew collection that never, ever return their books on time.

These creatures of the night, an' the aliens that think they can abscond wit books, an' that I won't find out what planet they're from, hey, they got another thing comin'. I got me da whole library to use as a resource. How to kill a hopin' Sciapod? Easy. I know all the answers 'cause I got da books.